Washington for Women

Photo by: Catherine Wetherfield
Standing Woman by Gaston Lachaise (American, born France, 1882-1935). Bronze.
Hirshhorn Museum and Sculpture Garden. Museum purchase with funds provided by
Smithsonian Collections Acquisition Program, 1981.

Washington for Women

*A Guide to Working and Living in the
Washington Metropolitan Area*

Jacci Duncan

MADISON BOOKS
Lanham • New York • Oxford

Published by Madison Books
4720 Boston Way
Lanham, Maryland 20706

12 Hid's Copse Road
Cummor Hill, Oxford OX2 9JJ, England

Distributed by National Book Network

Library of Congress Cataloging-in-Publication Data

Duncan, Jacci, 1964–
    Washington for women : a guide to working and living in the
Washington Metropolitan Area / Jacci Duncan.
        p.   cm.
    Includes index.
    ISBN 1-56833-088-X (paper : alk. paper)
    1. Women—Social networks—Washington Metropolitan Area—Directories.
    2. Women—Washington Metropolitan Area—Societies and clubs—Directories.
    3. Women—Services for—Washington Metropolitan Area—Directories. 4. Vocational
guidance for women—Washington Metropolitan Area—Directories. 5. Women—
Washington Metropolitan Area—Life skills guides. 6. Women in the professions—
Washington Metropolitan Area.   I. Title.
    HQ1439.W3D85   1997
    305.4'025'753—dc21   97-7164

ISBN 1-56833-088-X (paper : alk. paper)

⊛™ The paper used in this publication meets the minimum requirements of
American National Standard for Information Sciences—Permanence of
Paper for Printed Library Materials, ANSI Z39.48–1984.
Manufactured in the United States of America.

Contents

Preface.. ix

Part I: Professional

1 Business and Professional Networking Groups 3
Advertising/Marketing 6
Art/Design.. 6
Business/Entrepreneur... 8
Communications/Public Relations... 11
Computers/Data Processing... 12
Education 12
Environment/Energy 14
Financing/Banking 14
Government 15
Health Care/Pharmaceuticals 18
Human Resources 20
International 20
Legal 21
Media 22
Politics 26
Psychology/Sociology 27
Real Estate 28
Sales 28
Science and Technology 28
Sports 33
Trade Professions... 33
Transportation 34
Unions 34
Working Mothers 36
Writing/Publishing 36

2 Women's Career Guide to D.C. 37
Career and Employment Programs for Women 38
Getting a Job in Public Policy 41
Working on Capitol Hill 43

Getting a Job with the Government 44
The International Job Market 47
Job Search Strategies 49

3 The Woman Entrepreneur 55
Starting or Expanding a Business: Where to Find Help 56
Business Loan Assistance 64
Selling Your Goods or Services to the Government 68

4 Leadership 71
Leadership Programs for Women 72
Leadership Programs for Young Women 77

Part II: Politics

5 Political Involvement 83
Nonpartisan/Bipartisan Political Groups 86
Democratic Groups 90
Republican Groups 92

6 Advocacy 93
Advocacy Groups by Subject 94
Advocacy Groups 99
Policy Publications 110

Part III: Health Care

7 Women's Health Care Guide 113
Reproductive Health Services 113
Mammography 115
Women's Health Centers 116
Finding Quality Health Care Coverage 118
Finding a Physician 121

8 Women's Health Issues and Resources 123
General Women's Health Resources 123
Alcohol/Drugs 125
Autoimmune Diseases 126
Cancer 126
Breast Cancer 127
Eating Disorders 131
Heart Disease 131
HIV/AIDS 132

Immunization 133
Mental Health 134
Older Women's Health 135
Osteoporosis 136

Part IV: Mothers & Family

9 **Pregnancy Services**... 139
Information and Resources 139
Preparing for Birth 141
Hospitals Are Good Resources 141
Childbirth Education 143
After the Delivery 144
Services for Pregnant Teens 146

10 **Child Care** 149
Child Care Resources 150
Child Care Standards 153

11 **For Mothers ONLY!**... 157
Networks and Support Groups for Mothers 157
Publications for Parents 164

Part V: Education

12 **The Woman College Student**................................ 169
Organizations for College Women 169
Women's Colleges and Universities 171
Women's Studies Programs 173

13 **Internship Opportunities in Washington, D.C.** 177
Locating an Internship 177
Internships with Women's Organizations 178

Part VI: Social Services

14 **Violence Against Women**...................................... 185
Shelters and Services for Battered and Abused Women 188
Safety Tips for Women 190

15 **Housing** 193
Low-Cost Housing for Women and Families 193
Low-Cost Housing for Single Women 194

Housing for Women with HIV/AIDS 196
Housing for Women in Recovery from Substance Abuse 197
Housing and Services for Homeless Women 198

16 Legal Assistance.. 203
Employment Discrimination 203
Sexual Abuse/Domestic Violence 208
Pension Rights for Women 210

Part VII: Sports and Leisure

17 Sports and Fitness... 215
Sports Groups for Women 216
Exercise 222
Membership Groups 225

18 Arts and Literature.. 227
Art Groups for Women 227
Agencies for the Arts 228
Music/Dance Groups 230
Writing Groups for Women 231
Women's Journals 234
Women's Bookstores 234

19 Volunteer Opportunities.. 235
Community Service Groups 235
Social Service Agencies 238
Volunteer Clearinghouses 240
Mentor Opportunities 240
Women's Centers 241
Political Volunteerism 243

Index 245

About the Author 259

Part I

Professional

1

Business and Professional Networking Groups

Bridget Serchak, Consulting Editor

The number of business and professional networking groups for women in Washington has increased dramatically over the last two decades. Currently, there is a wide variety of groups that provide women with the needed resources, contacts and events for career success. And the number of groups keeps growing. Professional women's groups have become so popular that there is now an association or network for nearly every profession or area of expertise, such as Women in Mathematics and the Society of Women Geographers. Many groups provide networking opportunities, job banks and other career resources, such as professional training, educational events and professional seminars. Some even offer mentor programs.

The majority of networks and groups described in this chapter are predominantly for women. However, others have been included that have committees for women members or for the purpose of addressing industry issues pertinent to women.

You will find that most of the organizations have a national headquarters and a chapter office for the Washington region. Usually, two separate memberships are required. However, there are benefits to joining each. National membership generally provides access to annual events and national resources. Chapter membership usually offers networking opportunities, career development and access to local events. There are also regional groups, which are known for providing excellent career services, such as well-maintained job banks and programs and events for career development.

Networking Tips for Women
by
Anne Baber and Lynne Waymon

A Dozen of the Best Networking Tips for Women

Know what you want. Before attending a networking event, determine exactly what information you're looking for. Make a list of problems you're trying to solve, resources you need, or information you want.

Make small talk. Expert networkers are skillful at small talk. Anybody can learn small talk and use it to create valuable networking relationships.

Get into names. People rush introductions to get on to "the good stuff." However, names are "the good stuff." Teach people your name by providing a way for them to remember. For example, "I'm Sandy Jones. When you think about keeping up with the Joneses, think of me. I'm a financial planner."

Find a creative way to describe your profession. Forget your title. Find a dramatic way to explain what product or service you provide. Instead of "I'm president of Billing Services," say "I get the bugs out of your bills."

Find a reason to hand out your business card. Randomly handing out your business card at networking events is a waste of time. Instead, find a reason to exchange cards. Say something like, "I'd like to send you a copy of that article on quality management. May I have your card?"

Give first and freely. Always take the first step to build relationships. Listen to find out what information others need, and provide it.

Make yourself visible. Become visible in an organization. Volunteer for an activity or job that shows off your best skills and spotlights your business capabilities.

Say thank you. Come up with imaginative ways to thank people who help you, such as flowers, tickets, a sample of a product your company makes or a service you provide, a contribution to a charity or a handwritten note.

It's not who you know, but who knows you. People say, cynically, "It's not what you know, it's who you know." But what's really important in networking is who knows you. Get people to know you by telling short, vivid stories that illustrate your expertise. And continue to cultivate that relationship after the networking event ends.

Speak out. Speak to the local chapter of an association or civic group and be sure the program planner publicizes your speech. Provide a news release for her to send to the business calendar of your local newspaper.

Know that networking takes time. Networks don't happen overnight, but are nurtured over time. It usually takes six months to create a network of active relationships that are mutually advantageous. So start now.

Keeping Networking Alive: Following Up

Host a meeting. Want to show some influential people where your business is located and give them a clear image of what you do? Offer your business as a location place for a committee or board meeting.

Put out a newsletter. Produce a newsletter for customers, potential clients, professional colleagues and suppliers. Show how customers benefit from your business. Help contacts see how they could use your expertise.

Do a lunch bunch. Ask a few people you are trying to get to know better to lunch. Pick your lunch bunch carefully so that the benefits of their becoming better acquainted with you and each other are obvious.

Travel together. Going to a convention? Call a contact who you know is going and suggest that you travel together.

Pull up a chair. If you're going to a meeting or event that you know a contact will be attending, plan to sit next to each other. Call your contact before the event to arrange to spend time together.

Extend an invitation. Want to see someone more frequently? Encourage your contact to visit and perhaps join an organization in which you are a member.

Get feedback. Ask your contact to review something you've written. Your resume, a brochure or an article are all good materials to share. After the person has had a chance to review it, call or visit to discuss your contact's comments. If you make any changes, give the new copy to your contact and point out how their comments helped you.

Anne Baber and Lynne Waymon are business visibility experts, professional speakers and co-authors of Great Connections: Small Talk and Networking for Business People and 52 Ways to Reconnect, Follow Up & Stay in Touch...When You Don't Have Time to Network. To order call 800/352-2939.

Advertising/Marketing

Women in Advertising and Marketing (WAM)
301/369-7400
4200 Wisconsin Avenue, NW
Washington, DC 20016
WAM provides networking and career events, such as monthly networking dinners, speakers bureau and job bank.

Women's Direct Response Group (WDRG)
301/231-4098
WDRG holds a variety of monthly networking and professional development events for women in the direct marketing field.

Art/Design

American Institute of Architects/Women's Comm.
202/626-7300
1735 New York Ave., NW
Washington, DC 20006
The Committee offers networking and professional development to broaden opportunities for women in the field of architecture.

International Alliance for Women in Music (IAWM)
202/994-6338
George Washington University
Washington, DC 20052
http://music.acu.edu
IAWM is a coalition of women composers, conductors, performers and lovers of music for the purpose of networking, professional development and the promotion of women in music. IAWM promotes female artists through concerts, festivals, recordings, score calls, awards presentations and publications.

National League of American Pen Women
202/785-1997
1300 17th Street, NW
Washington, DC 20036
The League provides networking and resources to writers, composers, artists and others in related professions.

Women in Museums Network
202/357-3300
WiMN is a network of about 300 women who meet for monthly luncheons to discuss various issues, exchange information and share job leads.

Women's Caucus for the Arts
215/854-0922
Moore College of Art
1920 Race Street
Philadelphia, PA 19103-1178
The Caucus provides networking and professional development for women artists. Call the national headquarters for local contacts.

Wilhelmina Cole Holladay

**Founder
Chairman of the Board
National Museum of
Women in the Arts**

*Over a period of three decades, Mrs.
Holladay, together with her husband,
Wallace Holladay, assembled a significant collection of works by women
artists dating from the Renaissance
period to the present, which became
the seed for the National Museum of
Women in the Arts. The Holladays
founded the museum as a way to reveal and celebrate the hidden contri-
butions of women in the arts.*

Q. What career steps did you take to get where you are today?
A. I took responsible positions in volunteer work, such as president of my
son's private school. I studied history of art in the United States and
France. I cultivated associations that would be helpful.

Q. To what do you attribute your success?
A. Hard work, creative problem solving and commitment.

Q. What obstacles did you have to overcome along the way?
A. A tendency to procrastinate and difficulty in setting priorities.

Q. Who are your role models, or who were they earlier in your career?
A. Elizabeth Campbell, the founder of PBS; Margaret Thatcher and
Eleanor Roosevelt.

Q. What advice would you give other women interested in your profession?
A. Be prepared to work hard. Develop an ability to take criticism, both
deserved and undeserved. Establish goals. Be appropriately dressed at all
times and observe good etiquette.

Business/Entrepreneur

"9 to 5," National Association of Working Women
800/522-0925
402 Olympic Court
Ft. Washington, MD 20744
The Association offers career resources, networking opportunities, professional development and job resources.

Alexandria Professional Women's Network
703/549-1000
801 N. Fairfax Street, Suite 402
Alexandria, VA 22314
The Network provides networking, support and information services. It can be reached through the Alexandria Chamber of Commerce.

American Business Women's Association
816/361-6621
9100 Ward Parkway
Kansas City, MO 64114-0728
ABWA offers networking and professional development activities. Call the national headquarters for local contacts.

Business and Professional Women
202/293-1200
2012 Massachusetts Ave., NW
Washington, DC 20036
BPW works to create equality in the workforce by providing women with career resources. Members have access to a career resource center, and a variety of career and development programs.

Business Women's Network
202/466-8209, 800/48-WOMEN
1146 19th St., NW, 3rd Floor
Washington, DC 20036
BWN offers resources and career development events. BWN produces *The Business Women's Network Directory.*

Federation of Organizations for Professional Women
202/328-1415
1825 I Street, NW, Suite 400
Washington, DC 20006
FOPW is composed of individuals and groups working to support and promote women in the workforce through networking events, conferences, seminars and a job referral service.

National Association of Colored Women's Clubs, Inc.
202/726-2044
5808 16th Street, NW
Washington, DC 20001
The Association provides career development, networking, and community service opportunities.

National Association of M.B.A. Women
202/723-1267
3923 Georgia Ave., NW
Washington, DC 20011
The Association offers networking, career enhancement and job opportunities to support women with M.B.A. degrees.

Barbara Davis Blum
President
Chairwoman
Executive Officer
Adams National Bank

Q. What career steps did you take to get where you are today?
A. Before becoming president of Adams National Bank, I managed a proprietary multidiscipline mental health clinic; I owned and operated a chain of restaurants; I was Deputy Director of both the 1976 Carter-Mondale presidential campaign and presidential transition; I was the Deputy Administrator of the Environmental Protection Agency from 1977 to 1981; I was president of an international consulting firm and an advisor to the United Nations Environment Programme (UNEP).

Q. To what do you attribute your success?
A. Hard work and perseverance, but also a sensitivity to issues and understanding of human behavior. In addition, I have always been active as a volunteer. Much of my support has come from my nonprofit involvement. My activity and support continues.

Q. What obstacles did you have to overcome along the way?
A. Being female in a male-dominated profession.

Q. Who are your role models, or who were they earlier in your career?
A. I did not know many female role models when I was first starting out. I had to pave my own way and stick my neck out, and learn by my own experiences. Later, by the time I got into politics, there were many model women to learn from.

Q. What advice would you give other women interested in your profession?
A. Women have to jump on the bones of opportunity. Even though I had never run a bank, I lobbied for the top job by pressing my experience with women's groups; that I knew how to manage organizations; and that my social work background made me a good facilitator. In other words, I emphasized the transferability of my skills and networks to any setting.

National Association of Negro Business and Professional Women's Clubs, Inc.
202/483-4206
1806 New Hamp. Ave., NW
Washington, DC 20009
NANBPW is a coalition of 350 groups that offers employment and economic development, professional training, and community service.

National Association of Women Business Owners
301/656-1399
4424 Montgomery Ave., # 201
Bethesda, MD 20814
NAWBO offers resources, business development and professional development services for women business owners. NAWBO also offers a networking group for women who have been in business for themselves for more than eight years.

National Federation of Black Women Business Owners
202/833-3450
1500 Massachusetts Ave., NW
Suite 34
Washington, DC 20005
Support, networking and information clearinghouse for black women who own their own business. NFBWBO provides business and career development resources.

Network of Entrepreneurial Women (NEW)
703/425-3575
PO Box 2181
Reston, VA 22090-2181
Networking, education and resource group for women business owners that offers classes and seminars on business topics, such as financing, legal issues and networking.

Virginia Association of Female Executives
703/476-0089
30 Irving Place
New York, NY 10003
The Association provides professional development, resources and networking opportunities for women employed in executive positions in the Washington area.

Women Business Owners of Montgomery County
202/310-3222
PO Box 1281
Rockville, MD 20849
Membership includes women who own and operate businesses in Montgomery County for the purpose of networking, career enhancement and information exchange.

Women of Washington
202/296-5922
1828 L Street, NW, Suite 920
Washington, DC 20036
This regional organization sponsors numerous networking events, including panel discussions and luncheon speakers. Offers committees for young women and mentoring. Women of Washington publishes a monthly newsletter, which contains job listings, networking information and upcoming events.

**Women's Information
Network**
202/347-2827
1511 K Street, NW, Suite 428
Washington, DC 20005
http//www.eats.com/WIN
e-mail: win@eats.com/WIN
WIN is a Democratic group
that provides a variety of
networking events. The job
center has employment listings
and other career resources. WIN
offers one of the best
networking events for women
called "Women Opening Doors
for Women," in which high-
level professional women share
their experiences at informal
dinner parties.

Communications/Public Relations

**Association for Women In
Communications (AWIC)**
703/359-9000
10605 Judicial Drive, Suite A-4
Fairfax, VA 22030-5167
AWIC is composed of
women working in the communications field for the purpose of
professional development and
networking.

**Public Relations Society of
America (PRSA)/Women in
Public Relations Committee**
703/691-9212
11130 Main Street, Suite 305
Fairfax, VA 22030
The Committee offers net-
working opportunities and professional development events for
women working in public relations.

**Speech Communications
Association, Women's Caucus**
703/750-0533
5105 Backlick Road, St. E
Annandale, VA 22003
SCA's Women's Caucus
offers professional development,
educational resources and networking opportunities to address
the needs of women working in
the field of speech communications.

**Washington Women in Public
Relations (WWPR)**
202/310-1027
PO Box 65297
Washington, DC 20035-5297
WWPR is a regional group
for women working in the areas
of public relations, communications and advertising that provides networking opportunities,
industry resources and career
development.

**Women in Cable and
Television**
312/634-2330
230 West Monroe, Suite 730
Chicago, IL 60606
WICT works to empower
women in the fields of cable and
telecommunications through career resources and professional
development. Call the national
headquarters for local contacts.

Computers/Data Processing

Association for Women in Computing (AWC)
415/905-4663, Natl. HQs
e-mail: jfloy@aol.com
http://www.halcyon.com/monih/awc.html
AWC is composed of programmers, analysts, technical writers and entrepreneurs. Contact the local chapter through the listed e-mail address or contact the national headquarters.

DC Webgrrls
http://www.dcwebgrrls.org
dc@webgrrls.com
Support, resource and networking forum for women who are involved with the Internet. Members interact primarily on-line, but gather for monthly networking meetings, workshops and guest-speaker luncheons.

Education

American Assn. for Higher Education/Women's Caucus
202/293-6440
1 Dupont Circle, Suite 360
Washington, DC 20036
Education, information and networking forum for women's studies and issues in higher education.

American Assn. of University Professors/Committee on the Status of Women
202/737-5900
1012 14th Street, NW, Suite 500
Washington, DC 20005
Professional development and legal assistance for women in higher education.

American Association of University Women (AAUW)
202/785-7700
1111 16th Street, NW
Washington, DC 20036
http://www.aauw.org

AAUW serves women who hold a degree by providing leadership training, educational programs and networking.

American Council on Education, Women's Office
202/939-9390
1 Dupont Circle, NW, Suite 800
Washington, DC 20036
Supports and promotes women in higher education administration and female college students.

American Federation of Teachers/Women's Rights Committee
202/879-4400
555 New Jersey Avenue, NW
Washington, DC 20001
The Committee is active in research and education programs for women on campus, as well as in equality issues.

Women of Washington, Inc.

© Carol Rogers-Simpson 1996

Madeleine Kunin, Ambassador to Switzerland, Lynn Martin, former Secretary of Labor, Kathleen Kennedy Townsend, First Lt. Governor of Maryland, Rep. Connie Morella (R-MD) and Tara Sonenshine, *Newsweek* magazine, participate in Women on the Run: Life in the Political Fast Lane.

Women of Washington, Inc. is one of the most unique networking groups for women in Washington, D.C., with a membership that cuts across the lines of race, age, ideology and profession to unite women for the purpose of gender support through greater understanding of others.

Women of Washington, Inc. offers monthly events that focus on issues critical to women, such as forums of eclectic panels of leaders, ranging from conservative writer Arianna Huffington to liberal activist Betty Friedan. The intent is to encourage members to understand other points of view and experiences. Another popular event is "Conversation With...," which is an informal, one-on-one conversation with accomplished women.

"Women have become a strong force in the economy and we don't have time to reinvent the wheel. In order to access the wisdom and experience of others, women must reach out, share and organize," said Gail Berendzen, founder, president and CEO of Women of Washington, Inc. "Our organization was formed to do just that. Women of Washington, Inc. provides the venues which will help women in their professional and personal lives."

Association of American Law Schools/Women in Legal Education
202/296-8851
1201 Connecticut Ave., NW
Suite 800
Washington, DC 20036
Information and support network for female law professors and others in legal education. Operates a resource bank on gender issues.

Linguistic Society of America/ Committee on the Status of Women
202/835-1714
1325 18th Street, NW, Suite 211
Washington, DC 20036
The Committee works to develop guidelines for a nonsexist language, encourages research, education and information exchange.

National Association for Women in Education (NAWE)
202/659-9330
1325 18th Street, NW, # 210
Washington, DC 20036-6511
NAWE is composed of women working in education, administration, teaching and research positions, mostly in higher education for the purpose of professional development.

National Education Association (NEA)/Women's Caucus
202/833-4000
1201 16th Street, NW
Washington, DC 20036
The Women's Caucus works to promote equality in the education system by eliminating sexism and promoting programs such as Title IX.

Environment/Energy

Women's Council on Energy and the Environment
202/296-5085
PO Box 33211
Washington, DC 20033
Nonpartisan organization for women working in the environmental and energy fields. The group provides educational development, networking and career enhancement events.

Finance/Banking

American Society of Women Accountants (ASWA)
703/938-7114
11350 Random Hills Rd., # 800
Fairfax, VA 22030
Support, networking and career enhancement group for women working in the field of accounting. ASWA offers educational opportunities and leadership and skills.

American Women's Society of Certified Public Accountants
800/AWS-CPAI
401 N. Michigan Ave.
Chicago, IL 60601
Networking, information and support group for women working as certified public accountants. Contact national headquarters for local contacts.

Financial Women Intl. Inc.
703/807-2007
200 North Glebe Rd., # 814
Arlington, VA 22203
Formerly known as the National Association of Bank Women, FWI is composed of women working in banking and financial services for networking and professional development.

Insurance Professionals of Washington, D.C.
800/766-NAIW
1847 E. 15th Street
Tulsa, OK 74101
This is the local chapter of the National Association of Insurance Women. Membership primarily includes women working in the insurance industry and related fields for the purpose of professional enhancement and networking opportunities.

National Association of Professional Mortgage Women
206/778-6162
PO Box 2016
Edmonds, WA 98020-0999
National association for women working in the mortgage field that offers career development, industry resources and networking events. Contact the national headquarters for local officers.

Women in Housing and Finance (WHF)
703/536-5112
6712 Fisher Avenue
Falls Church, VA 22046
WHF offers monthly luncheons and special interest groups on insurance, securities, and technology. WHF also provides career resources, a job bank and trade seminars.

Women Life Underwriters Confederation
614/882-6934
Blendon Office Park 50085
Pine Creek Drive
Westerville, OH 43081
National organization for women working as underwriters, with a chapter in D.C. Contact the national headquarters for local contacts.

Government

American Federation of Govt. Employees/Women's Dept.
202/737-8700 x6418
80 F Street, NW
Washington, DC 20001-1583

The Women's Department deals with pay equity, sexual harassment, family issues and health care.

American Federation of State, County and Municipal Employees/Women's Rights
202/429-5090, 202/429-1000
1625 L Street, NW
Washington, DC 20036

The Department offers educational opportunities, such as workshops and seminars on issues of interest to women.

American Society for Public Administration/Section on Women in Public Admn.
202/393-7878
1120 G Street, NW
Washington, DC 20005

The Section holds awards ceremonies and offers various networking opportunities for women working in public administration.

Executive Women in Government (EWG)
6400 Naval Ave.
Lanham, MD 20706

EWG is composed of senior executive women in government. Membership is restricted to women in the senior executive service, presidential appointees, and former government professionals for networking events and career enhancement programs.

Federally Employed Women
202/898-0994
1400 Eye Street, NW, Suite 425
Washington, DC 20005-2252

FEW represents women employed in all levels of the federal government, including the military, and offers career training, networking events, a mentor program and other professional development activities, such as seminars on policy and legislative process.

National League of Cities/ Women in Municipal Government
202/626-3000
1301 Pennsylvania Ave., NW, Suite 550
Washington, DC 20004

Membership includes women who are elected or appointed to city positions, such as mayors, city administrators and council members, for the purpose of professional development and support.

Women Executives in State Government
202/628-9374
122 C Street, NW, Suite 840
Washington, DC 20001

Composed of elected and appointed women in the executive branches of state government for the purpose of professional development and networking.

Women in Government
202/333-0825
2600 Virginia Ave., NW, # 709
Washington, DC 20037-1905

Membership includes women elected to state, national and international positions with the government for the purpose of professional training, networking and resource services.

Dr. Sheila E. Widnall
Secretary of the U.S. Air Force

Q. What career steps did you take to get where you are today?
A. After I received a Ph.D. in science from MIT, I was appointed to the faculty as an assistant professor. Nearly three decades later, I had advanced to associate provost of the university. I've served on many boards, panels and committees in government, academia and industry, including the USAF Academy Board of Visitors. In 1993, I was appointed Secretary of the U.S. Air Force.

Q. To what do you attribute your success?
A. I would say my success results from always enjoying what I do. There has been a lot of luck and timing involved, as well. It also came from the willingness to take on additional assignments, volunteering.

Q. What obstacles did you have to overcome along the way?
A. Occasionally, my ideas were not recognized but attributed instead to others. But my main obstacles involved juggling a family and a career, and trying to do a good job with each.

Q. Who are your role models, or who were they earlier in your career?
A. I had six or seven mentors at various stages of my career, but I didn't really have any female role models, except my mother who worked as a juvenile probation officer. In terms of people who were helpful during my career, urging me on, encouraging me and also selecting me for various assignments, I clearly had quite a number of men who were extremely helpful.

Q. What advice would you give other women interested in your profession?
A. "Aim High" and have fun with your work. But most importantly, know that you probably shouldn't follow a career in a straight line. When my direction at MIT seemed a little stymied, I went outside and built a record so that when I returned, I came back at a different level. So I think for me it was a combination of inside-outside success that played off one another.

Women in Government Relations
202/347-5432
1029 Vermont Ave., NW, # 510
Washington, DC 20005
WGR offers job leads, legislative and career training seminars, White House briefings and leadership training. Membership requires sponsorship by a current member.

Women Officials of the National Association of County Officials
202/393-6226
440 First Street, NW
Washington, DC 20001
Comprised of women who serve at the county government level, the group offers professional development, educational seminars and networking opportunities.

Health Care/Pharmaceuticals

American Association of Immunologists/Committee on the Status of Women
301/530-7178
9650 Rockville Pike
Bethesda, MD 20814
Professional membership group for medical doctors and Ph.D.'s working in the field of immunology.

American Association of Women Dentists
312/644-6610
401 North Michigan Ave.
Chicago, IL 60611
Information, support and networking group for women working in the field of dentistry. Contact the national headquarters for local contacts.

American Association of Women Emergency Physicians
919/490-5891
21 West Colony Place, # 150
Durham, NC 27705
The Association offers networking, support and holds its

annual leadership conference in Washington.

American Association for Women Radiologists (AAWR)
703/648-8939
1891 Preston White Drive
Reston, VA 22091
AAWR provides a forum for information exchange and professional development for women working in the field of radiology.

American College of Nurse-Midwives
202/289-0171
818 Conn. Ave., NW, Suite 900
Washington, DC 20005
Support, resource and networking group for people working as nurse-midwives.

American College of Obstetricians and Gynecologists
202/638-5577
409 12th Street, SW
Washington, DC 20024
Support, resource and net-

working group for professionals working in the field of ob/gyn, or a related field.

American Medical Women's Association (AMWA)
703/838-0500
801 N. Fairfax Street, Suite 400
Alexandria, VA 22314
AMWA is composed of women health professionals for networking, professional development and resources.

American Nurses Association
202/ 554-4444
600 Maryland Ave., SW
Washington, DC 20024-2571
Professional support, resource and networking group for people working as registered nurses.

American Pharmaceutical Association (APA)/Committee on Women's Affairs
202/429-7500
2215 Constitution Ave., NW
Washington, DC 20037
APA offers professional development, educational and career opportunities to professionals working in the pharmaceutical industry.

American Public Health Association/Women's Caucus
202/789-5600
1015 15th Street, NW
Washington, DC 20005

The Caucus provides programs, information and educational resources to discuss women's issues within the field of public health.

Association of Women Surgeons
708/655-0392/0391
414 Plaza Drive, Suite 209
Westmont, IL 60559
National association for women surgeons, with a chapter in Maryland. Call the national headquarters for local contacts.

Association for Women Veterinarians
510/471-8379
32205 Allison Drive
Union City, CA 94587
National association for women working in the veterinary field. Call the national headquarters for local contacts.

Association of Women's Health, Obstetrics and Neonatal Nurses
202/662-1600
700 14th Street, NW, Suite 600
Washington, DC 20005
Formerly the Organization for Obstetric, Gynecologic and Neonatal Nurses, AWHONN offers training, support and networking events for professionals working in areas of women's health.

**District of Columbia Nurses
Association (DCNA)**
202/244-2705
5100 Wisconsin Ave., NW
Washington, DC 20016
    DCNA is a regional
support, information, resource
and networking group for
registered nurses working in the
Washington area.

**National Black Nurses
Association (NBNA)**
202/393-6870
1511 K Street, NW, Suite 415
Washington, DC 20005
    NBNA offers networking,
professional development and
career services for the support
and advancement of black
nurses.

Human Resources

**American Society for Training
and Development (ASTD)/
Women's Network**
703/683-8100
1630 Duke Street, Box 1443
Alexandria, VA 22313
    The Women's Network
provides a forum to discuss
issues of interest to women
working in the field of human
resources and training.

Women's HR Network
301/657-2838
3620 Raymond Street
Chevy Chase, MD 20815
    Support and information
group for self-employed women
working in the field of human
resources. The group offers
networking, referrals, resource
sharing and a mentor program.

International

**Association for Women in
Development (AWID)**
202/628-0440
1511 K Street, NW, Suite 825
Washington, DC 20005
    AWID offers networking
conferences and industry-related
information to people working
on international development
issues.

**Association of Women in
International Trade**
202/785-9842
    AWIT offers networking,

career services, international
trade events and professional
development for women working in the field of international
trade.

International Women's Forum
202/775-8917
1146 19th Street, NW, Suite 700
Washington, DC 20036
    Networking and career de-
velopment group for women
working in international affairs.
The Leadership Foundation links
women from around the world.

Organization of Women in International Trade
301/953-0676
1413 K Street, 1st Floor, NW
Washington, DC 20005-3303
OWIT offers professional development forums, an annual conference and access to contacts in international business for trade and business professionals.

Women in Intl. Security
301/405-7612
University of Maryland
College Park, MD 20742
WIIS is a network and professional development group for women in international security

fields, such as foreign and defense policy. WIIS serves as a clearinghouse on international issues.

Women's Foreign Policy Group
202/884-8597
1875 Connecticut Ave., NW
Suite 720
Washington, DC 20009
Provides information, professional development, mentor programs, networking opportunities and research projects for women working in the field of foreign policy.

Legal

American Bar Association Commission on Women in the Profession
202/662-1000
740 15th Street, NW
Washington, DC 20005
The Commission works to improve the status of women in the legal profession through professional development and awareness.

Association of American Law Schools/Women in Legal Education
202/296-8851
1201 Connecticut Ave., # 800
Washington, DC 20036
Membership is composed of law school faculty members across the nation.

International Association of Women Judges (IAWJ)
202/393-0955
815 15th Street, NW, Suite 601
Washington, DC 20005
e-mail: iwjf@aol.com
IAWJ supports women jurists and promotes the number of women judges at all levels of the judiciary.

National Association of Black Women Attorneys
202/637-3570
724 9th Street, NW, Suite 206
Washington, DC 20001
This national organization offers support, professional events, networking opportunities and career resources for black women attorneys.

**National Association of
Women Judges (NAWJ)**
202/393-0222
815 15th Street, NW, Suite 601
Washington, DC 20005
NAWJ supports women currently serving on the bench through networking, research and information.

**National Bar Association/
Women Lawyers Division**
202/842-3900
1225 11th Street, NW
Washington, DC 20001
The Women Lawyers Division promotes professional growth, awards honors and scholarships, and provides a forum for women to address issues pertinent to their gender.

**Women's Bar Association of
the District of Columbia**
202/785-1540
2000 L Street, NW, Suite 510
Washington, DC 20036
Regional group of attorneys, judges and law students that offers career networking events, professional development and career resources, such as a job bank and a job-seekers group that meets weekly.

Media

**American News Women's
Club**
202/332-6770
1607 22nd Street, NW
Washington, DC 20008
Membership includes high-level media professionals and newsworthy people. ANWC offers networking opportunities, seminars and panel discussions and distinguished speakers.

**American Women in Radio
and Television Inc. (AWRT)**
703/506-3290
1650 Tysons Boulevard, # 200
McLean, VA 22102
AWRT consists of women working in the electronic media and related fields for the purpose of professional development, job listings and networking seminars and conventions.

**International Women's Media
Foundation (IWMF)**
202/496-1992
1001 Connecticut Ave., NW,
Suite 1201
Washington, DC 20036
IWMF is mainly composed of women journalists for the purpose of networking, professional exchange, educational programs, career enhancement and leadership.

**National Federation of Press
Women (NFPW)**
913/341-0165
NFPW is composed of women working in press-related positions for the purpose of professional development, networking opportunities and job leads. Contact the national headquarters for local contacts.

Diane Rehm
Talk Show Host
The Diane Rehm Show
WAMU-FM

Q. What career steps did you take to get where you are today?
A. I began my career in radio as a volunteer producer at WAMU-FM. After 10 months, I was hired on a part-time basis and then worked to develop my skills and knowledge about the radio business.

Q. To what do you attribute your success?
A. Hard work, long hours, a supportive mentor, a supportive spouse and good luck.

Q. What obstacles did you have to overcome along the way?
A. Lack of self-confidence.

Q. Who are your role models, or who were they earlier in your career?
A. Irma Aandahl, my first boss, and Susan Harmon, former manager of WAMU-FM.

Q. What advice would you give other women who are interested in your profession?
A. Work hard and learn to be an attentive listener.

Susan Kidd
News Anchor
WRC-TV

Q. What career steps did you take to get where you are today?
A. I started out as a receptionist for a TV station in Atlanta. My first reporting job was in Greensboro, North Carolina. I also worked as a producer and a week-night anchor. From there I went to KTVI-TV in St. Louis as a news anchor. In 1983, I got the anchor job at WRC-TV in D.C.

Q. To what do you attribute your success?
A. My parents. My father was a college professor and my mother, a librarian. I grew up with a lot of books and a big emphasis on education. They set an example for me that I have to work hard to achieve. They defined "successful" as being happy with your career.

Q. What obstacles did you have to overcome along the way?
A. Being black and being a woman in some people's eyes are obstacles, but I have never felt that way. It's never been a problem.

Q. Who are your role models, or who were they earlier in your career?
A. My mentor in this business was the news director in Greensboro who taught me how to write well. He is my mentor, but I didn't model my career after anyone. Back then, there were only a few black network correspondents.

Q. What advice would you give other women interested in your profession?
A. Decide whether you want to be an actress or a journalist. Many young people just want to be on television. If your true interest is journalism, then read everything you can. You can't be a good writer unless you read good writing. Be open to new ideas and work hard to prove yourself.

Kathleen Matthews
News Anchor, WJLA-TV

Q. What career steps did you take to get where you are today?
A. If you had asked me 20 years ago when I graduated with a communications degree from Stanford University whether I'd be the prime time local news anchor in Washington, D.C., I'd say "No." My focus then was on writing and political reporting. My first job was writing editorials for radio, which led to a writing job in TV. I spent five years behind the scenes before asking for a chance to report on-camera as a general assignment news reporter. That eventually led to some opportunities to fill in at the anchor desk and finally the evening news anchor position.

Q. To what do you attribute your success?
A. When I was asked to anchor the evening news, people said, "This is the job you worked hard to get." I responded, "No, I worked hard and this is the job I got."

Q. What obstacles did you have to overcome along the way?
A. Jobs in journalism require long days and odd hours. I worked nights, early mornings and weekends. But the willingness to be where the news happened paid off for me. I've been able to move up within one news organization, get married and have three children along the way.

Q. Who are your role models, or who were they earlier in your career?
A. When I was studying journalism in college, I saw very few women's names in the local newspaper bylines. On television, the first "weather girls" were emerging on-camera. But Barbara Walters was co-hosting the *Today Show* on NBC and was a beacon for many of us.

Q. What advice would you give other women interested in your profession?
A. When I came to Washington searching for work, I was told to start in a small town. Perseverance paid off. Set your sights, work hard and make sure, as Stephen Covey writes, that once you put up your career ladder, it's resting on the building where you want it to be. You may need to shift your priorities and goals as you make your way.

Women in Film and Video
202/232-2254
PO Box 19272
Washington, DC 20036

WIFV consists of women who are active in film, video or related media for networking, and professional and educational support.

Politics

Capitol Hill Women's Political Caucus
202/986-0994
PO Box 599
Longworth House Office Bldg.
Washington, DC 20515

The Caucus provides networking events, professional development, job leads, a legislative hotline, and policy forums for women working in policy or legislative positions.

Democratic Women of Capitol Hill (DWCH)
703/280-4611
8113 Little River Turnpike
Annandale, VA 22003

DWCH functions as a networking, educational and spirit-building group for Democratic women working on Capitol Hill and in other professions.

League of Women Voters
703/522-8196
1229 N. Nash Street
Arlington, VA 22209

The League offers information and resources on candidates, issues, and voting, as well as other political activities and educational opportunities.

National Federation of Republican Women
703/54-9688
124 North Alfred Street
Alexandria, VA 22314

Women's political, education and volunteer arm of the Republican National Party that offers networking, policy forums and a variety of activities.

National Order of Women Legislators (NOWL)
202/337-3565
910 16th Street, NW, Suite 100
Washington, DC 20006

NOWL is composed of current and former women state legislators for the purpose of education, networking and resources.

National Political Congress of Black Women (NPCBW)
202/338-0800
600 New Hampshire Ave., NW
Suite 1125
Washington, DC 20037

NPCBW works to increase the role of African-Americans in the political process through leadership development, mentor programs, political support, advocacy and networking.

National Women's Political Caucus
202/785-1100
1211 Connecticut Ave., NW
Suite 425
Washington, DC 20036
NWPC works to increase the number of women in elected and appointed office in all levels of government through networking and educational opportunities.

Woman's National Democratic Club (WNDC)
202/232-7363
1526 New Hampshire Ave. NW
Washington, DC 20036
Networking, educational and resource group for women in the Democratic party that hosts public policy forums, speakers, social events, community involvement and information.

Psychology/Sociology

American Counseling Assn. Committee on Women
703/823-9800
5999 Stevenson Avenue
Alexandria, VA 22304
The Committee offers career information and educational opportunities as well as programs on gender equity and women's counseling issues.

American Mental Health Counselor Association/ Women's Committee
703/823-9800
5999 Stevenson Ave.
Alexandria, VA 22314
The Women's Committee deals with issues of concern to women working as mental health counselors and female patients.

American Psychiatric Assn./ Committee on Women and Women's Caucus
202/682-6000
1400 K Street, NW
Washington, DC
The Committee focuses on improving the status of women in the psychiatric profession and provides a forum for research and presentation of issues relevant to women.

American Psychological Association/Committee on Women in Psychology
202/336-6044
750 First Street, NE
Washington, DC 20002-4242
The Committee on Women in Psychology offers information, research and support to women working in the field of psychology.

American Sociological Association/Committee on the Status of Women
202/833-3410
1722 N Street, NW
Washington, DC 20036
The Committee works for the inclusion of women in sociological research, faculty and curriculum materials. Publishes a monthly newsletter.

Real Estate

National Association of Women in Construction
800/552-3506, Natl. HQs
Support, network and information group for women working in the field of construction, with a chapter in the D.C. area. Contact the national headquarters office for local contacts.

National Network of Commercial Real Estate Women
913/832-1808/1551, Natl. HQs
National networking group

for women working in all aspects of the real estate industry. Contact the national headquarters for local contacts.

Women's Council of Realtors (WCR)
312/329-8483, Natl. HQs
430 N. Michigan Ave.
Chicago, IL 60611
WCR is a professional support, network and resource group for women working in real estate. Contact the national headquarters for local contacts.

Sales

National Association of Professional Saleswomen
703/538-4390
712 W. Broad Street, Suite 5
Falls Church, VA 22046

Networking, career development and support group for women working in sales. The group offers a job bank, professional and social events, and monthly meetings.

Science and Technology

American Association for the Advancement of Science (AAAS)/National Network of Women in Science
202/326-6670
1333 H Street, NW
Washington, DC 20005
The Network promotes the advancement and awareness of women in the field of science.

American Astronomical Society/Committee on the Status of Women in Astronomy
202/328-2010
2000 Florida Ave., NW, # 400
Washington, DC 20009
The Committee functions as a resource, support and information forum that represents and promotes women astronomers.

Anna K. Behrensmeyer
Research Paleobiologist
National Museum of Natural History

Q. What career steps did you take to get where you are today?
A. Undergraduate major in geology; Ph.D. in geology, specializing in paleontology, from Harvard University; post-doctoral fellowships at U.C. Berkeley and Yale University; took a curator position at the National Museum of Natural History in 1981. Field work over the years includes taphonomy and paleoecology of fossiliferous deposits in the Turkana Basin, the Tugen Hills, Kanjera, and Olorgesailie in Kenya; study of fossil bone accumulations and Cretaceous plant-bearing rocks in North America; geological research at Lothagam Hill, Kenya; taphonomy and sedimentology in Miocene deposits in northern Pakistan; and study of modern vertebrate bone preservation in Amboseli Park, Kenya, and rivers in western North America.

Q. To what do you attribute your success?
A. Persistence; hard work; determination to excel; some great, inspiring teachers and colleagues; very supportive family, especially my mother; and curiosity! The thrill of discovering new things about life on earth.

Q. What obstacles did you have to overcome along the way?
A. Prejudice in graduate school about women doing field work. That was in the late 1960s and early 1970s.

Q. Who are your role models, or who were they earlier in your career?
A. Women teachers, from first grade through junior high; my mother and aunts; a few successful older female colleagues in geology and paleontology.

Q. What advice would you give other women who are interested in your profession?
A. Get the best undergraduate science education you can; pick a graduate school with exciting programs and people; and don't give up as long as you are excited by science. Know that there is time to do what you want, including a family.

Martha Krebs
Director, Office of Energy
Research
U.S. Dept. of Energy

Q. What career steps did you take to get where you are today?
A. After receiving a Ph.D. in physics from Catholic University, I began work as an analyst for the Library of Congress. I then became a science consultant for the House Committee on Science and Technology, and progressed to the position of staff director. From there I began work as an associate laboratory director at Lawrence Berkeley Laboratory in California. In 1993, I was appointed director of the Office of Energy Research.

Q. To what do you attribute your success?
A. I focus on the problem at hand and not how I may be perceived by my colleagues. I try to work for my colleagues' success both above and below me. I have a stake in the advancement of our larger institution.

Q. Who are your role models or who were they earlier in your career?
A. First and foremost was my mother who believed I could do anything I set my mind to. A physics teacher in college had an outstanding ability to speak of ccmplicated concepts in vivid terms that grounded them in everyday life. This has been critical to my success.

Q. What obstacles did you have to overcome along the way?
A. The first obstacle was to refocus myself on getting my doctorate after my son was born. The second obstacle was to insist that I receive appropriate compensation as I advanced in my career. For someone with a Ph.D. in physics, I have chosen an untraditional path. I moved early into policy, management and politics rather than spending much time practicing science.

Q. What advice would you give other women interested in your profession?
A. Gain substantive competence in some field or discipline. Build on that competence with communication and interpersonal skills. Work with people who can teach you something and work for their success as well as your own. Look for mentors (men are okay) and colleagues who share.

**American Chemical
Society/Women Chemists
Committee**
202/872-4600
1155 16th Street, NW
Washington, DC 20036
    The Women Chemists Committee works to promote women in the chemical field and monitor their status.

**American Physical Society/
Committee on the Status of
Women in Physics**
301/530-7164
1 Physics Ellipse
College Park, MD 20740-3844
    Research, support, information and network for women working in the field of physics.

**American Physiological
Society/Women in
Physiology Committee**
301/530-7164
9650 Rockville Pike
Bethesda, MD 20814-3991
    The Committee serves and promotes women in the field of physiology by offering information and educational forums and industry-related events.

**American Society of Bio-
Chemistry and Molecular
Biology/Committee on Equal
Opportunities for Women**
301/530-7145
9650 Rockville Pike
Bethesda, MD 20814
    Supports and promotes women in the field of bio-chemistry and molecular biology.

**American Society for Cell
Biology/Women in Cell Biology
Committee**
301/530-7153
9650 Rockville Pike
Bethesda, MD 20814
    The Committee promotes the interests and development of women in cell biology through publications, awards and events.

**American Society for Microbi-
ology/Committee on the Status
of Women in Microbiology**
202/737-3600
1325 Massachusetts Ave., NW
Washington, DC 20005
    The Committee provides support and educational services for women working in the field of microbiology.

**American Statistical Assn.
(ASA)/Committee on Women
in Statistics**
703/684-1221
1429 Duke Street
Alexandria, VA 22314
    The Committee works to increase the role of women in the field of statistics by encouraging publication and providing educational support.

**Association of American
Geographers/Committee on
the Status of Women in
Geography**
202/234-1450
1710 16th Street, NW
Washington, DC 20009
    Support, network and information resource for women working in the field of geography.

Association for Women in Mathematics (AWM)
301/405-7892
4114 Computer and Space
Science Bldg.
University of Maryland
College Park, MD 20742-2461
AWM is composed of mathematicians for the purpose of support and promotion of women mathematicians through awareness, career enhancement, professional resources and development.

Association for Women in Science (AWIS)
202/326-8940, 800/886-AWIS
1522 K Street, NW, Suite 820
Washington, DC 20005
e-mail: awis@awis.org
http://www.awis.org/awis
AWIS is composed of women representing all levels and areas of the science industry along with science students for networking opportunities, science resources, networking events and discounts on publications.

Biophysical Society/Committee on Profl. Opps. for Women
301/530-7114
9650 Rockville Pike
Bethesda, MD 20814
The Committee offers networking, resources, symposiums and a mentor program for women in the biophysical industry.

National Academy of Sciences Committee on Women in Science and Engineering
202/334-2709
2101 Constitution Ave., NW
Room TJ2017
Washington, DC 20418
The Committee supports and promotes women in the fields of science and engineering by providing resources and events.

The Society of Woman Geographers
202/546-9228
415 East Capitol Street, SE
Washington, DC 20003
The Society acts as a forum for professionals and serious enthusiasts in the fields of exploration and travel to present experiences and exchange ideas. The Society's Capitol Hill headquarters houses a museum, which displays the changing works of Society members.

Society of Women Engineers
212/509-9577
120 Wall Street
New York, NY 10005
The Society provides support, networking opportunities and resources for women working or interested in the field of engineering. Contact the national headquarters for local contacts.

Women in Aerospace
202/547-9451
922 Pennsylvania Ave., SE
Washington, DC 20003
Women in Aerospace offers networking opportunities, career resources and professional development to women working in the field of aerospace.

Women in Technology, Inc.
703/205-0930
2230 Gallows Road, Suite 130
Dunn Loring, VA 22027

Women in Technology, Inc. provides professional development and networking to women working in the field of high technology.

Sports

National Association for Girls and Women in Sport
703/476-3450
1900 Association Drive
Reston, VA 22091-1599

NAGWS offers professional development, educational opportunities, networking and sports-related events to women involved with sports.

Trade Professions

Institute of Electrical and Electronic Engineers/Task Force on Women and Minorities
202/785-0017
1828 L Street, NW, Suite 1202
Washington, DC 20036
The Task Force provides support and resources for women working as engineers.

National Association of Home Builders, Women's Council
202/822-0433, 800/368-5242
1201 15th Street, NW
Washington, DC 20005-2800
The Council promotes and supports the professional development and networking needs of women working in the home-building industry.

National Association of Minority Contractors (NAMC)
202/347-8259
1333 F Street, NW, Suite 500

Washington, DC 20004
NAMC offers training, education and special contracting opportunities to minority- and women-owned business owners.

National Association of Women in Construction
800/552-3506
327 South Adams Street
Ft. Worth, TX 76104
This group offers professional assistance and neworking to women working in the field of construction. Contact the national headquarters for local officers.

National Network of Commercial Real Estate Women
913/832-1808/1551, Natl. HQs
National networking group for women working in all facets of real estate, including construction.

Professional Women in Construction
212/687-0610
342 Madison Ave., Suite 451
New York, NY 10173

This group offers networking, support, resources and professional development to women working in all areas of the construction industry. Call the national headquarters for local contacts.

Women Construction Owners and Executives (WCOE)
202/745-9263, 800/788-3548
1615 New Hampshire Ave.
Washington, DC

WCOE promotes women working in the construction industry through education, events, information exchange and networking opportunities. Women have access to a credit union and reduced-rate loans.

Transportation

National Association of Railway Business Women
513/576-0902

National network and information group for women working in jobs associated with the railway. Call the national headquarters for local contacts.

Professional Women Controllers (PWC)
800/232-9PWC

PWC is a network, support and information group for women working in the field of air traffic control.

Women's Transportation Seminar (WTS)
617/367-3272

WTS offers monthly luncheons, tours of transportation-related sites and informal networking events and job leads for women working in transportation. Call the national headquarters for local contacts.

Unions

AFL-CIO/Standing Committee on Salaried and Professional Women
202/638-0320
815 16th Street, NW, Suite 707
Washington, DC 20006

The Committee focuses on the needs of women in technical occupations, such as pay equity, sex discrimination and ERA.

Alexandra Armstrong
CFP, Chairman
Armstrong, Welch & Macintyre, Inc.

Q. What career steps did you take to get where you are today?
A. I worked in the research department of a New York Stock exchange firm, where I eventually worked for one of the woman partners and got my brokerage license. When the same partner left to start her own firm, I went with her. At the age of 43, I decided to start my own firm. Then the market crashed and I had to make some changes. Fourteen years later I still own a financial planning/investment advisory firm.

Q. To what do you attribute your success?
A. A good liberal arts education; having a series of good mentors; continuing to expand my knowledge base; tenacity; good health; being single; willing to delegate authority: remembering to thank people for their help; being active in my professional association; communicating well to the press; being active in the community; ability to get on with people; having high standards; target marketing; writing a book.

Q. What obstacles did you have to overcome along the way?
A. My own fear of success. Initially I thought I might lose my femininity if I were successful. I also had to learn how men think. Men do think differently on many issues and there was a learning process.

Q. Who are your role models, or who were they earlier in your career?
A. Two of the female partners at the first brokerage firm I worked. Well before the debate started about "can you have it all?" these two women were successful in their careers, well dressed, articulate and fond of their families.

Q. What advice would you give other women interested in your profession?
A. Have a good educational background; be comfortable writing and speaking; be willing to work long hours; be able to adapt to change easily; realize you can't start at the top; acknowledge that success requires sacrifice; don't let adversity get you down; be responsive to your clients.

Coalition of Labor Union Women (CLUW)
202/466-4610
1126 16th Street, NW
Washington, DC 20036
   CLUW provides professional development, information, speakers forums and networking for women union members.

United Food and Commercial Workers International Union/Women's Affairs
202/223-3111
1775 K Street, NW
Washington, DC 20006
   Union for professionals who work in the food and service industries.

Working Mothers

Mother's Access to Careers at Home (MATCH)
703/205-9664
PO Box 123
Annandale, VA 22003
   Network, information and support group for mothers who have home-based businesses, including monthly meetings and lunch speakers.

Working Mother's Network
410/465-0183
1511 K Street, NW, Suite 428
Washington, DC 20005
   The Network holds support and networking events, and provides resources to working mothers to meet the needs of work and family. The Network is affiliated with the Women's Information Network.

Writing/Publishing

International Women's Writing Guild
212/737-7536
PO Box 810, Gracie Station
New York, NY 10028
   This national organization has many members in the Washington, D.C. chapter. Call the national headquarters for local contacts.

Women's National Book Association
703/587-4023
3101 Ravensworth Place
Alexandria, VA 22302
http://www.bentoni.com/wnba
   WNBA offers networking, professional development, career resources and support to women who have an interest in books or publishing, either as a profession or as a personal hobby.

2

Women's Career Guide to D.C.

Christine Onyango, Consulting Editor

Washington, D.C., has one of the best career markets for women in terms of job opportunities and wages. At last count, nearly one million women living in the nation's capital were employed, or 67 percent of the area's female residents, according to the U.S. Bureau of Labor Statistics. Studies also show that women tend to hold higher positions in D.C. and are paid more for their work than women in other parts of the country. These statistics should not seem too shocking. In fact, the D.C. job market has traditionally been a good friend to women. During World Wars I and II, women poured into Washington, D.C., to answer a call for duty. After the wars ended, many women chose to maintain careers in the nation's capital. Today, Washington's job market continues to offer women opportunities that are hard to match in other metropolitan areas. For one, there is a wide variety of career options. Where else can you find such a vast mixture of government, private and nonprofit jobs in all areas of interest? In D.C. you can work in a Congressional office, advocate for a cause you believe in, or choose from hundreds of thousands of jobs with the federal government.

Even though the job climate in Washington is attractive for women, unemployment and career transition remain a fact of life, especially with the '90s trend of downsizing. Fortunately, there are a number of job resources, training centers and networking groups to assist women in their job search. Whether you want to work on Capitol Hill, with the government, or in the private sector, there are literally hundreds of resources that can help lead you to the job. This chapter will help you locate the resources and programs that may be crucial in your job search, whether you are looking for your first job in Washington, D.C., or are wanting to improve your job status.

Career and Employment Programs for Women

Most resources in this section provide job banks, career development programs, conferences and career counseling. However, some offer training programs, such as Wider Opportunities for Women, which trains women in nontraditional professions. You will notice the inclusion of various women's centers in the Washington area, which should not be neglected during a job search.

Alexandria Office on Women
703/838-5030
110 N. Royal Street, Alexandria, VA 22314
The Alexandria Office on Women offers resources, programs and events for women wanting to improve or change careers. The Office provides an employment networking group, workshops on the job search process, a career changers program and counseling. Programs and services are arranged over the phone. This is not a walk-in center.

CASA of Maryland Center for Employment and Training
301/431-4177
734 University Blvd., East, Silver Spring, MD 20901
CASA offers a weekly information, educational and support group for Hispanic women called Mujeres de Hoy. The group meets on Mondays to discuss career and personal issues.

The Harrison Center for Career Education/YWCA
202/628-5672
624 Ninth Street, NW, 4th Floor, Washington, DC 20001
The Harrison Center offers three career training programs: the Non-traditional Employment for Women Training Program (NEW), a three-week course that trains women in traditionally male-dominated vocations, such as construction and transportation; the Practical Nursing Program, a 12-month program that prepares students for the national licensing exam to become a nurse or a physician assistant; and the Home Health Aide Program, which prepares students for the certification exam to become a home health aide.

Fairfax County Office for Women
703/324-5730
12000 Government Center Parkway, Suite 318, Fairfax, VA 22035
The Fairfax County Office for Women is a career resource and life skills center that offers a job bank, reference library, networking opportunities, career counseling, workshops and conferences. "Career

Television news anchors and reporters donate their clothing to raise money for *Suited for Change*, a group that helps low-income women succeed on job interviews.

Focus" is a seven-week workshop that helps women explore career options and establish career goals. The Office has a reentry program and publishes the *Job Loss Survival Guide*.

Jewish Social Service Agency/Jewish Vocational Services (JVS)
301/881-3700
6123 Montrose Road, Rockville, MD 20852
JVS offers an eight-week career assessment workshop, called *Vocational Opportunities for Women*, that helps women clarify career goals through group discussion, goal assessment, personality typing and skills evaluation. The Vocational Services also provides career counseling and other social service programs.

Montgomery County Commission for Women
301/279-1800
255 North Washington Street, Rockville, MD 20850
Montgomery County Commission for Women is a counseling and career development center primarily for Montgomery County residents. Job seekers have access to employment listings, career and personal counseling, career workshops, and a variety of programs, such as job search seminars. Out-of-county residents are charged higher fees.

Prince William County Office for Women
703/792-6611
Job Search: 703/792-6095
4370 Ridgewood Center Drive, Suite D, Woodbridge, VA 22192
The Office for Women offers a small employment center for women, which includes a job database and computer training courses. Women can access the database, "Job Search," that contains 15,000 government jobs in the D.C. area and elsewhere in the nation. The Commission also offers computer training courses. Appointments are required.

Suited for Change
202/293-0351
1712 I Street, NW, Suite B-100, Washington, DC 20006
Suited for Change is a not-for-profit organization that helps low-income women succeed on job interviews by providing career clothing and professional development training, such as interview techniques. Services are available at no charge, but women must have a referral, be seeking a job, and have completed a job training program.

Wider Opportunities for Women (WOW)
202/638-3143
815 15th Street, NW, Suite 916, Washington, DC 20005
WOW helps women break into nontraditional careers by providing on-site training, a career resource center and job placement. WOW offers courses in construction, machine repair, mechanics and other trades. WOW also offers basic literacy programs. There is no charge for any of these services. The only requirement is that women have the desire to work in the trade industry. WOW provides career counseling, employment information and a job bank to help women secure a job in their new profession.

Women Work! The National Network for Women's Employment
202/467-6346, 800/235-2732
1625 K Street, NW, # 300, Washington, DC 20006
Women Work! is a network of education, training and employment programs for women who are entering or reentering the workforce, or desiring to advance their career. Formerly known as the National Displaced Homemakers Network, Women Work! helps women achieve economic self-sufficiency through career resources, referrals, training and job leads. The network also provides a variety of job and family-related information, such as fact sheets on child support and health insurance continuation.

The Women's Center
703/281-2657
133 Park Street, NE, Vienna, VA 22180
The Women's Center is a career development and counseling center. Career resources include a job bank, job search workshops, a library of publications and activity listings and career counseling. The Center offers a program for displaced homemakers and a mentoring program called ICAN, The Information and Career Advisory Network. ICAN matches job seekers with middle management to top-level women for advice and guidance. The Center also offers a wide variety of professional development seminars and workshops on such topics as launching a job search, business writing and assertiveness training. Career testing is also offered, including the Myers Briggs Type Indicator (MBTI).

The Women's Center of Prince William County
703/281-4928, ext. 397
Pinekirk Presbyterian Church
13428 Dumfries Road, Manassas, VA 22111
This walk-in career and personal development center is open Saturdays and Wednesdays. The Center offers job listings and other resources. It operates on a drop-in basis and is not staffed.

The Women's Center and Referral Service
301/937-5265
3215 Powder Mill Road, Adelphi, MD 20783
This all-volunteer group offers programs, networks and support groups. It operates by appointment only and offers career workshops, referrals for professional services, community resources and a library. It also offers career testing, such as Myers Briggs. The Center sponsors the Business Advisory Council (BAC), which provides a forum for women business owners to share information. The Center cosponsors *FemNet*, an electronic bulletin board that can be accessed by calling 301/937-5266.

Getting a Job in Public Policy

Nearly every job in Washington, D.C., is associated with public policy. Whether it's a private company, a nonprofit organization or the government, there are a variety of jobs in public policy. Law firms, special-interest groups, research institutes, consulting firms, trade or professional associations, media outlets, federal agencies, or the U.S. Congress all have need of employees to perform policy work. Some policy

Working in a Congressional Office: What's Available

Chief of Staff/Administrative Assistant (AA). Acts as the Member's chief policy advisor; develops and implements all policy objectives, strategies and operating plans for the office; manages the functions of the office and the activities of staff members; acts as the Member's chief liaison.

Legislative Director. Advises the Member on all legislative issues; oversees the development of policy positions and legislative initiatives; manages and supervises the office's legislative staff; monitors legislative activity.

Legislative Assistant. Develops and plans legislative initiatives; monitors legislative developments; writes Floor speeches for the Member; meets with special interest groups and constituents on behalf of the Member.

Legislative Correspondent. Researches and responds to letters from constituents; provides administrative support to the legislative assistants.

Office Manager. Supervises the office staff; monitors personnel matters and compliance with rules of Congress; provides employee support services for staff; responsible for the maintenance of the office.

Press Secretary/Communications Director. Manages and coordinates media and other communications activities; acts as the formal spokesperson for the Member; creates media plans; writes speeches; writes op eds.

Scheduler/Executive Assistant. Schedules meetings and events; prepares itineraries for the Member; briefs the Member on all scheduled events.

Staff Assistant/Receptionist. Greets visitors to the office; answers the telephone; responds to constituent requests; performs general office duties, such as photocopying.

Systems Administrator. Maintains all office computers and troubleshoots problems; maintains the information management system for the office.

Intern. Assists with handling correspondence and office administration; performs research; attends hearings.

Source: Capitol Hill Women's Political Caucus

positions are more lobby oriented and focus on influencing the direction of policy by providing information and research to lawmakers, whereas other positions focus on monitoring, analyzing and reporting on national issues.

The key to getting a policy job is developing an area of expertise. Read as much as you can on a given topic and know what's going on in that policy area, not just in Washington, but across the nation as well. You can also start with this book to find the types of organizations that employ public policy positions. Special interest groups that focus on women's issues are listed in chapter 6. Women's political groups are listed in chapter 5. You can also find some good networking resources for women listed in chapter 1 under the subheadings Government, International and Politics. Also, refer to the following three sections in this chapter: Working on Capitol Hill, Getting a Job with the Government, and The International Job Market.

Working on Capitol Hill

Although competition is fierce, there are positions in more than 500 Congressional offices, with legislative committees and in leadership offices and support agencies. Positions can also be found with the two major political parties, the Democratic National Committee and the Republican National Committee, and through the parties' campaign committees. Washington is also home to thousands of special interest lobbying groups and satellite offices for public and private companies from all over the country, which employ lobbyists and legislative representatives to monitor and influence national policy. In addition, most Washington-based organizations, companies and associations have a legislative department that employs lawyers, policy workers and lobbyists to work on legislative activities.

To secure a position in Congress, contact the job placement offices at the U.S. Senate and the U.S. House of Representatives. These services help match potential employees to Congressional offices and committees with job openings. You can also find job listings in the legislative publications *Roll Call* and *The Hill,* and in the *House Action Reports.* Other good resources are the Democratic and Republican party headquarters and their campaign committees.

Capitol Hill Women's Political Caucus (CHWPC)
202/986-0994
PO Box 599, Longworth
Washington, DC 20515

CHWPC is a career, development and networking group for women working on Capitol Hill or in a policy position.

**Democratic Congressional
Campaign Committee**
202/863-1500
430 South Capitol Street, SE
Washington, DC 20003
   Provides job bank and resume referral service.

**Democratic National
Committee (DNC)**
202/863-8000
430 South Capitol Street, SE
Washington, DC 20003
   Provides job bank and resume referral service.

**National Republican
Congressional Committee**
202/479-7000
320 First Street, SE
Washington, DC 20003
   Provides job bank and resume referral service.

**Republican National Commit-
tee (RNC)**
202/863-8500
310 1st Street, SE
Washington, DC 20003
   Provides job bank and resume referral service.

**U.S. House of Representatives
Placement Office**
202/226-6731
3rd & D Streets, SW, Room 219
Washington, DC 20515
   Register with this office to
gain access to job listings in the
U.S. House of Representatives.

U.S. Senate Placement Office
202/224-9167
142 Hart Senate Bldg.
Room 142B
Washington, DC 20510
   Job seekers can register with
this office to gain access to job
listings in the U.S. Senate.

Roll Call
202/289-4900
900 2nd Street, NE
Washington, DC 20002

The Hill
202/628-8500
733 15th St., NW, Suite 1140
Washington, DC 20005

House Action Reports
202/546-3900
316 Penn. Ave., SE, Suite 301
Washington, DC 20003

Getting a Job with the Government

Federal jobs are known for offering competitive wages, good working conditions and job stability. To get information about federal jobs, start with
the U.S. Office of Personnel Management (OPM), which provides job
listings, application procedures, testing information and special job requirements.

Three Steps to Getting a Federal Job

STEP 1: Obtain job and employment information.

- Call the Federal Information Job Line at 202/606-2700, which provides information on application procedures, job vacancies, special requirements and exams. You can also call the 24-hour automated job information lines at individual federal departments.

- Use the self-service computers at OPM which allow job seekers to access employment information and application procedures. OPM is located at 1900 E Street, NW, Room 1416.

- Use your computer to access the Federal Job Opportunities Board to obtain information on the federal employment process and current job opportunities. Using your modem, dial the bulletin board at 912/757-3100. It can also be accessed through the Internet via Telnet at FJOB.OPM.GOV and File Transfer Protocol at FTP.FJOB.OPM.GOV.

- Use the FedFax system, by calling 202/606-2600, to access information about federal employment through your facsimile machine.

STEP 2: Obtain the Vacancy Announcement.
Once you have located a job that interests you, the next step is getting specific information about the application process and what the position entails, such as application deadlines and testing requirements. You can get copies of job announcements and application packages from most federal employment information systems. By calling the Federal Job Information Line and most automated information lines, you can listen to a listing of job announcements or have the listing faxed. You can also access vacancy announcements by using the self-service computers at OPM or by using the Federal Job Opportunities Board.

STEP 3: Apply for the position.
You can apply for most jobs with a resume or by filling out the Optional Application for Federal Employment (OF 612). Depending on the position, you may be required to fill out additional forms. Most forms will ask for personal information, education, work experience, and other job-related qualifications and skills. Some administrative positions may require a clerical test, which is offered weekly at locations throughout the metropolitan area. Exam information is available on the 24-hour Job Information Line.

Source: U.S. Office of Personnel Management

Office of Personnel Management (OPM)
202/606-2700, 24-Hour Job Information Line
1900 E Street, NW, Room 1416
Washington, DC 20415
Hours: M-F, 8 a.m. to 4 p.m.

OPM provides a variety of federal employment information through its automated phone system, facsimile service, computer bulletin board and on-site computers. Job seekers can use any of these methods to obtain job listings and descriptions, forms, application procedures and examination information. Job seekers can visit OPM to access all types of employment information from self-service computers. If you have your own computer and a modem, then the information can be accessed through the Federal Job Opportunities Board by dialing 912/757-3100. OPM also provides employment information through its FedFax service. By calling 202/606-2600, you can request information be sent via fax on a variety of topics, such as *Applying for a Federal Job* and *Federal Wage Grade Pay Scale*. To find out what information is available, start by selecting the *Index of Available Documents*.

Federal Job Information Lines

Many federal agencies have a 24-hour automated phone service to assist job seekers with vacant positions and application procedures.

Agriculture Dept.	
Food and Consumer Service	703/305-1474
Forest Service	703/235-2730
Central Intelligence Agency	800/562-7242
Commerce Dept.	202/482-5138
Bureau of the Census	301/457-4499
International Trade Admn.	202/482-1533
Natl. Institute of Stds. and Tech.	301/926-4851
Patent and Trademark Office	703/305-4221
Corporation for National Service	202/565-2800
Defense Dept./Dept. of the Army	703/325-8841
Defense Logistics Agency	703/274-7372
Energy Dept.	202/586-4333
Environmental Protection Agency	202/260-5055
Federal Communications Cmsn.	202/418-0101
Federal Deposit Insurance Corp.	202/942-3540
Federal Emergency Mgmt. Agency	202/646-3244
Federal Trade Commission	202/326-2020
General Accounting Office	202/512-6092

General Services Administration	202/273-3577
Health and Human Services Dept.	202/619-2560
Food and Drug Admn.	301/443-1969
National Institutes of Health	301/496-2403
Housing and Urban Development	202/708-3203
Interior Dept.	
U.S. Geological Survey	703/648-7676
Fish and Wildlife	703/358-2120
Justice Dept.	202/514-6818
Federal Bureau of Investigation	202/324-3674
Immigration and Naturalization Svc.	202/514-4301
Merit Systems Protection Board	202/254-8013
National Aeronautics and Space Admn.	202/358-1546
National Archives and Records Admn.	301/713-6760
National Endowment for the Arts	202/682-5799
National Endowment for the Humanities	202/606-8281
National Labor Relations Board	202/273-3980
National Library of Medicine	301/496-2403
National Science Foundation	703/306-0080
Office of Management and Budget	202/395-2892
Smithsonian Institution	202/287-3102
State Department	202/647-7284
Transportation Dept.	202/366-5668
Federal Aviation Admn.	202/267-8007
Treasury Dept./Internal Revenue Service	202/622-6340
U.S. Information Agency	202/619-4539
U.S. Postal Service	800/JOB-USPS
Veterans Affairs	202/273-5799
Voice of America	202/619-0909

Source: U.S. Office of Personnel Management

The International Job Market

Washington, D.C., is a hub of international activity. Not only is Washington home to a number of foreign embassies, but also to international special- interest organizations, businesses, research institutes, charitable and voluntary groups, consulting firms, educational and development groups. Getting a job in the international sector requires much more than determination and tenacity. Employers often require applicants to have an advanced degree, knowledge of more than one language, experience abroad and research skills. To find an international job, start with the membership groups listed in this section. Most provide job listings and leads, access to conferences, professional development and networking opportunities.

Association for Women in Development (AWID)
202/628-0440
1511 K Street, NW, Suite 825
Washington, DC 20005
Membership organization for professionals working in international development for networking, conferences, job leads and industry resources.

Association of Women in International Trade (AWIT)
202/785-9842
AWIT offers networking, career services and professional development for women working in the field of international trade. AWIT offers a job bank and a variety of trade events.

National Council for International Health
202/833-5900
1701 K Street, NW
Washington, DC 20006
Offers networking, career resources and job listings for jobs in international health.

Organization of Women in International Trade (OWIT)
301/953-0676
1413 K Street, 1st Floor, NW
Washington, DC 20005-3303
OWIT offers development forums, an annual conference, a job bank and monthly networking events.

Society for International Development (SID)
202/884-8590
1875 Connecticut Ave., NW
Washington, DC 20009-5728
SID posts international job vacancies in its newsletter, holds job fairs and other career resources.

Washington International Trade Association
202/293-4193
2025 I Street, NW, Suite 822
Washington, DC 20006
Offers networking, job leads and professional development.

Women in International Security
301/405-7612
Center for Intl. Security Studies
University of Maryland
College Park, MD 20742
WIIS serves as a network and career resource for women in the security field. WIIS also serves as a clearinghouse on international issues.

International Career Employment Opportunities
804/985-6444
Route 2, Box 305
Stanardville, VA 22973
Biweekly publication lists international job vacancies, including government, nonprofit groups and internships.

Job Search Strategies

Landing your first job in Washington may be difficult and time-consuming, but it's certainly not impossible. However, maneuvering your way into "the loop" could take months, even for a seasoned professional, as competition is fierce and jobs are limited. The good news is that once you're "in" you immediately become accessible to job leads and networking opportunities that will help you secure a better job later on. As you've probably already discovered, so much of hiring is done by word of mouth in the nation's capital, especially positions on Capitol Hill. Oftentimes, jobs are not publicly advertised, but are circulated through Washington's intricate networking system. And that's exactly where you want to be, connected to that system.

However, there are some things you can do to maximize your job marketability. Securing a job in Washington entails being prepared to go the extra mile—Washington style! And that simply means meeting people all the time and asking for help. It's a combination of networking, job-probing, circulating your resume and never giving up. It means going on informational interviews, participating in mentor programs, joining professional business groups or even working as an intern or volunteer to get your foot in the door. Here are some guidelines that could put you on the fast track to breaking into the Washington job market.

Networking

Networking is the art of meeting others for mutual career benefit. Let's face it, networking is the fast track to getting a job in Washington. It's making contacts, asking for more contacts and meeting people all the time. Sound difficult? It shouldn't when you consider that one of the first questions often asked in social situations is, "Where do you work?" This is now your job, to ask the same question, over and over again.

If you're new to the city or just beginning your career, it is critical to be prepared. Always have a resume on hand because you never know who you are going to meet or when. And when you do make contact, always ask for the person's business card. If they seem receptive, let them know you will call them in the very near future. That way when you do call, your chances will be greater of getting them on the phone or getting a return call.

Even though there is no sure-fire recipe for networking, look at it this way. It's simply the art of meeting people, finding out what they do for a living, who they know, and, ultimately, how they can help you profession-

professionally. If you're still unsure about how to initiate or expand your network, here are some ways to get started.

Make a list. Draw up a list of anyone and everyone you know in the D.C. area. Contact each person and explain your situation. Ask if they know of others who can be of assistance in your job search, or if they know of any job openings or career resources that would be helpful.

Join a business group. Join an association or networking group. There is an endless supply of professional groups that offer networking opportunities and career resources. These groups are great places to hear about job openings and meet others within your profession. Refer to chapter 1 for listings of networking groups for women.

Get political. Obviously, there are a number of political groups and events to choose from in the nation's capital—both partisan and nonpartisan. In a city that revolves around politics, you are sure to forge some strong bonds based on shared beliefs. Refer to chapter 5 for a listing of political groups of interest to women. You can find additional groups in local political guides.

Get active. Join an athletic league, a model of D.C. networking at its best. Softball and volleyball during the summer make way for football and indoor sports during the winter. Aside from bonding with your teammates on the court and field, you will likely cultivate some professional allies.

Volunteer. Volunteer your time to participate in a charitable event or become involved in a needy cause. There are many service and social groups looking for people to help take on a leadership responsibility. Refer to chapter 19 for volunteer opportunities in the community. While being a Good Samaritan and feeling the internal rewards, you might just meet others to include in your job-search network.

Improve your skills. Take a professional enhancement course. Courses on policy or legislative process are always readily available. Or how about a class in writing, editing or computers? Professional education will not only make you more marketable in the workforce, but it will also put you in touch with others who share your interests or expertise.

Join a special interest group. Washington is home to numerous special interest groups, such as the Children's Defense Fund, the Cystic Fibrosis

Preparing for a Job Search
by
Nan Siemer

The key to job-search success is being prepared, even at times when you're not actively looking for a job. Here are some ways to help you become more prepared for the inevitable.

Network before you need the connections. Too many people call their connections only when they need something. Call your professional contacts just to say hello. Don't forget that networking is give and take.

Be receptive to employment inquiries. Don't dismiss employment opportunities just because you already have a job. It may be worth your while to at least talk about the position. If you answer by suggesting an offer be made which you can't refuse, the request may become an offer.

Keep your resume up-to-date. Update your resume each time you win an award, join a professional group or gain new responsibilities at work.

Keep other job-related materials up to date. Keep all of your professional materials current, such as professional memberships, subscriptions, licenses, portfolios, or audio or video audition tapes.

Be aware of the latest developments in your field. It's important that you not only be aware of new developments within your company, but also within your industry. Read trade journals and talk with colleagues about new developments and trends.

Polish your job-seeking skills. Research possible job opportunities and decide which ones to pursue. Practice interviewing and negotiating techniques.

Be creative with your job search. Personnel departments and newspaper advertisements produce minimal results. Instead, get to know your industry and the people who run it. Get one-on-one with the people who do the hiring. Be personable, yet assertive.

Nan Siemer is a career strategist who lectures throughout the D.C. metropolitan area on job search strategies and negotiation skills.

Foundation and the Sierra Club. You will find that most of these groups are easily accessible and charge nominal membership fees. You are sure to find endless opportunities to participate in events and fundraisers that will likely yield invaluable networking opportunities.

Try something new. Get out and do something new. See an exhibit at one of Washington, D.C.'s many museums. Take a foreign language class or an art course. Attend a lecture series. Do something you ordinarily would not do. You never know who you might meet along the way.

Schedule Informational Interviews

Informational interviews are an excellent way to meet top-notch professionals within your career field without the added pressures of being considered for a job. The informational interview is a way to meet decision makers and ask for their assistance face-to-face. And it gives you the chance to conduct the interview. You are there to ask questions and learn, so come prepared with a list of questions. What often happens is that during the informational interview, the person offers you some pertinent advice or at best tells you of a job opening he or she has heard about recently. Either way, you win. Because there is no job available, the interview is more informal, relaxed and conversational. That works to your advantage because you can ask questions that would be considered inappropriate in a regular job interview. And it gives you a chance to shine while also getting to know the person and the profession.

There are a few standard rules of the informational interview process. The first is never ask for a job. Remember, the interview is for information only. Your primary purpose is to gather information and make professional contacts. You do not want the person to feel any pressure. Another rule that should not be neglected is that of requesting more contacts. Near the end of the interview (or if an appropriate time comes up sooner), ask if the person could provide you with more contacts to help you with your job search. You could say something like, "You have been so helpful. Do you know of anyone else who I can contact that might be willing to talk with me?" Before leaving the interview, make sure you leave a resume, and don't forget to follow up with a thank-you note.

Join a Professional Group

There are thousands of business associations and professional networking groups in Washington for almost any area of interest. You will be surprised at the career services offered for job seekers, such as job banks, networking events and professional development. Because there are so many groups to choose from, you may find it difficult to determine which groups to join. If you are looking for a networking or business group for women, then refer to chapter 1. Many offer seminars, meetings and happy hours specifically for networking and career development. Some groups also provide job listings, speakers bureaus, career events and mentor programs. One caution, however, some groups charge costly membership fees. If you're on a tight budget, some groups offer reduced rates to nonmembers for use of their career services. Nonmembers can sometimes attend an organization's events by paying a nominal fee. To locate these associations and networks, refer to one of the many local career guides and association books.

Apply for an Internship

If you haven't yet noticed, a significant portion of Washington's labor force works for little or no pay. Therefore, the word "intern" doesn't refer to a student working for school credit. In Washington, the term refers to people who are working for little or no pay, regardless of school affiliation, age or status. What's the tradeoff? An internship can sometimes be the golden opportunity to securing a good job or getting your foot in the door. And that is certainly a realistic hope.

Because Washington relies so heavily on interns, opportunities are abundant. This is especially true on Capitol Hill and with public policy organizations. You will also find that most private companies, nonprofit organizations and government agencies offer intern opportunities.

To find an internship, first decide on the type of group you would like to work for. You can start with this book. If you're interested in working for a special interest group that advocates for women's rights, then refer to chapter 6. If you would like to intern on Capitol Hill, contact a Congressional office or a legislative committee. Associations, political groups, research institutes, media outlets, social services, government offices and professional networking groups all hire interns, and many are listed in this book. Be aware that there are many small organizations, especially in the area of policy, that usually have need for assistance. These places are more likely to take on nonstudent volunteers. Also, don't neglect federal government offices and the Administration. Ever since the downsizing of government, volunteers have taken on a whole new role in government offices. Remember, the purpose of an internship or volunteer work is to get your foot in the door by filling a need.

You can also locate internship opportunities on the Internet. Many universities have web sites that list internship opportunities, such as the

University of Maryland, which offers a sizeable collection of progressive internships. The Feminist Majority provides a listing of internship opportunities on its web site (http://www.feminist.com).

Additionally, the *Internship Bible* (Princeton Review, 1996) is a great source for internship information. It identifies specific intern duties and quantifies into percentages the amount of substantive duties at each. It is important to know this beforehand. Some internships consist mostly of "grunt work," while others allow you more substantive exposure and skill-building opportunities. Obviously, you should opt for the latter. However, do not completely overlook the others, because the tradeoff may be a foot in the door. Refer to chapter 13 for more detailed information on internships.

Seek Out a Mentor

Mentor programs for women are becoming more common in Washington, D.C. Associations, networking groups and even companies and private organizations are now offering mentor programs for those who are new to the workforce, changing careers or starting their own business.

Mentoring is not a job and most likely will not lead to a job at the end of the program, at least not directly. Rather, it is the pairing of an experienced professional with a woman who is new to a given profession. The pair meets one to four times a month, usually at the place of employment. The idea is for the mentored woman to get an inside look at how her mentor operates within the profession and what her job entails. The pairing allows the mentored woman to benefit from her mentor's advice, guidance and personal experiences.

There are several networking and business groups that offer mentor programs, either formally or informally. Women of Washington and Federally Employed Women both offer mentor programs. The Women's Center sponsors the ICAN program, or the Informational and Career Advisory Network, a mentor program to assist women with career planning and development. One of the most unique mentor programs is called "Women Opening Doors for Women," and is sponsored by the Women's Information Network. High-level professional women speak at small dinner parties, giving participants the opportunity to ask questions and discuss their profession in an informal environment, while allowing them to get advice and insider information from women they see as mentors.

3

The Woman Entrepreneur

Amy Millman, Consulting Editor

Women-owned businesses are the fastest-growing segment of the economy. Not only are they increasing at nearly twice the rate of all businesses, but they now employ one out of every four American workers. In the decade leading up to 1996, women-owned firms in the United States grew by 78 percent, according to the National Foundation for Women Business Owners (NFWBO). During that same decade, women-owned firms increased by 59 percent in the nation's capital, 84 percent in neighboring Virginia, and 88 percent in Maryland.

With the explosion of women-owned businesses in Washington and across the nation, it's not surprising that there are a number of resources and business groups available to assist the woman entrepreneur. Whether you're just starting out or wanting to expand an existing business, help is available in the form of resource centers, counseling services, training programs, mentoring opportunities and networking groups just for women. This chapter will help guide you through three main areas of business ownership:

- Starting or Expanding a Business: Where to Find Help
- Business Loan Assistance
- Selling Your Goods or Services to the Federal Government

The federal government alone provides a wealth of resources for women business owners. The U.S. Small Business Administration (SBA) offers the most comprehensive resources for entrepreneurs. It would also be helpful to contact the U.S. Dept. of Commerce, which offers general business assistance for women and helps entrepreneurs acquire government contracts. In addition to federal resources, there are a variety of organizations that are excellent resources for women business owners, such as chambers of commerce, women's centers and professional groups.

Starting or Expanding a Business:
Where to Find Help

There are many programs, groups and services in the Washington metropolitan area to assist women business owners with all aspects of business ownership. Here are some of the most helpful:

● **The Small Business Administration**—Offers the most comprehensive resources, including a training center and a telephone referral service for women. You can also get assistance with business loans, individual counseling and access to information, publications and on-line resources.

● **The Department of Commerce**—Helps business owners sell their goods or services to the federal government and offers women business owners technical, financial and management assistance.

● **Chambers of Commerce**—Provide networking opportunities, business leads and resources. The D.C. Chamber of Commerce has a Women's Business Committee that is an excellent resource for women.

● **Women's Centers**—Provide development programs, networking events and various resources for women entrepreneurs.

U.S. Small Business Administration

The Small Business Administration offers the most comprehensive services and resources to entrepreneurs in the Washington area, including information, counseling, and special programs for women in all areas of business start-up and development. However, finding your way through the myriad of services may prove challenging. Know what's available and where to find the programs that best fit your business needs.

● A Good Place to Start
SBA Washington DC Office
202/606-4000
1110 Vermont Ave., Suite 900, Washington, DC 20043
    The District Office offers various services to business owners, including a variety of information resources, training and counseling programs and two services just for women: the Office of Women Business Ownership and the National Women's Business Center. It is important to

know what information and services are offered so that you can ask the right questions and get the help you need. The SBA District Office can help you locate the following seven services:

- **An Information and Referral Service for Women**

Office of Women Business Ownership, D.C. Representative
202/606-4000 (ask for the OWBO representative)
1110 Vermont Avenue, NW, Suite 900, Washington, DC 20005
    Contact the Washington representative of the Office of Women's Business Ownership (OWBO) by telephone for information on loan acquisition, counseling and special services for women. OWBO sponsors the Business Women's Roundtable, a networking and support group for women who have been in business for at least two years.

- **A Training and Counseling Center for Women**

National Women's Business Center (NWBC)
202/466-0544
1250 24th Street, NW, Suite 350, Washington, DC 20037
    The NWBC provides long-term training programs and one-day seminars in most aspects of business start-up and development. Topic areas include management, marketing, the Internet and procurement. NWBC is a public/private partnership with the SBA and serves all levels of women business owners.

- **Business Counseling Services**

Service Corps of Retired Executives (SCORE)
202/606-4000, x287
1110 Vermont Avenue, Suite 900, Washington, DC 20005
Hours: M-F, 9 a.m.-3 p.m.
    SCORE is staffed by retired business executives who offer individual and group counseling in all areas of business start-up and development. If you would like to be advised by a woman mentor, simply make your request when setting up the appointment. SCORE also offers classes on a variety of business ownership topics, such as writing a business plan, management skills and expanding a business.

- **Telephone Information Service**

Small Business Answer Desk
800/827-5722
    The Answer Desk is a telephone service to help guide entrepreneurs to the information, programs and services offered by the SBA. By using a Touch-Tone phone, you can access information in the following

categories: starting a business; financing a business; counseling and training programs; SBA publications and videotapes; assistance for minority small businesses; veterans' affairs; international trade; selling goods and services to the government; and business ownership for women. You can speak with a business counselor weekdays, 9 a.m. to 5 p.m.

● Information by Using Your Computer
Office of Women Business Ownership (OWBO)
http://www.sbaonline.sba.gov/womeninbusiness

The OWBO Web site provides business information for women business owners and links to other related sites. Browsers have access to a variety of resources including finances, selling goods or services to the federal government, importing and exporting, and technology.

SBA OnLine
202/205-6400, 800/697-4636 (limited access)
202/401-9600, 900/463-4636 (full access)
http://www.sba.gov
telnet://sbaonline.sba.gov

SBA OnLine can be accessed by the World Wide Web, Telnet, or an electronic bulletin board. It provides access to SBA information and materials in all areas of business start-up and development, including SBA publications, local events, e-mail forums and gateways to related sites.

U.S. Business Advisor
http://www.business.gov

The U.S. Business Advisor provides access to federal government business resources, including regulatory agencies, the SBA and the Dept. of Commerce. You can locate information on all aspects of business ownership, obtain and file government documents, and review regulations.

● Walk-in Information and Counseling Center
The Business Information Center
202/606-4000, x287
202/401-9600, on-line service
1110 Vermont Avenue, Suite 900, NW, Washington, DC 20005
Hours: M-F, 9 a.m.-4:30 p.m.

You can have most of your business planning and development needs met at this walk-in business center, which provides over 2,000 resources and small business planning tools for entrepreneurs. You can conduct research, create a business plan and use on-site computers to access information on starting and managing a business. You can also get on-site counseling from SCORE counselors.

● **Business Training at a College or University**

Small Business Development Centers, which are located at colleges and universities, provide counseling, in-depth management training and technical assistance to entrepreneurs. Services are provided by students under the guidance of professors.

Washington, D.C.

DC Office of Latino Affairs   202/939-3018
2000 14th Street, NW, # 202, Washington, DC 20010
East of the River Community Development Center   202/561-4975
3101 Martin Luther King Jr. Ave., SE, Washington, DC 20032
George Washington Univ. Small Business Clinic   202/994-7463
720 20th Street, NW, Washington, DC 20052
Howard University   202/806-1550
2600 6th Street, NW, Rm. 125, Washington, DC 20059
Marshall Heights Community Development Corp.   202/396-1200
3917 Minnesota Ave., NE, Washington, DC 20019
SBA Office   (x279) 202/606-4000
1110 Vermont Ave., NW, # 900, Washington, DC 20043-4500

Maryland

Small Business Dev. Center   301/883-6491
1400 McCormick Drive, # 282, Landover, MD 20785
Small Business Dev. Center   301/217-2345
101 Monroe Street, Suite 1500, Rockville, MD 20850
Small Business Dev. Center   301/932-4155
235 Smallwood Village Center, Waldorf, MD 20602-1852

Virginia

George Mason Univ. Small Business Dev. Center   703/277-7700
4031 University Drive, # 200, Fairfax, VA 22030
George Mason Univ. Small Business Dev. Center   703/993-8129
3401 North Fairfax Center, Arlington, VA 22201
Loudoun County Small Business Dev. Center   703/729-7555
45150 Russell Branch Pkwy., Ashburn, VA 22011

U.S. Department of Commerce

The U.S. Department of Commerce functions primarily as a point of entry for entrepreneurs to sell goods or services to the federal government. However, the Minority Business Development Agency offers some services to women and minority business owners.

Minority Business Development Agency (MBDA)
202/482-4671
14th & Constitution, NW, Rm 5701A, Washington, DC 20030
MBDA offers resources, programs and information to women and minority business owners through technical, financial and management assistance. MBDA recently began a new program intended to help minority women acquire franchises.

Chambers of Commerce

Chambers of Commerce are great resources for business development, information access and networking opportunities with other business owners. The District of Columbia Chamber of Commerce offers the Women in Business Committee, which hosts an annual showcase and trade show for women entrepreneurs, and provides support and networking opportunities for women.

Washington, D.C.
District of Columbia Chamber of Commerce   202/347-7201
1301 Pennsylvania Avenue, NW, # 309, Washington, DC 20004

Maryland
Greater Bethesda-Chevy Chase Chamber of Commerce   301/652-4900
7910 Woodmont Ave., # 1204, Bethesda, MD 20814
Greater Bowie Chamber of Commerce   301/262-0920
6770 Race Track Road, Bowie, MD 20715
Greater Gaithersburg Chamber of Commerce   301/840-1400
9 Park Ave., Gaithersburg, MD 20877
Maryland Chamber of Commerce   410/269-0642
60 West Street, Suite 100, Annapolis, MD 21401
Montgomery County Chamber of Commerce   301/424-6000
416 Hungerford Drive, Rockville, MD 20850
Potomac Chamber of Commerce   301/299-2170
10121 River Road, Potomac, MD 20854
Prince George's County Chamber of Commerce   301/731-5000
4640 Forbes Blvd., # 200, Lanham, MD 20706
Rockville Chamber of Commerce   301/424-9300
600 E. Jefferson Street, Rockville, MD 20852
Takoma Park Chamber of Commerce   301/270-1700
7500 Maple Ave., Takoma Park, MD 20912
Wheaton Chamber of Commerce   301/949-0080
2401 Blueridge Ave., Wheaton, MD 20902

Marketing Your Business
by
Linda Bolliger

A marketing program is fundamental to how you communicate your goods and services to consumers. Think of it as an interactive system of business activities that allows you to plan, price, promote and distribute products and services to satisfy consumer needs. Therefore, it is imperative your plan be flexible. Since consumers and their needs change constantly, your marketing program needs to reflect change too.

A marketing program consists of advertising, public relations, sales, market research, public affairs and general promotions. Before developing your marketing plan, consider these five areas:

Determine your target market area. Examine the market for your product or service. Get to know your customers and your competition. Visit your competition as a customer and survey potential customers. Review trade association literature.

Research consumer needs. What do consumers need or want? What will they spend their money on? To determine this, conduct research and gather data on trends, such as the buying habits of Baby Boomers or senior citizens. Track and predict market trends.

Prepare the product or service to meet consumer needs. Price and package your product or service so that it appeals to consumers. Determine how to add value to your commodity.

Hire and train personnel to address consumer needs. You might not be able to do it alone. It may be wise to hire some responsible employees to assist with customer satisfaction. Quantify their performance and then review it regularly.

Design a sales presentation. Recognize that sales materials are obsolete by the time they get to customers. With that in mind, try moderately priced materials with generic information and arranged creatively. And remember, simple can be elegant.

Linda Bolliger, a local business owner, chairs the Women in Business Committee at the D.C. Chamber of Commerce.

Virginia

Alexandria Chamber of Commerce	703/549-1000
801 N. Fairfax Street, # 402, Alexandria, VA 22314	
Arlington Chamber of Commerce	703/525-2400
20009 14th Street, # 111, Arlington, VA 22201	
Fairfax County Chamber of Commerce	703/749-0400
8230 Old Courthouse Road, # 350, Vienna, VA 22182	
Prince William County-Greater Manassas	703/368-4813
8963 Center Street, Manassas, VA 22110	
Virginia Chamber of Commerce	804/644-1607
9 South 5th Street, Richmond, VA 23219	

National

National Chamber of Commerce for Women	212/685-3454
10 Waterside Plaza, Suite 6H, New York, NY 10010	
U.S. Chamber of Commerce	202/659-6000
1615 H Street, NW, Washington, DC 20062	

Women's Centers

Most women's centers function as information and referral services for women in the areas of professional and personal needs. The following centers offer some services for women business owners, including training workshops and networking opportunities.

Fairfax County Office for Women
703/324-5730
12000 Government Center Parkway, Suite 318, Fairfax, VA 22035
Hours: M-F, 8 a.m.-4:30 p.m.

The Fairfax County Office for Women is a career resource and personal services center for women of Fairfax County. The Office offers some resources and programs for women business owners, such as referrals, training workshops and seminars.

Montgomery County Commission for Women
301/279-1800
255 North Washington Street, Rockville, MD 20850

Counseling and career development center that offers some resources and programs for women business owners, such as workshops on various business ownership topics, networking opportunities, referrals and publications.

© 1996 Olive Rosen

MarketPlace '96, sponsored by the DCCC, gave women entrepreneurs the opportunity to exhibit their products and services.

Prince William County Office for Women
703/792-6611
4370 Ridgewood Center Drive, Suite D, Woodbridge, VA 22192
The Office provides computer training courses, which are conducted by appointment.

The Women's Center
703/281-2657
133 Park Street, NE, Vienna, VA 22180
The Women's Center offers a variety of professional seminars and workshops on topics such as owning and launching a business. The programs are held in the evenings and on weekends. The Center also provides some career services for the woman entrepreneur, such as a library on business ownership and programs on assertiveness.

The Women's Center and Referral Service
301/937-5265
3215 Powder Mill Road, Adelphi, MD 20783
The Center assists women with career, business and personal growth through programs, seminars, networks and support groups. The Business Advisory Council (BAC) is a networking and resource group for women business owners to share information and encourage each other in all areas of business development.

Other Sources of Assistance

Conference for Women Entrepreneurs
The Dingman Center for Entrepreneurship
301/405-2148
Maryland Business School
University of Maryland, College Park, MD 20742-1815
   The conference features panel discussions, lectures and workshops for women business owners. The annual conference focuses on a variety of topics such as marketing, leadership skills, securing and maximizing capital, and the basics of how to succeed in business.

Legal and Business Information Center
202/857-4540
202/467-6910, fax
1120 19th Street, NW, 8th Floor, Washington, DC 20036-3684
e-mail: lbic@davhag.com
http://pages.prodigy.com/DC/lbic/lbic.html
   The Center provides information on legal issues and other business concerns to women business owners and other professionals by telephone, facsimile or e-mail. It also offers interactive workshops, educational programs, informal networking events, and business information. The Center, which is operated by a team of legal professionals, also functions as a referral network and a resource database.

U.S. Department of Labor, Women's Bureau
202/219-6652   215/596-1183
200 Constitution Ave., NW   3535 Market St., Rm. 2450
Washington, DC 20210   Philadelphia, PA 19104
http://www.dol.gov/dol/wb/
   The Women's Bureau publishes information about business ownership. The District Office in Philadelphia provides some direct services, such as conferences and trade shows.

Business Loan Assistance

Securing a small business loan is crucial to starting or expanding a business. It can also be one of the most difficult barriers to overcome for women entrepreneurs. According to the National Foundation for Women Business Owners (NFWBO), one-third of women business owners report some type of gender-based discrimination from lending institutions and two-thirds say they've had some difficulties working with lenders. Although disheartening, the statistics are an improvement from times past. It was less than three decades ago that women were required to have their husbands co-sign for loans. Today, obviously much has changed with more women than ever before gaining access to business loans.

To find help with securing capital for your business, start with the SBA. You can get individual and group loan consultations through the SCORE office and the Small Business Development Centers, which are listed in this chapter.

SBA Small Business Loans

The SBA offers several types of loan guarantee programs to help business owners attain loans from commercial lenders. The loans offer up to $750,000 and guarantee up to 80 percent of the amount. To qualify, the business must be a small business and operate as a for-profit entity. Entrepreneurs need to request an SBA-guaranteed loan from their banker, who in turn deals directly with the SBA. Some financial institutions have special relationships with the SBA and can offer expedited loan approval. In guaranteeing the loan, the SBA assures the lender that, in the event the borrower does not repay the loan, the government will reimburse the lending institution for some of its loss. As with any loan, the entrepreneur is responsible for the full amount of the loan and is required to make monthly loan payments directly to the lender. The length of time for repayment depends on the use of the proceeds and the ability of the business to repay. However, the standard is usually five to 10 years for working capital and up to 25 years for fixed assets.

Types of SBA Small Business Loans
The SBA's primary lending program, the *Loan Guaranty Program*, consists of various lending programs, which target specialized business needs. Each has different requirements, allocation purposes and terms.

- **LowDoc—The Low Documentation Loan Program.** One of the newest, quickest and most simplified SBA loan programs is LowDoc, which allows business owners to secure a small business loan for as much as $100,000. LowDoc offers a simple, one-page SBA application form. Completed applications are usually processed within two or three days.

- **FASTRAK.** FASTRAK loans make capital available quickly to businesses seeking loans of up to $100,000 by relying primarily on the lender's application. Repayment is usually five to seven years for working capital and up to 25 years for real estate or equipment. Your local SBA office can provide you with a list of FASTRAK lenders.

● **CAPLines.** CAPLines are short-term loans for short-term needs, with revolving lines of credit. A CAPLine loan can be for any dollar amount. The SBA guarantees 75 percent up to $750,000.

● **DELTA. Defense Loan and Technical Assistance Program.** The DELTA program assists small businesses adversely affected by defense cuts. The maximum gross loan amount is $1.25 million. The loans may require special handling because of their complicated credit analyses.

● **The Export Working Capital Program (EWCP).** Intended to assist exporters seeking short-term working capital, the SBA guarantees 75 percent of a loan up to $750,000. The EWCP uses a one-page application and streamlined documentation, which results in turnaround usually within 10 days. Interest rates are negotiated between you and your lender.

● **The International Trade Loan Program.** The SBA guarantees as much as $1.25 million in combined working capital and fixed-asset loans for the purposes of purchasing, building or renovating land and buildings, purchasing machinery, or making other capital improvements.

How to Apply for an SBA Loan

If you are starting a new business, then you will have to prepare a business plan that contains business and financial information about the proposed business. The plan should describe in detail the type of business to be established, your business experience and your management capabilities. You will also need to prepare an estimate of how much cash you and others will be able to invest in the business and how much you will need to borrow. As a general guideline, lenders award a maximum ratio of two to one for every dollar you invest. In order to apply for an SBA loan, you will need to prepare the following.:

● Prepare a loan proposal, including a business financial statement, or balance sheet, which lists all of the company's assets and liabilities. If you are starting a new business, then you will also have to list your personal assets and liabilities.

Tips for Securing a Business Loan
by
Deattra Perkins

Before you even sit down with the lender, find out whether the bank or lending institution is a good match for your type of business. You can determine this by inquiring whether the bank has previously conducted business with a similar firm of similar size.

Make sure your loan package is complete. Check to make sure you have all the appropriate loan documents, such as a business plan, tax returns and financial statements. Most banks will want to see your personal tax returns for the last three years.

Know exactly how much you want to borrow. Don't give an estimate. This amount should be contained in your cover letter for the initial loan request. You can determine your cash need by completing a cash flow statement, which will determine the costs of overhead, salary and other expenses.

Be prepared to answer questions about all aspects of your business. Research your business and the market for your product or service. If you have a CPA prepare your financial statement, have that person explain it to you so that you can talk authoritatively during the interview. If you still do not know an answer, tell the lender that you will check with your CPA.

Be prepared to put up collateral to guarantee a loan. If you are a first-time entrepreneur, then lenders will want you to put up equity. You can describe your collateral in the executive summary of your business plan.

Be aware that bankers will review your credit. Find out beforehand what is contained in your credit report by requesting a copy from your local credit reporting agency. If it contains anything negative, try to get it removed or have an explanation attached.

Deattra Perkins is the director of training for the National Women's Business Center.

- Prepare a business profit and loss statement for the previous three years, and if available, for the current year. Be prepared to provide copies of your signed business Federal Income Tax Returns for the same period of time. If you are starting a new business, then you will need to prepare a detailed projection of business earnings for the first year of business operation or until your business reaches a projected break-even point.

- Prepare a personal financial statement of the owner(s), partner(s) or stockholders owning 20 percent or more of the corporate stock or ownership in the business.

- Make a list of your collateral that will be offered as security for the loan. Estimate the present market value of each item and list the liens, if any, against each item. Itemize by category, such as real estate, machinery and equipment, furniture and fixtures and inventory.

- State the total amount of the loan you are requesting. Substantiate this amount by listing the purposes for which the money will be used by category and dollar amount.

- Make an appointment with the SCORE office so that your proposal can be reviewed by a trained professional (see prior section).

Take all of the above materials to your banker and request a direct bank loan. If declined, ask for a loan under SBA's Guaranty Loan Program. If your banker needs assistance or would like to review your loan with the SBA, have the lender contact the SBA Financing Division at 202/606-4000, ext. 253, 240 or 259. The SBA will deal directly with the bank.

Selling Your Goods or Services to the Federal Government

The federal government spends nearly $200 billion annually on goods and services. Unfortunately, less than 2 percent is awarded to women-owned businesses. To improve this number, Congress has established a 5 percent procurement goal for women-owned businesses. In response, federal agencies are offering conferences, training sessions and fairs to help women businesses sell their products or services to the government. In addition to these opportunities, you can maximize your potential for securing contracts by taking advantage of the resources listed in this section.

Office of Government Contracting
U.S. Small Business Administration
202/205-6469
409 3rd Street, SW, Washington, DC 20024

The Office provides a variety of services, resources and publications for businesses wanting to sell goods or services to the government. The office has two helpful publications available at no cost: *Procurement Assistance: A Practical Guide for Businesses Seeking Federal Contracts*, and *The 25 Most Asked Questions About Federal Procurement*. You can also register with the Procurement Automated Source System (PASS), a database of small businesses that is accessed by government buying entities.

Offices of Small and Disadvantaged Business Utilization (OSDBU)
202/482-3387
14th Street and Constitution Ave., NW, Washington, DC 20230

Most federal agencies have an Office of Small and Disadvantaged Business Utilization (OSDBU) Representative to assist women business owners with procurement. These representatives can help lead you to the appropriate personnel to market your product or service. Some federal agencies also have Women-Owned Business Representatives (WOBREP), who assist women in acquiring contracts and subcontracts.

Minority Business Development Agency (MBDA)
202/482-4671
14th & Constitution, NW, Rm 5701A, Washington, DC 20030

MBDA provides resources and information to women and minority business owners on procurement, as well as an on-line directory of contractors that is viewed by government and private sector purchasing agencies.

Commerce Business Daily
202/512-1800
Superintendent of Documents, Dept. of Commerce

The *Commerce Business Daily* lists contracts offered by the government. *CBS* is available by subscription or at SBA offices, regional GSA Service Centers and some libraries. It is published weekdays.

Six Steps to Government Procurement

Step 1—Verify that the agency you wish to do business with actually buys the goods or services your company can provide.

Step 2—Locate the buying offices that purchase your product or service and ask the OSDBU or procurement official for a forecast or acquisition plan of their contracting opportunities for the current year. Also request the names of contacts within the procurement office who can provide further assistance.

Step 3—Visit small purchase chiefs or buyers. Find out how often your products or services are purchased; how officers maintain their bidders' mailing list; how many firms are on the bidders' list; and how often the list is rotated.

Step 4—List your capabilities on various bidders' mailing lists. Commerce OSDBU uses these three lists to identify firms for small business set-asides:

- Solicitation Mailing List Application (SF-129). A standard bidders' list used by most federal government agencies to identify potential contractors.
- Procure Automated Source System (PASS). A database of small businesses, which is used by federal agencies, state governments and prime contractors to identify prospective contractors.
- Automated Business Enterprise Locator System (ABELS). A national computer system containing information on minority-owned businesses interested in selling to the government.

Step 5—Submit capability statements to small purchasing and procurement offices and to OSDBU personnel. Your statement should include specifics on the types of products or services your company provides, a listing of your standard industrial classification codes (SIC), and references from previous customers. Use the SIC Manual to identify your SIC code. The manual is available at public libraries and through NTIS at 703/487-4650.

Step 6—Marketing in person to the small purchasing office is always the best approach. Check bulletin boards for posting of small purchasing activity. Interview the buyers and the program personnel to further explain your company's capabilities.   Source: U.S. Dept. Of Commerce

4

Leadership

Women are slowly gaining ground in business and professional roles with increasing responsibilities. Although the numbers are still fairly low, more women than ever before are winning seats on boards and commissions, running for and winning public offices, owning their own businesses and heading companies and organizations. And for the first time, women are attaining the most senior levels of leadership and responsibility. Studies reveal that a current trend among top Fortune companies is having multiple female board members. From 1994 to 1995, there was an 11 percent increase in the number of women serving on Fortune 500 boards. During that same period there was a 40 percent increase in the number of Fortune 500 companies with at least three women on their boards. Although the numbers are encouraging, it is important to note that women are only 9.5 percent of all people serving on Fortune 500 boards, and they number only four of all the CEO's of Fortune 1000 companies. As entrepreneurs, women now own one-third of the nation's businesses. Over the last decade, the number of women-owned firms increased by 78 percent, bringing the total to nearly eight million businesses and generating nearly $2.3 trillion in sales.

The same trend holds true for women in public office, a slow increase of a relatively small number. In the 105th U.S. Congress, women are 11 percent of the U.S. Congress and 20 percent of state legislatures. Although still far from equality, the numbers reflect a slight progression of even smaller numbers from years past.

To meet the growing demand for women in leadership roles and to encourage even greater participation, there are an increasing number of organizations in Washington that offer leadership training programs to professional women and college students. Several of the programs listed in this chapter are available to women entrepreneurs and business leaders, while others offer training services for women in public policy and campaign skills training.

Leadership Programs for Women

Fifty plus One
301/587-8061
817 Silver Spring Avenue, Suite 302, Silver Spring, MD 20910
   Fifty plus One offers classes on campaign training for women who are interested in running for elective office or managing a campaign. The two-day training sessions cover such topics as campaign research, fundraising, budgeting, media exposure, public speaking, grassroots organizing, polling, and the roles of the Democratic or Republican parties. Courses are taught by women elected officials and seasoned campaign professionals.

Gillian Rudd Leadership Institute for Women Business Owners
301/495-4975
1100 Wayne Avenue, Suite 830, Silver Spring, MD 20910-5603
   The Institute offers an annual four-day leadership program for women business owners. The program offers workshops and panel discussions to help women enhance their business skills to meet their personal goals in profitability and growth. The Institute is sponsored by the National Foundation for Women Business Owners.

Leadership America, Inc.
703/549-1102
700 N. Fairfax Street, Suite 610, Alexandria, VA 22314
   Leadership America, Inc. is a national not-for-profit leadership organization that recognizes, educates and connects accomplished women. It offers advanced leadership development programs for women who have already shown outstanding leadership abilities. The programs consist of three four-day sessions over the span of one year. These professional development sessions analyze the complexities of national and international issues, and focus on leadership styles that embody individual values, vision, creativity, motivation, management and organizations.

Leadership Conference/The Women's Center
703/281-2657
133 Park Street, NE, Vienna, VA 22180
   The annual Leadership Conference is a one-day program that offers skills development, networking opportunities and educational growth. The Conference features some of the nation's most distinguished women in politics, business and other fields. Speakers from the 1996 program included Madeleine Kunin, U.S. Deputy Secretary of Education, Sen. Dianne Feinstein (D-CA) and author Deborah Tannen.

Local Leadership Roundtable
202/939-8083
2000 14th Street, NW, Suite 354, Washington, DC 20009
Established by the DC Commission for Women, the Local Leadership Roundtable is composed of presidents, executive directors and other top management of women's groups. The Roundtable provides a forum for these leaders to examine and develop policy issues to improve conditions for women in the D.C. area.

National Foundation for Women Legislators, Inc. (NFWL)
202/337-3565
910 16th Street, NW, Suite 100, Washington, DC 20006
NFWL provides leadership training programs for women legislators. The Leadership College for Women State Legislators helps women enhance their leadership skills while also focusing on personal strategies through individualized sessions. Campaign College provides a learning forum for incumbents on how to successfully run a campaign and win re-election. The College examines such topics as fundraising, political debating, campaign themes and getting out the vote. The program also offers individual political consultation.

National Hispana Leadership Institute
703/527-6007
1901 N. Moore Street, # 206, Arlington, VA 22206
Professional leadership development program for Hispanic women that consists of four one-week sessions. Each session focuses on a different topic, such as creating a national network, working toward effective change in public policy, and leadership assessment. Each year, 20 professionals who have demonstrated outstanding achievement are selected to participate in the leadership program.

National Leadership Institute
301/985-7195
University College
University Blvd. at Adelphi Road, College Park, MD 20742
The National Leadership Institute, which is located at the University of Maryland, offers a variety of leadership programs, including leadership application workshops for senior level executive women. The workshops focus on such topics as how women can improve their opportunities for advancement in the workplace; how to be a good leader; and how to overcome gender barriers.

Leadership Tips for Women
by
Katha Kissman

Women leaders are needed at all levels of service and the best way to develop such skills is to get involved. You can start by volunteering for a nonprofit organization or serving on a government committee or commission. By doing this you will learn to work with a variety of different people, while providing an important community service. In addition, you will build confidence, which is a crucial element of leadership.

Leadership success depends on whether these skills are recognized, nurtured and developed. Whether you are a corporate executive, public office holder, manager of a nonprofit organization or a volunteer, there are some basic skills that apply to all leadership roles.

Personalize a mission. Come up with your own mission and live it.

Lead by example. Set a good example for others by your behavior. It's not "do as I say," but "do as I do."

Learn to listen. Make sure you are hearing what is being said and when appropriate apply it to your work.

Know when to follow. Sometimes leaders are so busy leading they don't see when it's valuable to follow.

Be self-motivated. Don't rely on others to motivate your actions.

Validate feelings and opinions of others. Respect that people have a right to their opinion. You can validate someone's feelings without agreeing.

Develop empathy. Try to put yourself in the other person's shoes.

Think creatively. A creative plan or approach to a project could yield excellent results.

Be positive. A good attitude can go a long way. Don't blame. Rather, focus on solving problems.

Give to others. Leading isn't always leading, but sometimes giving. Open yourself up to the joys of giving.

Follow your passion. Find out what lights your fire and go after it.

Mentor colleagues. You would be surprised at what you may gain from doing this.

Pick your fights wisely. Not everything is worth the time and effort spent pushing your point. Sometimes it's okay to choose not to win.

Try new things. Be open-minded. Don't limit yourself.

Embrace change. Change is constant, so you have to learn to work with it, rather than fight it. Most leaders are even exhilarated by change.

Let the small stuff go. Always, keep the big picture in mind.

Honor your commitments. Be reliable. Have integrity.

Know when to say no. Sometimes leaders take on too many responsibilities. You will get more respect if you say "no" than if you say yes and don't follow through.

Focus on the process as well as the end result. The process is important. The end doesn't always justify the means.

Leave perfection to others. No one is perfect, so don't try to be.

Strive to learn at all times. Learning new things means a more capable leader.

Well-being is just as important as professional skills to your leadership success. It's imperative you make time for yourself. Enrich yourself. Pamper yourself. Forgive yourself. Like yourself. And, most important, have a life.

Katha Kissman is executive director of Leadership America, a not-for-profit leadership organization for women.

National Political Congress of Black Women, Inc. (NPCBW)
202/338-0800
600 New Hampshire Ave., NW, Suite 1125, Washington, DC 20037
   NPCBW provides leadership training for women professionals, campaigners and activists in Washington, D.C. and in other cities around the nation. NPCBW works to increase the role of African-Americans in the political process through leadership development, mentor programs, political support, advocacy and networking.

National Women's Economic Alliance Foundation (NWEA)
202/393-5257
1440 New York Ave., NW, Suite 300, Washington, DC 20005
   NWEA offers leadership seminars, workshops and panel discussions for female executives. Members receive a monthly newsletter that lists upcoming events and pertinent publications, activities and related information. NWEA also offers management programs, forums, research, seminars and a mentor program. NWEA sponsors the annual "A Seat at the Table," a learning series.

National Women's Political Caucus (NWPC)/Campaign Training
202/785-1100
1211 Connecticut Ave., NW, Suite 425, Washington, DC 20036
   NWPC offers campaign skills workshops, which examine all aspects of starting and running a political campaign. These regional workshops cover topics such as raising money, developing a campaign plan and message, motivating volunteers, and addressing the news media. NWPC is a national organization dedicated to increasing the number of women in elected and appointed office.

Policy Leaders Action Network
202/387-6030, 800/935-0699
1875 Connecticut Ave., NW, Suite 710, Washington, DC 20009
http://www.cfpa.org/pub/cfpa/
   The Policy Leaders Action Network is a bipartisan network of progressive elected state leaders for the purpose of generating new ideas and strategies for pragmatic policies. The Network provides publications, information, educational seminars and networking events. The Network is offered by the Center for Policy Alternatives.

WGR Leader Foundation
202/347-5432
1029 Vermont Ave., NW, # 510, Washington, DC 20005

The WGR Leader Foundation offers a variety of training and education programs in government relations. The Foundation offers a "Women in Leadership" Program, an interactive public policy training and professional development program intended to give women the knowledge and skills to create and implement public policy initiatives. The program consists of bimonthly meetings and one weekend retreat over a seven-month period. The Foundation is sponsored by Women in Government Relations.

Wider Opportunities for Women/Leadership Development Project
202/638-3143
815 15th Street, NW, Suite 916, Washington, DC 20005
The Leadership Development Project trains women leaders and service providers in the public policy system. The two-day training program focuses on budget negotiations and general skills development for advancing women's policies at local, state and national levels. The program also develops networks of women advocates who can work together for change.

Women's Campaign Research Fund (WCRF)
202/393-8164
734 15th Street, NW, Suite 500, Washington, DC 20005
WCRF offers a variety of leadership training programs for women in public office and those planning to seek office. The Political Leadership Workshops teach leadership development skills for public office. The Leadership 2000 Program is a three-day conference that provides political and public policy-making assistance to the nation's top women office holders. The "Making It to the Top" seminars offer strategic long-term political career training to women in public office. WCRF also offers communications training courses, which provide instruction on media skills and refining campaign messages.

Leadership Programs for Young Women

Campaign Skills Training for Young Women
202/785-1100
1211 Connecticut Avenue, NW, Suite 425, Washington, DC 20036
Presented by the National Women's Political Caucus, this training seminar teaches students and young women campaign skills. It is designed to get young women involved in public service and the political process.

National Clearinghouse for Leadership Programs (NCLP)
301/314-7174
1135 Stamp Student Union
University of Maryland, College Park, MD 20742
NCLP functions as a national resource center for leadership programs on college campuses in the D.C. area and throughout the nation. Hours of operation are Monday through Friday, 9 a.m. to 5 p.m.

National Conference for College Women Leaders
202/659-9330
1325 18th Street, NW, # 210, Washington, DC 20036-6511
Sponsored by the National Association for Women in Education, the Conference assists women college students in leadership roles to improve their leadership skills.

Public Leadership Education Network (PLEN)
202/872-1585
1001 Connecticut Ave., NW, Suite 900, Washington, DC 20036
PLEN is a consortium of women's colleges that prepares female students for public leadership roles. PLEN offers weekend and one- and two-week seminars and internship programs on the public policy process. Programs are taught by women leaders who serve as mentors and role models to the students. PLEN publishes a helpful guide to internships called *Preparing to Lead, a College Woman's Guide to Internships and Other Public Policy Learning Opportunities in Washington, DC.*

Women As Leaders Seminar
The Washington Center
202/336-7600
1101 14th Street, NW, Suite 500, Washington, DC 20005
Offers two-week seminars for college women that focus on leadership skills for public service and business. The seminars include workshops, panel discussions and distinguished women of achievement.

Young Women's Project (YWP)
202/393-0461
923 F Street, NW, 3rd Floor, Washington, DC 20004
The YWP helps girls and women develop leadership skills and self-esteem. The Bodies Project offers weekly skills training workshops, discussion groups and community-based team projects, such as working in an adolescent health care clinic. The Peer Technical Assistance Project (PTAP) trains young women for advocacy roles and offers leadership skills training, information and other support services.

College Women: Developing Your Leadership Potential
by
The Public Leadership Education Network (PLEN)

Get involved on campus. Gain practical leadership experience on your campus by chairing a student government committee or by identifying a problem on your campus and organizing a group to try to solve it.

Seek a mentor. Identify a woman leader on your campus who is effective in working with people and ask her to be your mentor. Volunteer in her office in exchange for the opportunity to learn from her.

Volunteer for community service. Sign up for a service project at your campus or in your community. Find a project that allows you to exercise some responsibility as you observe those in leadership roles.

Public speaking. Take every opportunity to gain experience speaking in front of a group of people. The more you do it, the more confident and effective you will become.

Write it down. Practice expressing yourself in writing on why you support a particular policy or issue. Write letters to your campus or local newspaper, or your state or national elected officials.

Get political. Volunteer to work in a political campaign. You will be able to observe different leadership styles and make connections that will help you find further leadership roles in the office of an elected official.

Take a leadership course. Sign up for a leadership program, such as PLEN's Public Policy Programs. You will learn crucial skills from national women leaders and from other student leaders from around the country.

Do an internship. Locate an internship at an organization where you will be able to observe its leaders. Watch carefully and notice which leadership behaviors are the most effective and which styles appeal most to you.

PLEN is a consortium of women's colleges preparing women students for public leadership roles through seminars and internship programs.

Part II
Politics

5

Political Involvement

Marjorie Sims, Consulting Editor

Even before all women had the legal right to vote, they were involved in the political process and even elected to public office. Take Jeanette Rankin, a Republican from the state of Montana. She was elected to the U.S. House of Representatives in 1916, a full four years before the 19th Amendment granted all American women the right to go to the polls. But in those days and for decades beyond, women were scarce in public office. Today much has changed. There is a record number of women serving in the U.S. Congress and in elected positions around the country. Women have permeated state legislatures and local government offices.

It was the '70s that brought significant advancements for women in the political arena. In that decade, two groups formed—the National Women's Political Caucus (NWPC) and the Women's Campaign Fund (WCF)—that would change the way women became involved in the political process. The groups worked to increase the role of women in public office through campaign financing, leadership training and volunteer support networks. It wasn't long before these support groups produced the first real signs of national recognition. Women began running for and winning seats in federal, state and local offices. It wasn't long before we began witnessing a series of "Years of the Woman" in the nation's capital and across the country. One of the most memorable of these years was 1992, when the elections of Sen. Dianne Feinstein (D-CA) and Sen. Barbara Boxer (D-CA) marked the first time women held both of any state's two senate positions. That year also produced the first African-American woman Senator, Carol Moseley-Braun (D-IL), and elevated a record number of women to elected and appointed positions all across the country.

But even though women have made great strides in gaining public office and securing a place in politics, they still have quite a way to go to attain equality. In the 105th Congress, only 9 percent of the U.S. Senate seats were held by women and 12 percent of the seats in the U.S. House of Representatives were held by women. And the nation is still far away from electing a woman to the highest office in the country. But statistics show that women are a gaining force, both as candidates and as voters. For the last three decades, women have proved their commitment to the suffrage movement by making up the majority of U.S. voters—53 percent—and turning out to the polls in greater numbers than men. In the 1996 Presidential election, 54 percent of all voters were women.

The resources in this chapter are intended to give women the tools and the insight to become involved in the political process, whether it's running for office, assisting with a campaign, participating in a get-out-the-vote project, working for a public officeholder, or advancing a public policy issue.

How to Get Involved in Politics
by
Anita Perez Ferguson
National Women's Political Caucus

Imagine yourself reading the Sunday newspaper or watching the evening news and being enraged by something that is going on in your community. The news story may be about schools that are unable to open because of poor maintenance; it may be about businesses that are closing due to neighborhood conditions; or it may be a story of a woman being beaten or robbed. Whatever it is, it makes you mad. That is the perfect time to think about getting involved in politics.

Only you can determine when an issue or event really motivates you to get involved. The interest and energy you feel at that moment is what you will need to keep you involved when the going gets rough and the task of changing your community seems daunting. But before jumping into a campaign of your own, it is important to prepare yourself by learning some crucial skills that will make your chances of succeeding even greater.

Get Political Experience
In addition to the initial motivation, another necessary ingredient for running for office is experience in the political world. Your work for other candidates, as a spokesperson for an issue or an advocate for a community project are all experiences that will help you develop a more realistic idea of what to expect and how to proceed in your own campaign.

Take a Leadership Training Program

Taking a campaign training program allows women to get an overall picture of the campaign process by enhancing hands-on experience. Campaign programs with the National Women's Political Caucus (NWPC) cover decision-making criteria for getting into a race, research, planning and strategy. Potential candidates also learn about fund raising and media relations, as well as public policy formation. During the last two years, the NWPC has trained over 2,500 women for campaign work and thousands more over our 25-year history.

Get Involved in Your Community

If you are in the early stages of the process and just thinking that serving in public office may be in your future, the best plan is to get involved now. Don't hesitate to take action in your community. Join the local branch of the NWPC to get started in political activity. You may also want to consider the many organizations that are dedicated to specific issues, such as education, business development and environmental protection. The experience you gain will be valuable and you will be surprised how quickly you will be called upon to take on even larger responsibilities.

Seek a Mentor Opportunity

If your interest is in state, national or international issues, find a current leader whom you may assist and learn from. There is always more work to be done than there are people willing to work. Your expressed interest and consistent follow-through will boost your involvement faster than you can imagine.

Focus on the Three R's

Finally, don't forget your old school day trio of reading, writing and arithmetic. Read everything you can on the subject of special interest. Write your opinions down and distribute them to policy makers and news editors. Learn the money side of your issue. What drives the budgets? Who benefits from the status quo? Combined, these three focus areas will help you develop into a knowledgeable spokesperson for your perspective and help you gain the needed skills for a candidate for public office.

The National Women's Political Caucus is a nonpartisan, grassroots organization dedicated to increasing the number of women in elected and appointed office at all levels of government.

Nonpartisan/Bipartisan Political Groups

Black Women's Roundtable on Voter Participation
202/659-4929
1629 K Street, NW, Suite 801, Washington, DC 20006
Sponsored by the National Coalition on Black Voter Participation, the purpose of the Roundtable is to organize voter registration and education programs within the black community to increase voter participation.

Capitol Hill Women's Political Caucus
202/986-0994
PO Box 599, Longworth House Office Bldg., Washington, DC 20515
Networking, professional development and information group for women working with congressional offices, public interest groups, lobbying organizations and the federal government. The group, which is affiliated with the National Women's Political Caucus, meets monthly, holds programs and events of interest to women policy workers and provides job listings and several bipartisan task forces that deal with issues of interest to women. The Caucus publishes the newsletter *Capitol Hill Report* and provides a legislative hotline.

Fifty plus One
301/587-8061
817 Silver Spring Ave., Suite 302, Silver Spring, MD 20910
Fifty plus One works to train and encourage pro-choice women to run for elective national, state or local offices with the intent of making officeholders more representative of the population they serve. The name represents the percentage of women that make up the total U.S. population, which is 51 percent. Fifty plus One holds candidate training seminars in locations along the east coast. The group also offers information to assist women who want to run for elective office.

League of Women Voters, National Headquarters
202/429-1965
1730 M Street, NW, Washington, DC 20036
http://www.lwv.org/ ~ lwvus/
The League of Women Voters is a nonpartisan organization that promotes informed and active participation in the political process. The League provides a variety of information on the political process and major public policy issues for informed decision making. The League's chapters provide networking opportunities, events and educational programs.

Photo: Susan Noonan/Maryland Public Television
Rep. Eleanor Holmes Norton (D-DC), host Bonnie Erbe, Geraldine Ferraro, U.S. Ambassador to the U.N. Human Rights Commission, and Susan Au Allen of the Pan Asian American Chamber of Commerce appear on a segment of *To The Contrary*, an all-women weekly political talk show that airs on WETA (Saturdays at 11 a.m.) Maryland Public Television (Sundays at 11:30 p.m.) And WHMM-TV (Sundays at 5:30 p.m.).

League of Women Voters of the National Capital Area
703/522-8196
1229 N. Nash Street, Arlington, VA 22209
The National Capital Chapter represents a dozen leagues in the Washington metropolitan area, which include the following:

Washington, DC
202/331-4122
2025 Eye Street, NW, Rm 917
Washington, DC 20006

Alexandria, VA
703/549-3240
206 S. Fayette Street
Alexandria, VA 22314

Fairfax, VA
703/658-9150

4026 Hummer Road
Annandale, VA 22003

Montgomery County, MD
301/984-9585
12216 Parklawn Drive
Rockville, MD 20852

Prince George's County, MD
301/864-1016
8309 Rosette Lane
Adelphi, MD 20783

National Association of Minority Political Women (NAMPW)

202/686-1216

6120 Oregon Ave., NW, Washington, DC 20015

Political group devoted to research and education of issues of concern to minority women. NAMPW also sponsors activities and networking events.

National Political Congress of Black Women, Inc. (NPCBW)

202/338-0800

600 New Hampshire Ave., NW, Suite 1125, Washington, DC 20037

NPCBW works to increase the role of African-Americans in the political process through leadership development, mentor programs, political support, advocacy and networking.

National Woman's Party

202/546-1210

144 Constitution Avenue, NE, Washington, DC 20002

The National Woman's Party was established in 1913 to promote woman suffrage. Its primary goal is the passage of the Equal Rights Amendment.

National Women's Political Caucus (NWPC)

202/785-1100

1211 Connecticut Ave., NW, Suite 425, Washington DC 20036

NWPC works to increase the number of women in public office in all levels of government by recruiting, training and supporting women candidates. NWPC offers publications and services to assist women candidates and others interested in supporting women candidates. NWPC offers special training seminars for students, executives and women of color. NWPC has a network of state and local chapters across the country that function as a networking forum for women in politics.

Susan B. Anthony

703/683-5558

919 Prince Street, Alexandria, VA 22314

Nonpartisan political action committee that supports pro-life women candidates on the national level.

Women's Campaign Fund (WCF)

202/393-8164

734 15th Street, NW, Suite 500, Washington, DC 20005

WCF is a nonpartisan organization that supports pro-choice women candidates of both parties at the national, state and local levels. WCF pro-

Sewall-Belmont House

H.C. Duriton '92

The Sewall-Belmont House is a tribute to the women's suffrage movement that led to the ratification of the 19th Amendment. The two-story museum located on Capitol Hill contains relics, portraits, busts, political cartoons and other memorabilia honoring the movement and the leaders who led the fight that gave American women the legal right to vote. Among the relics are a faded purple and yellow banner the suffragists used in 1917 and 1918 to picket the White House, the desk used by Susan B. Anthony to write the woman suffrage amendment, a life-size marble statue of Joan of Arc, and marble busts of four prominent suffragists: Lucretia Mott, Susan B. Anthony, Elizabeth Cady Stanton and Alice Paul.

The Sewall-Belmont house is the headquarters for the National Woman's Party. It was designated a National Historic Landmark in 1972 and is now part of the National Park Service.

The Sewall-Belmont House is located at 144 Constitution Ave., NE, 202/546-3989. It is open Tuesday through Friday from 10 a.m. to 3 p.m. and Saturdays from noon to 4 p.m.

vides campaign financing, training programs and other forms of support for women candidates all over the country.

Democratic Groups

Democratic National Committee (DNC), Office of Women's Outreach
202/488-5017, 202/863-8183
430 South Capitol Street, SE, Washington, DC 20003
This office is concerned with women's policy issues within the DNC.

Democratic Women of Capitol Hill (DWCH)
703/280-4611
8113 Little River Turnpike, Annandale, VA 22003
DWCH is a networking, educational and spirit-building group for Democratic women working on Capitol Hill. The group is loosely organized and offers luncheon speakers and networking events.

Emily's List (Early Money Is Like Yeast)
202/326-1400
805 15th Street, NW, Suite 400, Washington, DC 20005
Emily's List raises money for Democratic pro-choice women candidates.

Woman's National Democratic Club
202/232-7363
1526 New Hampshire Ave., NW, Washington, DC 20036
Political, networking, educational and social group for women Democrats. Membership benefits include forums, featuring high-profile political speakers, seminars on current issues, political action events and community service projects.

Women's Council of the Democratic Senatorial Campaign Committee
202/224-2447
430 S. Capitol Street, SE, Washington, DC 20003
Supports Democratic, pro-choice women candidates for the Senate.

Women's Information Network (WIN)
202/347-2827
1511 K Street, NW, Suite 428, Washington, DC 20005
Democratic pro-choice group for young women that provides support for elections, political events and voter registration, as well as networking events and social activities.

Continuing the Legacy
by The League of Women Voters

Women fought for 72 years for the right to vote. In 1920, they finally had it. That same year Carrie Chapman founded the League of Women Voters to teach women how to use the vote and to encourage them to participate in the political process.

But the suffrage movement was not just about women gaining the right to vote. It was about making our democratic system serve all the citizens. It was about giving women a say in the government by whose rules they had to abide. After 75 years, these goals have not yet been fulfilled.

With experience and woman power working for us, we're ready for phase two—increasing the number of women and minorities in elected office.

Only 26 women have served in the U.S. Senate since 1789, compared to about 1,800 men. Only 187 women have served in the U.S. House of Representatives compared to 9,300 men. Only 13 women in American history have served as governor. As of April 1995, 21 percent of all state legislators were women. Twenty-one percent is still a long, long way from being proportional to the population. This tells us how exclusive our system has been and how many barriers we have to overcome.

The first barrier is money. In 1996, a seat in the House cost on average $660,000 and a Senate seat cost $3.6 million. The problem is that the current campaign finance laws place challengers at a disadvantage. When 90 percent of Congress is male, women are by definition challengers. Although 1994 saw a record number of women candidates for House seats, nearly half were challengers. On average, the 52 female challengers were outspent by their incumbents by a ratio of three to one.

The second barrier is time. More and more women are taking on the responsibility not only for children, but also for their parents. And they have to work. They're trying to do it all.

The third and most troubling barrier is the changing political climate. Campaigns are growing nasty. The practice of politics is becoming uglier. Not only the candidate, but even the candidate's children and spouse are subjected to sniping attacks. We are finding that civility—the common rules of decency—have seriously eroded. People no longer respectfully disagree. This intolerance for differing opinions has poisoned the political climate.

These are all serious barriers. Money is scarce. Time is just as scarce. It's no wonder that only one in nine women even thinks about running for public office. And there are still other challenges. Women have few role models, most do not view themselves as office holders, and no community-based programs exist to ensure that potential women and minority candidates come forward or gain the experience necessary to run and hold office effectively.

Now our challenge is to overcome these barriers to fulfill the entire legacy of our foremothers, the suffragists.

The League of League of Women Voters is a nonpartisan political organization that encourages the active and informed participation of citizens of government.

Republican Groups

League of Republican Women of the District of Columbia
202/452-7414
Political, social and networking group for Republican women.

National Federation of Republican Women
703/548-9688
124 North Alfred Street, Alexandria, VA 22314
Political education, community involvement and networking group for Republican women. The goals of the Federation are based on the Republican platform.

Republican National Committee (RNC), Women's Division
202/863-8500
310 First Street, SE, Washington, DC 20003
The Women's Division deals with policy issues of interest to women, based on the Republican platform.

Republicans for Choice
703/960-9882
2900 Eisenhower Ave., # 202, Alexandria, VA 22314
Advocacy group and political action committee for pro-choice Republicans.

RENEW—Republican Network to Elect Women
703/836-2255
1555 King Street, Suite 200, Alexandria, VA 22314
Mailing: PO Box 22313
RENEW works to elect Republican women through recruitment, training and the funding of candidates in all levels of government offices.

The WISH List—Women in the Senate and House
202/342-9111
3205 N Street, NW, Washington, DC 20007
Fundraising network to elect Republican pro-choice women candidates to the U.S. House of Representatives and the U.S. Senate.

6

Advocacy

Susan Lowell Butler, Consulting Editor

In times past, it had been referred to as "Chiffon Politics," the behind-the-scenes political influence wielded by Washington's prominent women. Tea parties, society dinners and evenings of bridge provided ideal forums to promote ideas and advance their political agendas. Eventually, however, the Chiffon politicians began moving in greater numbers to the more visible role of testifying at committee hearings. Women had already learned how to lobby their cause in public from their foremothers who ran a highly visible suffrage campaign that eventually led to the passage of the 19th Amendment. In the '60s and '70s, women continued to gain ground in the Capitol when the tide of social change and strong female leadership energized the advent of the women's movement. Women became a visible force with the formation of the National Organization for Women (NOW), the National Women's Political Caucus (NWPC) and other groups that championed women's rights.

Today, women's advocacy groups form a considerable force in the legislative arena. Hundreds of women's groups and both-gender groups advocate for issues of interest to women in almost every area of social and political concern. In recent years alone, women have made significant advancements. In 1991, a strong lobby of women's health advocates ensured the passage of the Women's Health Research Provision, which required the government to redress gender inequities in government-sponsored medical research. The Family Medical Leave Act of 1993 gave workers in businesses with 50 or more employees the right to take up to 12 weeks per year of unpaid job-protected leave for the purpose of tending to family health needs. The Violence Against Women Act improved conditions for the prevention and prosecution of sexual assault and other violent crimes against women.

Advocacy Groups by Subject

General Women's Issues
Alexandria Office on Women
Association of Junior Leagues
Center for Advancement of Public
    Policy
Center of Concern, Women's
    Project
Center for Development of
    Population Activities
Center for Policy Alternatives
Center for Women Policy Studies
Clearinghouse on Women's Issues
    Council of Presidents
DC Commission for Women
Fairfax County Commission for
    Women
Feminist Majority
General Fed. of Women's Clubs
Institute for Women's Policy
    Research
Intl. Center for Research on Women
Montgomery County Commission
    for Women
National Organization for Women
National Women's Law Center
Prince William County Commission
    for Women
Virginia Women's Network
Women Leaders Online
Women's Legal Defense Fund
Women's Research and Education
    Institute
YWCA

Business/Women in the Workforce
9 to 5, National Association of
    Working Women
AFL-CIO, Women's Rights Project
American Assn. of Univ. Women
American Fed. of Govt. Employees
Association for Women in Science
Center for Policy Alternatives
Centre for Development and
    Population Activities

Coalition of Labor Union Women
Federally Employed Women
Fed. of Orgs. for Profl. Women
Feminist Majority
Metropolitan Women's Org. Project
National Association of Negro
    Business and Profl. Women
National Assn. of Women Business
    Owners
National Committee on Pay Equity
National Fed. of Business and
    Professional Women
National Organization for Women
National Women's Law Center
Pension Rights Center
Wider Opportunities for Women
Women in Government
Women in Government Relations
Women Work!
Women's Action for Good
    Employment Standards
Women's Legal Defense Fund

Communications/Media
Intl. Women's Media Foundation
Women in Film and Video
Women's Institute for Freedom of
    the Press

Conservative
Concerned Women for America
Independent Women's Forum
Renaissance Women

Education
American Assn. of Univ. Women
American Council on Education
National Education Association
Women's College Coalition

Equality/Civil Rights
ERA Summit
National Woman's Party
National Women's Law Center
Women's Legal Defense Fund

"I believe that, on the eve of a new millennium, it is time to break our silence. It is time for us to say here in Beijing, and the world to hear, that it is no longer acceptable to discuss women's rights as separate from human rights. These abuses have continued because, for too long, the history of women has been a history of silence.

"It is a violation of human rights when babies are denied food, or drowned, or suffocated, or their spines broken, simply because they are born girls. It is a violation of human rights when women and girls are sold into the slavery of prostitution. It is a violation of human rights when women are doused with gasoline, set on fire and burned to death because their marriage dowries are deemed too small. It is a violation of human rights when individual women are raped in their own communities and when thousands of women are subjected to rape as a tactic or a prize of war. It is a violation of human rights when a leading cause of death worldwide among women ages 14 to 44 is the violence they are subjected to in their own homes by their own relatives. It is a violation of human rights when young girls are brutalized by the painful and degrading practice of genital mutilation. It is a violation of human rights when women are denied the right to plan their own families and that includes being forced to have abortions or being sterilized against their will.

"If there is one message that echoes forth from this conference, let it be that human rights are women's rights. And women's rights are human rights, once and for all."

First Lady Hillary Rodham Clinton
Fourth World Conference on Women, Beijing, September 1995

Family and Children

Advocates for Youth
Child Welfare League of America
Children's Defense Fund
Children's Foundation
Coalition for America's Children
Girl Scouts of the USA
Girls, Incorporated
National Assn. of Child Advocates
National Child Support Advocacy
  Coalition
National Women's Law Center
Women's Legal Defense Fund

Feminist

The Feminist Institute
The Feminist Majority
National Organization for Women

Health

American College of Nurse
  Midwives
American Medical Women's
  Association
American Nurses Association
Healthy Mothers, Healthy Babies
Jacobs Institute of Women's Health
Natl. Black Women's Health Project
National Breast Cancer Coalition
National Coalition for Cancer
  Survivorship
National Women's Health Network
Society for the Advancement of
  Women's Health Research
Virginia Breast Cancer Foundation

Human Rights/Peace

Amnesty International Women's
  Program
Eleanor Roosevelt Institute
Human Rights Watch
Sisterhood Is Global Institute
Women's Action for New
  Directions
Women's American ORT
Women's Fed. for World Peace
Women's Strike for Peace

Lesbian

Human Rights Campaign Fund
Natl. Gay and Lesbian Task Force
P-FLAG

Legal

Center for Law and Social Policy
NOW Legal Defense and Educ.
  Fund
Professional Women's Legal Fund
Women's Legal Defense Fund

Older Women

American Association of Retired
  Persons/Women's Initiative
Gray Panthers
Older Women's League

Politics

Democratic National
  Committee/Women's Division
Emily's List
League of Women Voters
National Fed. of Republican Women
National Women's Political Caucus
Republican National Committee/
  Women's Division

Religious

Church Women United
Jewish Women International
National Council of Catholic
  Women
National Council of Jewish Women
Women's Alliance for Theology,
  Ethics & Ritual

Reproductive Issues

Alan Guttmacher Institute
Catholics for a Free Choice
Centre for Development and
  Population Activities
Eagle Forum
Feminists for Life
National Abortion Federation
National Abortion Rights Action
  League (NARAL)

© Rick Reinhard

"We stand today at the Lincoln Memorial as American families and as an American community to commit ourselves to putting our children first, to building a just America that leaves no child behind, and to ensuring all our children healthy and safe passage to adulthood. We stand to affirm our belief that each of us individually and collectively as citizens of a great nation can do better in protecting and improving the quality of life for all children.

"This day is about unity and community, not about controversy. It is about rekindling our children's hope and renewing our faith in each other and in our nation's future. It is about America's ideals, not about any single group's ideology. It is about what we can do and are doing to make a difference for our children, and not about what we can't do. It is about principles of justice and compassion and not about personal or partisan politics. It celebrates our youth, family and community strengths rather than problems and seeks to turn our pain into the power of our collective healing—into a movement to leave no child behind."

Marian Wright Edelman
Stand for Children Day, Washington, D.C., June 1996

National Family Planning and
Reproductive Health Association
National Organization for Women
National Right to Life Committee
Planned Parenthood Federation Pro-
Life Alliance of Gays and
Lesbians
Religious Coalition for
Reproductive Choice
Republicans for Choice
Voters for Choice
Women's Legal Defense Fund

Natl. Coalition Against Domestic
Violence
National Council on Child Abuse
and Family Violence
National Network to End Domestic
Violence
National Organization for Women
National Organization for Women,
Legal Defense Fund
Women's Action for New
Directions
Women's Legal Defense Fund

Sports
National Association for Girls and
Women in Sport

Transportation
Maryland Association of Women
Highway Safety Leaders

Violence Against Women
Center forWomen Policy Studies
DC Coalition Against Domestic
Violence
Maryland Network Against
Domestic Violence

Women of Color
Black Women United for Action
Black Women's Agenda Inc.
Intl. Black Women's Congress
Mexican American Women's
National Association
National Assn. of Negro Business
and Profl. Women's Clubs
Natl. Conf. of Puerto Rican Women
National Council of Negro Women
Natl. Political Congress of Black
Women, Inc.
Org. of Chinese-American Women

"Integrating women, and issues of concern to them, into the mainstream of society and its institutions can be very difficult work. So too the application of a gender perspective to the identification, analysis and solution of problems. Adopting a gender perspective means changing much more than policies and programs on papers. It cannot be done by fiat, although it certainly helps to have the support and direction come from the highest level. It means changing the way we think, changing our world view, internalizing and assimilating this perspective into the body politic so that never again will women be marginalized and their issues put on the agenda as an afterthought, something to be considered only if time and resources allow."

Linda Tarr-Whelan
U.S. Representative
U.N. Commission on the Status of Women
United Nations, March 1996

Advocacy Groups

9 to 5, National Association of Working Women
800/522-0925
238 West Wisconsin, # 700
Milwaukee, WI 53203

Advocates for Youth
202/347-5700
1025 Vermont Ave., NW, # 200
Washington, DC 20005

AFL-CIO Women's Rights Project
202/638-0320
815 16th Street, NW, Suite 707
Washington, DC 20036

Alan Guttmacher Institute
202/296-4012
1120 Conn. Ave., NW, # 460
Washington, DC 20036

Alexandria Office on Women
703/838-5030
110 N. Royal Street, Room 201
Alexandria, VA 22314

American Association of Retired Persons (AARP) Women's Initiative
202/434-2400
601 E Street, NW
Washington, DC 20049

American Association of University Women (AAUW)
202/785-7700
1111 15th Street, NW
Washington, DC 20036

American College of Nurse Midwives
202/289-0171
818 Connecticut Ave., NW
Suite 900
Washington, DC 20006

American Council on Education, Office of Women in Higher Education
202/939-9390
1 Dupont Circle, NW, Suite 800
Washington, DC 20036

American Federation of Govt. Employees/Women's Dept.
202/737-8700
80 F Street, NW
Washington, DC 20001

American Medical Women's Association
703/838-0500
801 Fairfax Street, Suite 400
Alexandria, VA 22314

American Nurses Association
202/544-4444
600 Maryland Ave., SW
Washington, DC 20024-2571

Amnesty International Women's Program
202/775-5161
1118 22nd Street, NW
Washington, DC 20037

Equality Within the Law

U.S. Supreme Court Justice Ruth Bader Ginsburg

Even at an early age, U.S. Supreme Court Justice Ruth Bader Ginsburg recognized the inequities of society. Her true inspiration was her mother Celia, who would see to it that her daughter got the chance she never had. And she viewed education as the key. Celia took her daughter on frequent trips to the library and saved her pin money for a college fund. And Celia's encouragement paid off. Young Ruth excelled in high school and won scholarships to college. Tragically, Celia Bader died of cancer the day before Ruth's high school graduation ceremony.

Celia's legacy of a better life for her daughter was a theme that would play throughout the life of the future U.S. Supreme Court Justice, who has spent most of her life working to redress gender inequities within the law so that future generations of girls and women would have even greater opportunities than herself. This is how she remembered her mother in 1993 after being nominated to the U.S. Supreme Court.

"I have one last thank you. It is to my mother, Celia Amster Bader, the bravest and strongest person I have known, who was taken from me much too soon. I pray that I may be all that she would have been had she lived in an age when women could aspire and achieve, and daughters are cherished as much as sons."

When she entered Harvard Law School, Ruth Bader Ginsburg was already married and the mother of a 14-month-old daughter. She was one of only nine women in the class of 1959. She transferred to Columbia Law School for her final year of law studies. She graduated at the top of her law class but still had a difficult time securing a clerkship.

"My status as a woman, a Jew and a mother to boot was a bit much for prospective employers in those days," said Justice Ginsburg.

But Justice Ginsburg eventually gained a clerkship with a New York District Court judge. Next, she accepted a position as researcher, then associate director of Columbia Law School's Project on International Procedure. In 1963, she was hired as the second woman on the law faculty at Rutgers University in New Jersey, where she worried about retaining her job once she became pregnant with her second child and even hid the pregnancy by wearing loose-fitting clothing.

Justice Ginsburg's study of the law and her own personal experiences with second-class treatment shaped her feeling that the inequalities were a symptom of broader social conditions that denied women choices and opportunities that were available to men. She believed law could be used to help redress those inequities. Ginsburg joined the New Jersey affiliate of the ACLU and began litigating cases on behalf of New Jersey teachers who were forced to forfeit their jobs when they became pregnant.

After being asked to teach a course on sex-based discrimination at Rutgers University, she began researching gender discrimination within the law. She found there was a series of laws that treated women unfairly by forbidding them to work at certain professions. The rationale was that women were "the gentler sex" and in need of special protection from life's hardships. Justice Ginsburg believed that gender discrimination should be included in the Fourteenth Amendment, which prohibits the denial of the equal protection of the law to any person. At the time, gender discrimination was not considered an acceptable topic of discussion.

"Race discrimination was immediately perceived as evil, odious, and intolerable. But the response I got when I talked about sex-based discrimination was 'What are you talking about? Women are treated ever so much better than men.' I was talking to an audience that thought I was somehow critical about the way they treated their wives and their daughters," said Ginsburg.

It was then that Justice Ginsburg launched her campaign that would later earn her the title of "the Thurgood Marshall of gender equality law." She joined forces with the ACLU's national office, and helped write the ACLU's brief in the key Supreme Court gender-discrimination case, *Reed v. Reed* (1971), and continued litigating cases on gender-based discrimination. Her reasoning that it harmed not only women, but all of society, won her many cases. She argued that the well-being of families was at stake when women received differential treatment. Eventually, the Court accepted Ginsburg's view that challenges to gender-based legal distinctions deserved close scrutiny. Today, prohibition of gender discrimination is well established within the law.

The efforts of Justice Ginsburg were not overlooked. In 1980, she was appointed to the U.S. Court of Appeals for the District of Columbia Circuit. Thirteen years later, she was appointed to the highest court in the nation, the U.S. Supreme Court.

Assn. for Women in Science
202/408-0742
1522 K Street, NW, Suite 820
Washington, DC 20005

Association of Junior Leagues
202/393-3364
1319 F Street, NW, Suite 604
Washington, DC 20004

Black Women United for Action
703/922-5757
6551 Loisdale Court, Suite 714
Springfield, VA 22150

Black Women's Agenda Inc.
202/387-4166
3501 14th Street, NW
Washington, DC 20010

Catholics for a Free Choice
202/986-6093
1436 U Street, NW, Suite 301
Washington, DC 20009

Center for Advancement of Public Policy
202/797-0606
1735 S Street, NW
Washington, DC 20009

Center of Concern Women's Project
202/635-2757
3700 13th Street, NW
Washington, DC 20017

Center for Development and Population Activities
202/667-1142
1717 Mass. Ave., NW, # 200
Washington, DC 20036

Center for Law and Social Policy
202/328-5140
1616 P Street, NW
Washington, DC 20036

Center for Policy Alternatives/Women's Economic Justice Program
202/387-6030
1875 Connecticut Avenue, NW
Suite 710
Washington, DC 20009
http://www.cfpa.org/pub/cfpa

Center for Women Policy Studies
202/872-1770
2000 P Street, NW, # 508
Washington, DC 20036

Centre for Development and Population Activities
202/667-1142
1717 Massachusetts Ave., NW
Washington, DC 20036

Child Welfare League of America, Inc.
202/638-2952
440 First Street, NW, Suite 300
Washington, DC 20036

Children's Defense Fund
202/628-8787
25 E Street, NW
Washington, DC 20001

Children's Foundation
202/347-3300
725 15th Street, NW, Suite 505
Washington, DC 20005

Church Women United
202/544-8747
110 Maryland Avenue, NE
Washington, DC 20002

Clearinghouse on Women's Issues
202/362-3789
PO Box 70603
Friendship Heights, MD 20813

Coalition for America's Children
202/638-5770
1634 Eye Street, NW, 12th Fl.
Washington, DC 20006

Coalition of Labor Union Women
202/296-1200
1126 16th Street, NW
Washington, DC 20036

Concerned Women for America
202/488-7000
370 L'Enfant Promenade, SW
Suite 800
Washington, DC 20024

Council of Presidents
202/331-7343
c/o National Committee on Pay Equity
1126 16th Street, NW
Washington, DC 20036

DC Coalition Against Domestic Violence
202/387-5630
513 U Street, NW
Washington, DC 20001

DC Commission for Women
202/939-8083
2000 14th Street, NW, Suite 354
Washington, DC 20009

Democratic National Committee/Women's Division
202/863-8183
430 South Capitol Street, SE
Washington, DC 20003

Eagle Forum
202/544-0353
316 Pennsylvania Ave., SE
Washington, DC 20003

Eleanor Roosevelt Institute
202/387-3713
2023 Q Street, NW
Washington, DC 20009

Emily's List
202/326-1400
805 15th Street, NW, Suite 400
Washington, DC 20005

ERA Summit/Americans for Democratic Action
202/785-5980
1625 K Street, NW, Suite 210
Washington, DC 20006

Fairfax County Commission for Women
703/324-5730
12000 Government Center Parkway, Suite 318
Fairfax, VA 22035

Federally Employed Women
202/898-0994
1400 Eye Street, NW, Suite 425
Washington, DC 20005

**Federation of Organizations
for Professional Women**
202/328-1415
2001 S Street, NW, Suite 500
Washington, DC 20009

The Feminist Majority
703/522-2214
1600 Wilson Blvd., Suite 801
Arlington, VA 22209
http://www.feminist.org

Feminists for Life
202/737-FFLA
202/393-3352, Action Line
733 15th Street, NW, Suite 1100
Washington, DC 20005

**General Federation of
Women's Clubs**
202/835-0246
1734 N Street, NW
Washington, DC 20036

Girls, Incorporated
202/463-1881
3101 New Mexico Ave., NW
Suite 240
Washington, DC 20016

Girl Scouts of the USA
202/659-3780
1025 Connecticut Ave., NW
Suite 309
Washington, DC 20036

Gray Panthers
202/466-3132
2025 Pennsylvania Ave., NW
Suite 821
Washington, DC 20006

**Healthy Mothers, Healthy
Babies**
202/863-2458
409 12th Street, SW, # 309
Washington, DC 20024

**Human Rights Campaign
Fund**
202/628-4160
1101 14th Street, NW, Suite 200
Washington, DC 20005

**Human Rights Watch
Women's Rights Project**
202/371-6592
1522 K Street, NW, Suite 910
Washington, DC 20005

Independent Women's Forum
703/243-8989
2111 Wilson Blvd., Suite 550
Arlington, VA 22201
http://www.iwf.org

**Institute for Women's Policy
Research**
202/785-5100
1400 20th Street, NW, # 104
Washington, DC 20036

Intl. Black Women's Congress
202/234-4292
1212 New York Ave.
Washington, DC

**International Center for
Research on Women**
202/797-0007
1717 Mass. Ave., NW, # 302
Washington, DC 20036

International Women's Media Foundation (IWMF)
202/496-1992
1001 Connecticut Ave., NW
Suite 1201
Washington, DC 20036

Jacobs Institute of Women's Health
202/863-4990
409 12th Street, SW
Washington, DC 20024

Jewish Women International
202/857-1370
1828 L Street, NW, Suite 250
Washington, DC 20036

League of Women Voters
202/429-1965
1730 M Street, NW
Washington, DC 20036

Maryland Assn. of Women Highway Safety Leaders
301/868-7583
7206 Robinhood Drive
Upper Marlboro, MD 20772

Maryland Network Against Domestic Violence
301/942-0900
11501 Georgia Ave., Suite 403
Silver Spring, MD 20902-1955

Metropolitan Women's Organizing Project
202/659-9589
PO Box 65883
Washington, DC 20035

Mexican American Women's National Association (MANA)
202/833-0060
1725 K Street, NW, Suite 501
Washington, DC 20006

Montgomery County Commission for Women
301/279-1800
255 North Washington Street
Rockville, MD 20850

National Abortion Federation
202/667-5881
1436 U Street, NW, # 103
Washington, DC 20009

National Abortion Rights Action League (NARAL)
202/973-3000
1156 15th Street, NW, Suite 700
Washington, DC 20005

National Assn. of Child Advocates
202/289-0777
1522 K Street, NW, Suite 600
Washington, DC 20005

National Assn. for Girls and Women in Sport (NAGWS)
703/476-3452
1900 Association Drive
Reston, VA 22091-1599

National Association of Negro Business and Profl. Women
202/483-4206
1806 New Hampshire Ave.,
NW
Washington, DC 20009

National Association of Women Business Owners (NAWBO)
301/608-2590
1100 Wayne Ave., Suite 830
Silver Spring, MD 20910

National Black Women's Health Project
202/835-0117
211 Connecticut Avenue, NW
Suite 310
Washington, DC 20036

National Breast Cancer Coalition
202/296-7477, 800/935-0434
1707 L Street, NW, Suite 1060
Washington, DC 20036
http://www.natlbcc.org

National Child Support Advocacy Coalition
703/799-6559
PO Box 4629
Alexandria, VA 22303

National Coalition Against Domestic Violence
202/638-6388
PO Box 34103
Washington, DC 20043

National Coalition for Cancer Survivorship
301/650-8868

National Committee on Pay Equity
202/331-7343
1126 16th Street, NW, Suite 411
Washington, DC 20036

National Conference of Puerto Rican Women
202/387-4716
5 Thomas Circle, NW
Washington, DC 20005

National Council of Catholic Women
202/682-0334
1275 K Street, NW, Suite 975
Washington, DC 20005

Natl. Council of Jewish Women
202/296-2588
1707 L Street, NW, Suite 950
Washington, DC 20036

National Council on Child Abuse and Family Violence
202/429-6695
1155 Connecticut Ave., NW
Washington, DC 20036

Natl. Council of Negro Women
202/737-0120, 202/463-6680
633 Pennsylvania Ave., NW
Washington, DC 20004

National Education Association
202/822-7300
1201 16th Street, NW
Washington, DC 20036

National Family Planning and Reproductive Health Association (NFPRHA)
202/628-3535
122 C Street, NW, Suite 380
Washington, DC 20001-2109

National Federation of
Business and Professional
Women, Inc.
202/293-1100
2012 Massachusetts Ave., NW
Washington, DC 20036

National Federation of
Republican Women
703/548-9688
124 North Alfred Street
Alexandria, VA 22314

National Gay and Lesbian
Task Force
202/332-6483
2320 17th Street, NW
Washington, DC 20009

National Network to End
Domestic Violence
202/434-7405
701 Pennsylvania Ave., NW
Washington, DC 20004

National Organization for
Women (NOW)
202/331-0066
1000 16th Street, NW, # 700
Washington DC 20036

National Political Congress of
Black Women, Inc.
202/338-0800
600 New Hampshire Ave., NW
Suite 1125
Washington, DC 20037

National Right to Life
Committee
202/626-8800
419 Seventh Street, NW, # 500
Washington, DC 20004

National Woman's Party
202/546-1210
144 Constitution Ave., NE
Washington, DC 20002

National Women's Health
Network
202/347-1140
514 10th Street, NW, Suite 400
Washington, DC 20004

National Women's Law Center
202/588-5180
11 Dupont Circle, Suite 800
Washington, DC 20036

National Women's Political
Caucus
202/785-1100
1211 Connecticut Ave., NW
Washington, DC 20036

NOW Legal Defense and
Education Fund (NLDF)
202/544-4470
120 Maryland Ave.
Washington, DC 20002

Older Women's League
202/783-6686
666 11th Street, NW, 7th Floor
Washington, DC 20001

Organization of Chinese-
American Women
202/638-0330
1300 N Street, NW, Suite 100
Washington, DC 20005

P-FLAG
202/638-4200
1101 14th Street, NW, # 300
Washington, DC 20005

Pension Rights Center
Women's Pension Project
202/296-3776
918 16th Street, NW, Suite 704
Washington, DC 20006

Planned Parenthood
Federation
202/785-3351
1120 Conn. Ave, NW, Suite 461
Washington, DC 20036

Prince William County
Commission for Women
703/792-6611
4370 Ridgewood Center Dr., #D
Woodbridge, VA 22192

Pro-Life Alliance of Gays and
Lesbians
202/223-6697
PO Box 33292
Washington, DC 20033

Religious Coalition for Repro-
ductive Choice
202/628-7700
1025 Vermont Ave., NW,
1130
Washington, DC 20005

Renaissance Women
202/546-4142
205 Third Street, SE
Washington, DC 20003

Republican National Commit-
tee /Women's Division
202/863-8500
310 First Street, SE
Washington, DC 20003

Republicans for Choice
703/960-9882
2900 Eisenhower Ave., # 202
Alexandria, VA 22314

Sisterhood Is Global Institute
301/657-4355
4343 Montgomery Ave., # 201
Bethesda, MD 20814

Society for the Advancement
of Women's Health Research
202/223-8224
1920 L Street, NW
Washington, DC 20036

Virginia Breast Cancer Foun-
dation
804/285-1200
PO Box 17884
Richmond, VA 23226

Virginia Women's Network
703/938-8316
617 John Marshall Drive, NW
Vienna, VA 22180

Voters for Choice
202/588-5200
2604 Connecticut Avenue, NW
Washington, DC 20008

Wider Opportunities for
Women (WOW)
202/638-3143
815 15th Street, NW, Suite 916
Washington, DC 20005

The Woman Activist Fund
703/573-8716
2310 Barbour Road
Falls Church, VA 22043

Women in Government
202/333-0825
2600 Viginia Ave., NW, # 709
Washington, DC 20037-1905

**Women in Government
Relations**
202/347-5432
1029 Vermont Ave., NW, # 510
Washington, DC 20005

Women Leaders Online
wlo@wlo.org

Women Work!
202/467-6346, 800/235-2732
1625 K Street, NW, # 300
Washington, DC 20006

**Women's Action for Good
Employment Standards**
202/483-8643
1616 18th St, NW, Suite 109-B
Washington, DC 20009

**Women's Action for New
Directions**
202/543-8505
110 Maryland Ave., NE, # 205
Washington, DC 20002

**Women's Alliance for
Theology, Ethics & Ritual**
301/589-2509
8035 13th Street
Silver Spring, MD 20910

Women's American ORT
301/424-7541
356 Hungerford Drive
Rockville, MD 20850

Women's College Coalition
202/234-0443
125 Michigan Ave., NE
Washington, DC 20017

**Women's Federation for
World Peace**
202/291-4977
4224 16th Street, NW
Washington, DC 20011

**Women's Institute for
Freedom of the Press**
202/966-7783
3306 Ross Place, NW
Washington, DC 20008-3332

Women's Legal Defense Fund
202/986-2600
1875 Conn. Ave., NW, # 700
Washington, DC 20009
e-mail: info@wldf.org

**Women's Research and
Education Institute**
202/328-7070
1700 18th Street, NW, 4th Floor
Washington, DC 20009

Women's Strike for Peace
202/543-2660
110 Maryland Ave., NE, # 302
Washington, DC 20002

YWCA
202/628-3636
624 9th Street, NW, 2nd Floor
Washington, DC 20001

Policy Publications

Action Bulletin for Women's Rights
703/573-8716
2310 Barbour Road
Falls Church, VA 22043-2940
Newsletter published by the Woman Activist that contains information on policy issues and other developments affecting women's rights.

Alert
202/328-1415
1825 I Street, NW, Suite 400
Washington, DC 20006
Bi-monthly newsletter published by the Federation of Organizations for Professional Women that reports on policy activities that affect women.

CWI Newsletter
301/871-6106
PO Box 70603
Friendship Heights, MD 20813
Newsletter published monthly by the Clearinghouse on Women's Issues that monitors activities and policy developments that affect the women's movement.

Political Woman Hotline
wlo@wlo.org
E-mail alert service offered by Women Leaders Online that reports activist information on issues of interest to women.

The Source
202/554-2323
409 12th Street, SW, Suite 705
Washington, DC 20024
Bimonthly newsletter published by Women's Policy, Inc. that tracks legislative developments in the U.S. Congress on issues of interest to women and families. *The Source* monitors bill introductions, floor actions, mark-ups and committee actions and relevant legislative activities.

Washington Feminist Faxnet
202/265-6245
1735 S Street, NW
Washington, DC 20009
Weekly faxed update compiled by the Center for Advancement of Public Policy on happenings in Congress and around the nation that affect the feminist movement.

The Women's Quarterly
703/243-8989
2111 Wilson Blvd., Suite 550
Arlington, VA 22201-3057
http://www.iwf.org
Quarterly journal published by the Independent Women's Forum which contains articles and commentary on issues of interest to women, including commentary and investigative essays.

Part III
Health Care

7

Women's Health Care Guide

Valerie Gwinner, Consulting Editor

Washington, D.C., is home to a wide variety of health care professionals who treat women or specialize in women's health. But which is right for you? Finding the right doctor may consist of examining qualifications or getting a recommendation from someone you trust. The decision might also depend on your health plan. Some allow patients to choose any doctor and others require that you choose a physician from an established list.

Most women refer to a primary care provider for their general medical care, such as annual physicals and treatment for illnesses. These include general practitioners, internists, and family practitioners. Many women use their ob/gyn as their primary health provider. Nurse practitioners, who are becoming more popular, especially among HMO patients, can also perform physical exams and treat common illnesses and diseases.

Once you have decided on the type of care provider, you may want to consider these questions. Do you want a female provider? Does location of the practice play a role in your decision? Do you want a provider who focuses on women's health? What type of setting do you prefer—private practice, group office or clinic setting? To get even more detailed information, you can research the credentials and backgrounds of possible providers, so that you feel comfortable with your selection.

Reproductive Health Services

Many women get their basic reproductive health care services from a general practitioner, ob/gyn or nurse-midwife. Ob/gyns and nurse midwives specialize in providing prenatal care and delivering babies.

Women's Periodic Health Tests

	Routine Tests	How Often
Ages 19-39	Pelvic Exam, including	
	Pap Test and STD tests	Annually
	Cholesterol	Every 5 years
	Tetanus-Diphtheria booster	Every 10 years
Ages 40-64	All the above tests plus:	
	Mammography	Every 1-2 years until age 50, then annually
	Fecal occult blood test	Annually
	Sigmoidoscopy	Every 3-5 years after age 50, then annually at 55
Ages 65+	All the above tests plus:	
	Cholesterol	Every 3-5 years
	Thyroid-stimulating hormone	Every 3-5 years
	Urinalysis	Annually
	Pneumococcal vaccine	Once

Sources: American College of Obstetricians and Gynecologists, National Preventative Task Force

Women should receive a reproductive health exam—or wellness exam—on an annual basis, especially if they are sexually active. If a woman has special risk factors, then more frequent visits are required. Here is what to expect from a typical wellness exam.

Physical Exam. The doctor will check your weight and blood pressure, listen to your heartbeat, and feel your abdomen and neck.

Breast Exam. Your doctor will check your breasts for signs of lumps to help prevent breast cancer. You should also be performing breast self exams on a regular basis. If you do not know how to perform a breast self exam, then this is a good time to ask your physician to show you how.

Pelvic Exam. Your doctor will examine your outside genitals and then insert a slender instrument called a speculum into the vagina to view the vagina and cervix. With a swab, the doctor will remove samples from your cervix that will be analyzed in the lab to test for cervical cancer and any other irregularities. The doctor checks the size, position and shape of your uterus and ovaries by reaching into your vagina with one or two fingers and pressing down on the lower abdomen with the other hand.

Mammography

Mammography is a life-saving technique that can locate tumors too small for you or your doctor to feel. Annual mammograms are recommended for women over the age of 50. Although mammography guidelines are in the process of being reevaluated, many health groups recommend women 40 years and older get a mammogram every one to two years.

In 1992, the Food and Drug Administration (FDA) adopted strict requirements for mammography facilities across the nation, ensuring women access to safe and reliable mammography in their communities. The guidelines require that facilities pass inspection by providing approved equipment and trained technicians to administer mammograms. Certificates of compliance should be on display at sites that have been approved by the FDA. To locate an approved facility in your area or for more information about breast cancer detection services, contact the FDA Mammography Information Service at 800/4-CANCER.

Low-Cost Mammography Programs in the D.C. Area

Unfortunately, not all women get a mammogram. If money is the barrier, then there are a number of reduced-cost and even no-cost mammography programs available at hospitals and health centers in the D.C. area. County facilities require women live in the county. For more information about reduced-cost mammography programs, contact the Komen Foundation at 800/I'M-AWARE. For information about Medicare coverage of mammography, call 800/638-6833. The following health centers offer low-cost or no-cost mammography programs.

Alexandria Hospital
703/504-3000
4320 Seminary Road
Alexandria, VA 22304

Bailey's Health Center
703/931-3606
5827 Columbia Pike

Falls Church, VA 22041

Columbia Hospital for Women
Betty Ford Comprehensive
Breast Center
202/293-6654
2425 L Street, NW
Washington, DC 20037

Fairfax County Health Dept.
South County Health Center
703/660-9542
7692 Richmond Highway
Alexandria, VA 22306

Greater Southeast Community
Hospital
202/574-6000
1310 Southern Ave., SE
Washington, DC 20032

Montgomery Co. Health Dept.
301/217-1750
100 Maryland Ave.
Rockville, MD 20850

Prince George's County
Health Department
301/856-9470, 9480

9314 Piscataway Road
Clinton, MD 20735

Prince George's Hospital
Center
301/275-2000
3001 Hospital Drive
Cheverly, MD 20785

Shady Grove Adventist
Hospital
301/279-6000
9901 Medical Center Drive
Rockville, MD 20850

Washington Adventist Hospital
301/891-7600
7600 Carroll Ave.
Takoma Park, MD 20912

Women's Health Centers

Women's health centers offer annual wellness exams and other related services, such as contraception, testing for sexually transmitted diseases or abortion services. In addition to the listed resources, you can also find services at hospitals and community health centers.

Columbia Hospital for Women Medical Center
202/293-6540
2425 L St., NW, # 330
Washington, DC 200037

301/309-9116
9707 Medical Center Drive
Rockville, MD 20850

Columbia Hospital offers comprehensive health services for women, girls and newborns. It is the only women's hospital in the country established and chartered by Congress. The hospital provides general health care, reproductive exams, surgery services, breast cancer screening and many other specialty areas, such as a Women's Wellness and Community Education Program and cosmetic surgery.

Alexandria Women's Health Clinic
703/370-0550
101 S. Whiting Street
Alexandria, VA 22304

Annandale Women and Family Center
703/751-4702
2839 Duke Street
Alexandria, VA 22314

Capitol Women's Center
202/338-2772
1339 22nd Street, NW
Washington, DC 20037

Commonwealth Women's Clinic
703/533-3700
916 W. Broad Street
Falls Church, VA 22046

Femme Care Medical Center for Women
703/385-6400
10565 Lee Highway
Fairfax, VA 22030

Hillcrest Women's Surgi-Cntr.
202/829-5620
7603 Georgia Ave., NW
Washington, DC 20012

202/584-6500
3233 Pennsylvania Ave., NW
Washington, DC 20020

Metropolitan Family Planning Institute
301/474-5300
5915 Greenbelt Road
College Park, MD 20740

301/423-3313
5625 Allentown Road
Camp Springs, MD 20746

New Summit Medical Center
202/337-7200
1630 Euclid Street, NW
Washington, DC 20009

Nova Women's Medical Center
703/280-1500
9900 Main Street
Fairfax, VA 22031

Planned Parenthood
202/347-8512
1108 16th Street, NW
Washington, DC 20036

202/581-5710
2811 Pennsylvania Ave., SE
Washington, DC 20020

703/820-3335
5622 Columbia Pike, Suite 303
Falls Church, VA 22041

703/385-3404
10875 Main Street, Suite 208
Fairfax, VA 22030

301/468-7676
4701 Randolph Road, Suite 209
Rockville, MD 20852

301/773-5601
Landover Mall, East, Suite 203
Landover, MD 20785

301/588-7933
8605 Cameron Street, Suite 204
Silver Spring, MD 20910

301/208-1300
19650 Clubhouse Road
Gaithersburg, MD 20879

Potomac Family Planning Center
301/251-9124
966 Hungerford Drive
Rockville, MD 20850

Prince George's Reproductive Health Services
301/434-2300
7411 Riggs Road
Hyattsville, MD 20783

Takoma Women's Health Center
301/270-8880
7005 Carroll Ave.
Takoma Park, MD 20912

202/331-9293
2141 K Street, NW
Washington, DC 20037

Washington Free Clinic
202/667-1106
1525 Newton Street, NW
Washington, DC 20010

Washington Surgi-Clinic
202/659-9403
1018 22nd Street, NW
Washington, DC

Woman Care of Washington
301/869-5550
803 Russell Ave., Suite 2A
Gaithersburg, MD 20879

Women's Clinic
202/877-6037
110 Irving Street, NW
Washington, DC

Women's Comprehensive Health Center
202/483-4400
1700 17th Street, NW
Washington, DC

Finding Quality Health Care Coverage

An estimated 40 percent of women living in Washington, D.C. do not have health insurance. That's a staggering number. However, it's less shocking when you consider Washington's high rate of part-time and transitional employment, which often leaves employees without health coverage. The result is that women are having to purchase health insurance on their own or go without. Finding a health plan that meets your needs and your price range may be a challenge. Here are some resources that can help you make a selection.

Center for the Study of Services
202/347-7283
733 15th Street, NW
Washington, DC 20005
Publishes the *Consumer's Guide to Health Plans* that rates HMOs and provides information on selecting a health care plan.

Health Insurance Association of America
202/824-1600
1025 Connecticut Ave., NW
Washington, DC 20036
Provides basic information on health coverage.

Maryland Insurance Administration
800/492-6116
Provides some consumer information about health insurance.

National Committee for Quality Assurance
202/955-3515
2000 L Street, NW, # 500
Washington, DC 20036
Offers information on selecting a health plan.

Virginia Bureau of Insurance
800/552-7945
Provides some consumer information about health insurance.

Virginia Insurance Counseling and Advocacy Project
804/225-2271
700 E. Franklin Street
Richmond, VA 23219
Sponsored by the Virginia Department for Aging, this group assists the elderly on insurance matters and programs.

Medicaid

Medicaid is government health care assistance for low-income residents. For information and eligibility requirements for Medicaid, contact your county health department.

Arlington County
703/358-5620

800 S. Walter Reed Drive
Arlington, VA 22204

District of Columbia
Dept. of Human Services
202/724-5236
2100 Martin Luther King Jr.
  Ave., SE
Washington, DC 20032

Fairfax County
703/324-7500
12011 Govt. Center Parkway
Fairfax, VA 22035

Montgomery County
301/468-4386
5630 Fishers Lane
Rockville, MD 20852

Prince George's County
301/422-5077
6111 Ager Rd.
Hyattsville, MD 20782

Comparing Health Insurance Plans

Think carefully about your health care situation. Do you want coverage for your whole family or just yourself? Do you want protection for a catastrophic illness or disability? Are you concerned with preventative care and checkups? Do you want to choose your providers or would you be comfortable in a managed care setting that might restrict your choices? Here are some issues to consider when comparing health plans.

- Inpatient hospital services
- Outpatient surgery
- Physician visits (in the hospital)
- Office visits
- Skilled nursing care
- Medical tests and X-rays
- Prescription drugs
- Psychiatric and mental health care
- Drug and alcohol abuse treatment
- Home health care visits
- Rehabilitation facility care
- Physical therapy
- Hospice care
- Maternity care
- Chiropractic treatment
- Preventative care and checkups
- Well-baby care
- Dental care
- Wellness programs (e.g., nutrition counseling, smoking cessation)

Cost-Related Questions to Ask

*   How much is the premium (monthly, quarterly or annually)?
*   Are there any discounts available for good health or healthy behaviors?
*   How much is the annual deductible?
*   What coinsurance or copayments apply?
*   Is there an annual "out-of-pocket" maximum amount of coinsurance that is paid per year for covered services? How much?
*   Is there a lifetime maximum benefit?
*   What cost containment and quality assurance procedures are included (e.g., utilization review, precertification, second surgical opinions)?

Service-Related Questions to Ask

*   Are there any medical service limits, exclusions, or preexisting conditions that will affect you or your family?
*   How will service needs be handled? Is there a local or toll-free phone number?
*   Will you fill out claim forms? How long will it take for claims to be processed?
*   Is the insurance company a solid one? Does it have good references? Is it licensed by the state? What is its financial stability/rating?
*   Can you be seen on evenings or weekends, or do you have to go to the emergency room during those times?

Source: Health Insurance Association of America

Finding a Physician

Once you have decided on a health care plan, the next step is locating a physician to care for your health needs. Local physician guide books can help you make a selection. Medical societies also provide consumers with some information to help make wise decisions. Many offer physician lists and individual merits, such as board certification and hospital privileges.

Guide to Women Physicians in the Washington DC Area, by Judy Grande, Rocky Run Publishing, McLean, VA.

Directory of 540 female physicians, including their credentials, where they received training, board certification, languages and other related information to compare and contrast doctors.

Guide to Physicians in the Washington DC Area, by Judy Grande, Rocky Run Publishing, McLean, VA.
Directory of physicians working in the Washington Area, including credentials, training, areas of expertise and specialties.

Health Care Choices in the Washington Area, by Families USA, Families USA Foundation, 1334 G Street, NW, Washington, DC 20005.
Book contains information on locating health care providers and physicians plus other health resources of interest to women and parents.

Alexandria Medical Society
703/751-4611
101 South Whiting Street, # 210
Alexandria, VA 22304

Arlington Medical Society
703/528-0888
4615 Lee Highway
Arlington, VA 22207

Fairfax County Medical Society
703/560-4855
8100 Oak Street
Dunn Loring, VA 22027

Howard County Medical Society
410/781-6300
PO Box 1340
Elicott City, MD 21041

Loudoun Co. Medical Society
703/430-7884
PO Box 230
Leesburg, VA 22075

Maryland Medical and Chirurgical Society
800/492-1056
1211 Cathedral Street
Baltimore, MD 21201

Medical Society of the District of Columbia
202/466-1800
1707 L Street, NW, Suite 400
Washington, DC 20036

Montgomery County Medical Society
301/921-4300
15855 Crabbs Branch West
Rockville, MD 20855

Prince George's County Medical Society
301/341-7758
6307 Landover Road
Cheverly, MD 20785

Prince William County Medical Society
703/368-6505
PO Box 1447
Manassas, VA 22110

8

Women's Health Issues and Resources

Valerie Gwinner, Consulting Editor

Throughout the life course, men and women face very different health issues and conditions—even discounting reproductive issues. Although women generally live longer than men, they are more susceptible to chronic ailments, such as autoimmune diseases and depression. Women are the fastest growing group to contract the AIDS virus and they comprise nearly all cases of breast cancer and eating disorders. They are also far more likely than men to suffer from rape and physical abuse. This chapter contains numerous organizations to help women make informed health decisions. Many of the organizations provide information, referrals, and other services that address women's health needs.

General Women's Health Resources

National Black Women's Health Project (NBWHP)
202/835-0117
1211 Connecticut Ave., Suite 310, NW, Washington, DC 20036
NBWHP provides information on women's health issues of interest to black women. NBWHP offers links to self-help groups in all areas of mental and emotional well-being in the D.C. community and nationally.

National Maternal and Child Health Clearinghouse
703/821-2098
2070 Chain Bridge Rd., Suite 450, Vienna, VA 21182-2536
Provides information and referrals for reproductive and child health needs.

National Women's Health Information Center (NWHIC)
http://www.4woman.org

The NWHIC provides information on a variety of women's health concerns for consumers and health care professionals. Topics include mental illness, osteoporosis, eating disorders, heart disease, HIV/AIDS and issues pertinent to older and younger women. NWHIC is provided by the U.S. Public Health Service's Office on Women's Health and the U.S. Department of Defense.

National Women's Health Resource Center
202/293-6045
2425 L Street, NW, Washington, DC 20037

Operated by Columbia Hospital for Women, the Center provides information, referrals and publications on women's health issues for consumers and health care professionals. NWHRC operates a health information library which can be accessed by request over the phone, in writing, or in person. Members receive services at no cost and others pay a nominal fee.

Office of Minority Health Resource Center
800/444-MHRC (6472)
Office of Minority Health, DHHS
PO Box 37337, Washington, DC 20013

The Office of Minority Health Resource Center is the largest resource and referral service on minority health in the nation. The Center provides information, publications, referrals and other resources on health issues of interest to women and minorities.

Women's Health Information Clearinghouse
National Women's Health Network (NWHN)
202/628-7814, Clearinghouse
202/347-1140, NWHN
514 10th Street, NW, Suite 400, Washington, DC 20004

The Women's Health Information Clearinghouse provides information on a variety of women's health issues to the public and health care professionals. The clearinghouse is operated by the National Women's Health Network (NWHN), a membership group that provides publications and services to members at no cost and to nonmembers for a nominal fee. Information can be accessed over the phone or from an on-site library. NWHN publishes reports and other health materials and provides health referrals.

Alcohol/Drugs

Women are at greater risk than men for developing health problems—such as liver disease and reproductive complications—as a result of abusing drugs or alcohol. Women who abuse drugs and alcohol also put themselves at greater risk for contracting tuberculosis, breast cancer, oral and pharynx cancer, HIV/AIDS and sexually transmitted diseases.

Alcohol, Drugs and Pregnancy Healthline
800/638-2229
Information line for expecting mothers that provides assistance on the effects of using drugs or alcohol while pregnant.

American Council for Drug Education
800/488-DRUG
204 Monroe Street, Suite 110, Rockville, MD 20850

Center for Substance Abuse Treatment
800/662-4357

National Clearinghouse for Alcohol and Drug Information
800/729-6686
PO Box 2345, Rockville, MD 20847-2345

National Drug Information Treatment and Referral Line
800/662-HELP
11426-28 Rockville Pike, Suite 410, Rockville, MD 20852

Washington Area Council on Alcohol and Drug Abuse
202/783-1300
Information and referrals on treatment and other services on alcohol and drug abuse.

Women's Services Center
202/727-5166
1905 E Street, SE, Building 13, Washington, DC 20003
Counseling and treatment center for women of childbearing years who are on drugs.

Autoimmune Diseases

Autoimmune diseases, in which the body produces antibodies against its own healthy tissues and organs, represent the fourth-largest cause of disability among American women. Three-quarters of autoimmune diseases—such as lupus, diabetes, rheumatoid arthritis and multiple sclerosis—occur in women.

Alzheimers Association of Greater Washington
301/652-6446
7970 Old Georgetown Road, Suite 1100, Bethesda, MD 20814

Lupus Foundation of Greater Washington
703/684-2925
515-A Braddock Road, Alexandria, VA 22314

National Institute of Arthritis and Musculoskeletal and Skin Diseases
301/496-8188
10 Center Drive, Bethesda, MD 20892-1905

National Multiple Sclerosis Society
202/296-5363
2021 K Street, NW, Suite 100, Washington, DC 20006-1003

Cancer

Each year, cancer claims the lives of hundreds of thousands of women. Some of the more common cancers among women include lung, breast, cervical, ovarian, uterine, colon and skin. Lung cancer is the number one cancer killer among American women, due largely to cigarette smoking. Breast cancer (see the following section) is the second most frequent cause of cancer deaths among women. Uterine and ovarian cancers claim the lives of about 50,000 women each year.

American Cancer Society
800/ACS-2345
1875 Connecticut Ave., NW, Suite 730, Washington, DC 20009
    Information on all types of cancer.

American College of Obstetricians and Gynecologists (ACOG)
202/638-5577
409 12th Street, SW, Washington, DC 20024-2188
Information on cervical cancers.

American Lung Association
800/LUNG-USA
475 H Street, NW, Washington, DC 20001

National Cancer Institute
800/4-CANCER
9000 Rockville Pike, Bldg. 31, Room 10A24, Bethesda, MD 20892

Breast Cancer

Two decades ago, one in 20 women developed breast cancer, compared with one in eight today. Although there is no cure, the best method of prevention is early diagnosis and treatment. Annual exams from your physician, breast self exams and mammography are the best known methods to detect cancerous lumps. For information on mammography, refer to chapter 7.

American Cancer Society
800/ACS-2345
1875 Connecticut Ave., NW, Suite 730, Washington, DC 20009
    Provides patient services, support groups, information and referrals for victims of breast cancer and other cancers.

Arlington Hospital Cancer Center
703/558-5555
1701 N. George Mason Drive, Arlington, VA 22205
    Offers support groups for women living with cancer.

Betty Ford Comprehensive Breast Center
Columbia Hospital for Women
202/293-6654
2425 L Street, NW, Washington, DC 20037
    Offers screening, diagnostic and treatment programs for breast cancer patients. Offers a mammography program and surgical consultation for low-income women. To schedule mammograms, call 202/293-6372.

Breast Cancer Prevention

Age 20-40	Have a health care professional check your breasts every three years. Conduct monthly breast self exams.
Age 40	Have your first mammogram. Conduct monthly breast self exams.
Age 40-50	Have a health care professional check your breasts every year. Have a mammogram every 1-2 years, or as recommended by your physician. Conduct monthly breast self exams.
Over age 50	Have a health care professional check your breasts every year. Have a mammogram every year. Conduct monthly breast self exams.

Source: American Cancer Society

Breast Cancer Resource Committee
202/463-8020
1765 N Street, NW, Washington, DC 20036
Provides counseling, support groups and referrals for victims of breast cancer.

Caring and Sharing
703/444-4460
14 Pidgeon Hill Drive, Suite 130, Sterling, VA 20165
Sponsored by Loudoun Hospital, "Caring and Sharing" is a twice-monthly support group for women diagnosed with any type of cancer.

Fairfax Hospital: "Life with Cancer"
703/698-2841
3300 Gallows Road, Falls Church, VA 22046
Offers classes, seminars, workshops, counseling, information, referrals and support groups for breast cancer and other types of cancer.

Greater Washington Coalition for Cancer Survivorship
202/364-6422
Provides education, information and support services for women with any type of cancer.

National Race for the Cure

© Marty LaVor

Nearly 30,000 people turned out for the National Race for the Cure and raised over $1 million. Most of the money went to local facilities for research, education and treatment of breast cancer. The Washington race was held in conjunction with races in 30 other states, making it the largest private fundraiser for breast cancer research.

"This is a disease that touches everyone in our society. We all know someone who has been affected by breast cancer: Our mother, sister, wife, daughter or friend. The National Race for the Cure empowers people. It provides a mechanism for hope and through the Race for the Cure, we will find a cure for breast cancer."

Mary McAuliffe, Chair
1996 Race for the Cure, Washington, D.C.

Howard University Cancer Center
202/806-7697
2041 Georgia Ave., NW, Washington, DC 20060-0001
Prevention, screening, diagnosis and support services.

Lombardi Cancer Helplink
202/784-4000
3800 Reservoir Road, NW, Washington, DC 20007
Sponsored by Georgetown University Hospital, Helplink offers information and referrals for screenings, diagnostics and treatment.

The Mautner Project for Lesbians with Cancer
202/332-5536
1707 L Street, NW, Suite 1060, Washington, DC 20036
Offers support services, programs, and educational services for Lesbians with any type of cancer.

My Image After Breast Cancer
703/461-9595, 800/970-4411, 703/461-9616, Hope Line
6000 Stevenson Ave., Suite 203, Alexandria, VA 22304
Resource center that provides information, seminars, referrals and support services on breast cancer. Hope Line is a 24-hour telephone support service staffed by volunteers who are breast cancer survivors.

National Cancer Institute
800-4-CANCER
9000 Rockville Pike, Bldg. 31, Rm. 10A24, Bethesda, MD 20892
Provides over-the-phone information and counseling about breast cancer screening and treatment.

National Women's Health Resource Center (NWHRC)
202/293-6045
2440 M Street, NW, Suite 325, Washington, DC 20037
Offers a breast cancer information package as well as other information and resources.

Providence Hospital's Wellness Institute
202/269-7275
1150 Barnum Street, NE, Washington, DC 20017
Provides information on breast cancer awareness, detection and assessment.

Eating Disorders

About 5 million American women—mostly young women—suffer from some type of eating disorder. The most common disorders are anorexia nervosa, bulimia and overeating, or binge eating. Eating disorders kill up to 10 percent of their victims and cause serious medical complications for many others. Early treatment increases survival rates and reduces long-term health complications.

American Anorexia/Bulimia Association
212/501-8351
293 Central Park West, Suite 1-R, New York, NY 10024
Information and referrals.

Eating Disorder Program/Washington Adventist Hospital
800/542-5096
7600 Carroll Ave., Takoma Park, MD 20912
Meets weekly at Washington Adventist Hospital and is free of charge.

National Association of Anorexia Nervosa and Associated Disorders
708/831-3438
PO Box 7, Highland Park, IL 60035
Information and referrals.

National Institute of Mental Health
301/443-4513
5600 Fishers Lane, Room 7C-02, Rockville, MD 20857

Shady Grove Eating Disorder Center
301/977-7782
16220 Frederick Road, Suite 512, Gaithersburg, MD 20877
The Center offers support groups for people with eating disorders. Classes meet monthly and are offered free of charge.

Heart Disease

Although many people don't realize it, heart disease is the number one killer of American women. Compared with men, women are generally older and sicker when they are diagnosed with heart disease. Medical experts have found that lifestyle and behavioral factors play a significant role in heart disease, including smoking, poor nutrition, and lack of exercise.

American Heart Association
202/686-6888
5335 Wisconsin Ave., NW, Washington, DC 20015
   The American Heart Association offers programs and information on cardiac health, including symposiums on women with heart conditions.

National Heart, Lung and Blood Institute Information Center
800/575-WELL, 301/251-1222
PO Box 30105, Bethesda, MD 20824-0105

Office of Disease Prevention and Health Promotion
800/336-4797, 202/727-2600
PO Box 1133, Washington, DC 20013-1133

HIV/AIDS

Since 1984, women have been the fastest-growing group to be infected with HIV, the virus that causes AIDS. The disease is the third leading cause of death among women of reproductive age. Since there is no cure for the disease, a woman's best defense is to not become infected. The two main ways women become infected is through unprotected sex and needle sharing among drug users.

DC AIDS Information Line
202/332-2437

National AIDS Hotline/Centers for Disease Control and Prevention
800/342-AIDS, (800/243-7889, TDD)
PO Box 13827, Research Triangle Park, NC 27709

National AIDS Information Clearinghouse
800/458-5231
PO Box 6003, Rockville, MD 20850

National Association of People with AIDS
202/898-0414
1413 K Street, NW, 7th Floor, Washington, DC 20005
   Information, referrals and bimonthly newsletter.

National Minority AIDS Council
202/483-6622
1931 13th Street, NW, Washington, DC 20009
Information and referral service for women and minorities.

Teen AIDS Hotline
800/234-8336
Information and referrals about HIV/AIDS and safe sex.

Whitman-Walker Clinics
202/332-AIDS
1407 S Street, NW, Washington, DC 20009
Offers therapy and support services for lesbians and gays with AIDS and their caregivers at four clinics in the Metropolitan Area. There is a women-only HIV testing day every other month.

Women's Council
202/296-6525
1129 20th Street, NW, Suite 400, Washington, DC 20036-3403
Information, education and prevention resources on HIV/AIDS.

Immunization

Vaccinations are a crucial part of women's preventative health care to guard against a variety of deadly diseases at home and when traveling abroad. Women in their reproductive years should have a tetanus-diphtheria booster every 10 years and MMR (measles, mumps, rubella) once if not immune. Vaccines for hepatitis B, influenza, pneumococcal infection and diseases like cholera are given as needed based on risk factors.

National Immunization Information Hotline
800/232-2522
Provides general information on vaccinations and referrals to providers in your community.

District of Columbia Commission of Public Health
202/576-7130
1660 L Street, NW, Washington, DC 20036

Maryland Dept. of Health and Mental Hygiene
410/225-6679
201 West Preston Street, Baltimore, MD 21202

Virginia Dept. of Health
804/786-6246
PO Box 2448, Richmond, VA 23218

Mental Health

Women are twice as likely as men to experience a major depression during their lifetimes, and one in 10 women will experience a mood disorder. Mental illness is a disease and not a personality flaw. However, many of these disorders go untreated even though effective treatment exists. In addition to the following resources, there are numerous mental health counseling centers in the Washington, D.C. area that are just for women.

Anxiety Disorders Association of America
301/231-9350
6000 Executive Blvd., Rockville, MD 20852

Crisis Hotline
202/561-7000
   Twenty-four-hour crisis and referral service, provided by the U.S. Dept. of Health and Human Services.

Depression and Related Affective Disorders Association
410/955-4647, 202/955-5800
600 N. Wolfe Street, Meyer 3-181, Baltimore, MD 21287-7381

National Alliance for the Mentally Ill
800/950-NAMI
200 N. Glebe, Suite 1015, Arlington, VA 22203

National Institute for Mental Health
301/443-4513
5600 Fishers Lane, Rm 7C-02, Rockville, MD 20857

Panic Disorder Education Program
800/64-PANIC
5600 Fishers Lane, Rockville, MD 20857

Self-Help Clearinghouse of Greater Washington
703/941-5465
7630 Little River Turnpike, # 206, Annandale, VA 22003
Sponsored by the Mental Health Association of Northern Virginia, the Clearinghouse offers information and referrals for mental health issues.

Older Women's Health

Even though women on average live longer than men, they experience poorer health and health care attention. Studies show that women receive less medical treatment than men, and older women are less likely to have health insurance policies that supplement Medicare expenses. Older women are grappling with certain diseases, such as osteoporosis, arthritis and Alzheimer's disease.

Hysterectomy Educational Resources and Services (HERS)
215/667-7757
422 Bryn Mawr Avenue, Bala Cynwyd, PA 19004

National Institute of Aging
301/496-1752
9000 Rockville Pike, Bethesda, MD 20892

Older Women's League
202/783-6686
666 11th Street, Suite 700, Washington, DC 20001
Provides fact sheets on health issues for older women.

Women in Midlife and Menopause (WMM)
301/345-0566
7337 Morrison Drive, Greenbelt, MD 20770
Networking, information, referral and support group for women to share menopause experiences and coping mechanisms.

The Women's Initiative
Association of American Retired Persons
202/434-2400
601 E Street, NW, Washington, DC 20049
Provides information and resources on older women's health issues.

Osteoporosis

Osteoporosis is a debilitating bone disease that affects 20 million American women. The disease causes bone mass to deteriorate, which results in bone fractures and disabling disfigurement. Although it primarily affects older women, the foundation for osteoporosis begins early in life when bones are developing. Women can help offset the risk of osteoporosis by building bone density at every age with a calcium-rich diet and by engaging in weight-bearing exercises. In addition to milk, other products that contain calcium include broccoli, yogurt, almonds, cheese, tofu, salmon and fruit juice.

National Osteoporosis Foundation
202/223-2226
1150 17th Street, NW, Suite 500, Washington, DC 20036
The Foundation provides information, referrals, and activities for patients and professionals.

Osteoporosis and Related Bone Disorders
National Resource Center
800/624-BONE
1150 17th Street, NW, Suite 500, Washington, DC 20036
Provides information on bone disorders.

Calcium Recommendations

Age Group	Optimal Daily Calcium Intake
Birth-6 mo.	400 mg
6 mo.-1 year	600 mg
1-5 years	800 mg
6-10 years	800-1,200 mg
11-24 years	1,500 mg
25-50 years	1,000 mg
Pregnant & nursing	1,200-1,500 mg
50-65 years	1,000 mg (if on estrogens)
50-65 years	1,500 mg (if not on estrogens)
65+ years	1,500 mg

Source: National Institutes of Health

Part IV

Mothers and Family

9

Pregnancy Services

KellyAnne Gallagher, Consulting Editor
Buffy Beaudoin-Schwartz, Consulting Editor

Having a baby is one of the most significant events in a woman's life. It's also a time in which a lot of very important decisions have to be made. These are just some of the issues to consider: Should I have the baby delivered by a doctor or a nurse-midwife? Should I deliver at the hospital, a birthing center, or even at home? What hospitals have delivery and postpartum services? Should I take a class to prepare for the delivery? Once I have the baby, how do I learn about breast-feeding or the basics of infant care? These are just some of the issues that will have a great impact on your birthing experience and your new baby. Fortunately, there are a number of resources, services and programs to help with these decisions.

This chapter contains a variety of resources on these important issues, including childbirth education courses, breast-feeding and postpartum assistance. Hospitals are also good resources that usually provide comprehensive maternity services, such as child birthing classes, new baby courses and infant education. This chapter also includes special programs and services for pregnant and mothering teens.

Information and Resources

The American College of Nurse Midwives
202/728-9860
818 Connecticut Ave., NW, # 900, Washington, DC 20006
Provides local referrals for certified midwives and a national directory of registered nurses who are certified as midwives.

The Confinement Line Telephone Support Network
703/941-7183
PO Box 1609, Springfield, VA 22151
Support and information service for women confined to bed during pregnancy due to complications, sponsored by the Childbirth Education Association.

District of Columbia Office of Maternal and Child Health (OMCH)
202/547-BABY (2229)
202/727-0393
OMCH provides information and referrals for expecting and new moms in the D.C. area, such as a newborn screening program, nutrition programs and pregnancy risk assessment.

M.O.M. Program (Matters on Maternity)
703/504-3636
Sponsored by Alexandria Hospital, the M.O.M. Program is a question-and-answer hotline on all aspects of being a new mom. The service is staffed by nurses.

National Center for Education in Maternal and Child Health
703/524-7802
2000 15th Street, Suite 701, Arlington, VA 22201
The Center offers consumer information on maternal and child health, as well as referrals to national sources of information.

National Maternal and Child Health Clearinghouse
703/821-8955
2070 Chain Bridge Road, Suite 450, Vienna, VA 22182
The Clearinghouse provides information, publications and referrals on prenatal and infant care.

Parent Helpline of Montgomery County
301/929-2025
Telephone help line for parents in need of information on child development and parenting. Hours of operation are 8:30 a.m.to 5:00 p.m.

Zacchaeus Free Clinic/Bread for the City
202/265-2400
1525 7th Street, NE, Washington, DC 20001
Phone service that provides mothers and expecting mothers with information on pregnancy and childbirth. Hours of operation are 9 a.m. to 4 p.m.

Publications

Beltway Baby
by Evelyn Goldstein
First edition, Oct. 1994, Washington Book Trading Co. $10.95.
Comprehensive book on information about having a baby in the D.C. area, including prenatal decisions, choosing a doctor, finding a childbirth class, hospital selection, health programs and locating stores that sell new and used baby goods.

Capital Baby
by Lisa K. Friedman, 1990
PO Box 15045, Chevy Chase, MD 20825, 301/608-0524
Resource guide for new parents in the D.C. area, which includes information on social activities, diaper services, products and classes.

Maternity and Infant Resource Guide
703/631-4MOM
PO Box 1345, Fairfax, VA 22030
Published by the Maternity Network, the guide contains resources for health care, child care, retail, and support groups for moms.

Preparing for Birth

Hospitals Are Good Resources

In addition to delivery services, many hospitals in the Washington metropolitan area provide a number of other services for pregnant women and new moms, such as childbirth education, parenting classes, lactation consultants and counseling for postpartum depression. Many hospitals have "New Mom" programs, prenatal courses, general health programs for mothering, sibling classes and support groups for new mothers.

Washington, D.C.
Columbia Hospital for Women   202/293-6500
2425 L Street, NW, Washington, DC 20037
DC General Hospital   202/675-5000
19th & Massachusetts, SE, Washington, DC 20003

Fort Washington Hospital 301/292-7000
11711 Livingston Road, Ft. Washington, MD 20744
George Washington University Medical Center 202/994-1000
901 23rd Street, NW, Washington, DC 20037
Georgetown University Medical Center 202/784-2000
3800 Reservoir Road, NW, Washington, DC 20007
The Greater Southeast Community Hospital 202/574-6000
1310 Southern Ave., SE, Washington, DC 20032
Howard University Hospital 202/865-6100
2041 Georgia Ave., NW, Washington, DC 20060
Mt. Vernon Hospital 703/664-7000
2501 Parkers Lane, Alexandria, VA 22306
Providence Hospital 202/269-7000
1150 Varnum Street, NE, Washington, DC 20017
Sibley Memorial Hospital 202/537-4000
5255 Loughboro Road, NW, Washington, DC 20016
Walter Reed Army Medical Center 202/782-1000
6900 Georgia Ave., NW, Washington, DC 20307

Maryland

Frederick Hospital 301/698-3300
406 West 7th Street, Frederick, MD 21701
Greater Laurel Beltsville Hospital 301/497-7977
7100 Contee Road, Laurel, MD 20707
Holy Cross Hospital 301/905-BABY
1500 Forest Glen Road, Silver Spring, MD 20910
Howard County General Hospital 410/740-7890
5755 Cedar Lane, Columbia, MD 21044
Montgomery General Hospital 301/774-8882
18101 Prince Phillip Drive, Olney, MD 20832
Prince George's Hospital Center 301/275-2000
3001 Hospital Drive, Cheverly, MD 20785
Southern Maryland Hospital 301/868-8000
7503 Surratts Road, Clinton, MD 20735
Washington Adventist Hospital 301/891-7600
7600 Carroll Ave., Takoma Park, MD 20912

Virginia

Alexandria Hospital 703/504-3000
4320 Seminary Road, Alexandria, VA 22304
Arlington Hospital 703/558-5000
1701 N. George Mason Drive, Arlington, VA 22205
Fairfax Hospital 703/698-1110

3300 Gallows Road, Falls Church, VA 22046	
Fair Oaks Hospital	703/391-3600
3600 Joseph Siewick Drive, Fairfax, VA 22033	
Loudoun Hospital	703/478-1801
224 Cornwall Street, Leesburg, VA 20176	
Potomac Hospital	703/670-1313
2300 Opitz Blvd., Woodbridge, VA 22191	
Prince William Hospital	703/369-8000
8700 Sudley Road, Manassas, VA 20110	

Childbirth Education

**American Society for Psychoprophylaxis in Obstetrics
(ASPO/Lamaze)**
800/368-4404
703/549-2226
1200 19th Street, NW, Suite 300, Washington, DC 20036-2422
ASPO/Lamaze promotes the Lamaze delivery method of coaching, breathing and relaxing. Courses are taught in nearly two dozen locations in the Washington metropolitan area. ASPO/Lamaze also provides a number of other service and support groups on topics such as new mothers, breast-feeding and labor support.

The Bradley Method
800/423-2397
The Bradley Method is based on natural child delivery. Call this toll-free number to locate local courses.

Childbirth Education Association (CEA)
703/941-7183
PO Box 1609, Springfield, VA 22151
CEA offers classes on the Lamaze birthing method that are taught by nurses. Provides information on other pregnancy-related services, such as breast-feeding, baby care and dealing with postpartum depression. CEA also operates a telephone hotline for pregnant women who are confined to bed due to pregnancy complications.

Family Life and Maternity Education (FLAME)
703/276-9248, 800/776-9248
PO Box 379, Dunn Loring, VA 22027
FLAME offers classes and information on the Lamaze method of childbirth delivery. Classes are held at sites in Virginia and Maryland.

After the Delivery

Breast-Feeding

Breast-Feeding Consultants of NOVA
703/207-9091
7245 Arlington Blvd, Suite 319, Falls Church, VA 22042
Certified lactation consultants and breast pump equipment rentals.

Breast-Feeding Counseling Services
301/907-2616
Certified lactation consultants and breast-feeding equipment rentals.

La Leche League International (LLL)
703/534-8548
LLL promotes the practice of breast-feeding and functions as a support and information group for mothers. The LLL information line will provide you with contacts for all the LLL chapters in the metropolitan area. Meetings cover not only breast-feeding, but also subjects such as nutrition, child care and other parenting information.

Mother's Matters
703/620-3323
11800 Sunrise Valley Drive, # 305, Reston, VA 20191
Breast-feeding information and supplies.

The National Capital Lactation Center and Cmty Human Milk Bank
202-784-MILK (6455)
Sponsored by Georgetown University Hospital, the Center provides information about breast-feeding, breast pump rentals, childbirth education and parenting classes at three locations in the D.C. area.

Nutrition

Office of Nutrition Programs
Women and Infant Children's Program (WIC)
202/645-5662
2100 Martin Luther King Ave., Suite 409, SE, Washington, DC 20020
WIC provides nutritional counseling and supplemental food to low-income mothers, expecting mothers and their children (under the age of five).

Postpartum

Depression After Delivery
703/938-0247
800/944-4PPD
Telephone answer service and support group for women experiencing postpartum depression.

Maternity Center
301/530-3300
6506 Bells Mill Road, Bethesda, MD 20817
Offers postpartum support groups and other pregnancy services for new and expecting moms.

Bereavement

Jewish Social Service Agency
301/881-3700
6123 Montrose Road
Rockville, MD 20852

703/750-5400
7345 McWhorter Place
Annandale, VA 22003

Offers bereavement support groups and counseling on parenting and personal issues. Offers a single mothers support group as well as social services for both genders.

Miscarriage, Infant Death and Stillbirth (MIS)
301/460-6222
9715 Medical Center Drive, Rockville, MD 20850
Self-help support group for parents who have experienced the loss of a fetus or baby. There are a number of support groups throughout the Washington metropolitan area. Other services include telephone counseling, a lending library and a speakers program.

Perinatal Loss Support Group
703/369-2071
PO Box 1284, Manassas, VA 20110
Mutual help support group for parents who have experienced a pregnancy loss, still birth or early infant death. Monthly meetings and a lending library.

Services for Pregnant Teens

Columbia Hospital for Women/Teen Health Center
202/546-TEEN
650 Pennsylvania Ave., SE, Washington, DC 20003
The Teen Health Center provides health care, nutritional counseling and social service programs for pregnant teens. The Center also offers general health services and birth control to teens.

Community of Caring
202/673-7702
2250 Champlain Street, NW, Washington, DC 20009
Community of Caring provides health care and support services for pregnant teens. Dental and pediatric services are also offered.

Edward C. Mazique Parent Child Center
202/462-3375
1719 13th Street, NW, Washington, DC 20009
The Center operates a "Junior Parents Program" which offers day care and other educational services for pregnant or parenting teens.

Family Place
202/265-0149
3309 16th Street, NW, Washington, DC 20010
The Family Place recently discontinued special programs for pregnant and mothering teens, but has integrated teens in all-age classes, counseling sessions and discussion groups. Spanish/English staff.

Latin American Youth Center/Teen Parenting Program
202/234-4549, 202/483-1140
3045 15th Street, NW, Washington, DC 20009
The Teen Parenting Program provides social services, counseling and education, such as pre-GED classes, to encourage teen parents to stay in school. The majority of clients are Hispanic, but services are open to all races.

Mary's Center for Maternal and Child Health/The Teen Program
202/483-8196
2333 Ontario Road, NW, Washington, DC 20009
The Teen Program provides medical, social and support services to pregnant teens. Services include prenatal care, parenting programs, in-home consultations and general guidance. The Center has a pediatrician on staff to care for infants. Spanish/English staff.

NE Place Health Center
202/635-6535
1731 Bunker Hill Road, NE, Washington, DC 20017
Provides support and prenatal services to pregnant teens. Case managers assist the teens prior to delivery and then help them with the transition to the hospital setting for delivery.

Outreach for Parent Teens
703/358-5819
816 South Walter Reed Drive, Arlington, VA 22204
Outreach for Parent Teens is a service of the Arlington County Career Center that encourages and helps teenage moms return to school. The program helps link participants with appropriate social service programs to help address immediate financial, nutritional, child care, housing and health care needs.

Sasha Bruce Youthwork/Teen Mothers Program
202/675-9340
1022 Maryland Ave., NE, Washington, DC 20002
The Teen Mothers Program provides housing and other social services for teen mothers, including career and educational guidance, legal assistance, parenting programs and counseling.

St. Ann's Infant and Maternity Home
301/559-5500
4901 Eastern Ave., Hyattsville, MD 20782
Services include education and counseling for pregnant or parenting teens, day care, residential maternity and mother-baby services.

Teenage Mothers
202/675-9380
701 Maryland Ave., NE, Washington, DC 20002
Offers housing and social services for teenage moms who are in the foster care system. This program provides educational and career guidance, parenting and life skills, and medical assistance.

Young Parents Network
703/771-5186
102 Heritage Way, NE, Suite 200, Leesburg, VA 22075
Information, support and counseling network for teenage parents. The program is sponsored by the Loudoun County Dept. of Social Services.

10

Child Care

KellyAnne Gallagher, Consulting Editor
Buffy Beaudoin-Schwartz, Consulting Editor

More mothers than ever before are in the workforce, and Washington, D.C. is certainly no exception. In fact, the nation's capital is one of the top spots for working mothers. According to the Washington Child Development Council, 67 percent of women with children under the age of six are in the labor force. And it's a trend that has slowly increased over the years. In 1970, 39 percent of mothers with children were employed in the workforce and in 1990, that number grew to 62 percent. Currently, approximately half of mothers with infants—under the age of one—worked outside of the home at least on a part-time basis. Given these numbers, which are likely to grow even more in coming years, the demand for quality child care is at its highest ever. Whether mothers work outside of their home or from their home office, the need for affordable child care has become one of the top issues for working women.

Parents who work long or nontraditional hours are oftentimes faced with finding child care options that fit their time schedules. According to Care Around the Clock, in 1990, 72 million mothers worked nonstandard hours. And the numbers continue to grow as companies become more family-friendly and offer flex-time options. The following resources and guidelines are intended to help mothers locate quality and affordable child care based on their individual needs.

Child Care Resources

Independent Referral Agencies

Child Care Aware
800/424-2246
1319 F Street, NW, Suite 810, Washington, DC 20004
Child Care Aware connects parents with child care referral agencies in the D.C. area and in other regions of the nation. It is a great initial resource to help parents locate referral agencies in regions not listed in this book. The service is operated by the National Association of Child Care Resources and Referral Agencies and is a helpful resource if you're moving and need to locate a child care referral agency in your new city.

Metropolitan Washington Council of Governments (MWCOG)
202/962-3256
777 North Capital Street, NE, Washington, DC 200002-4239
MWCOG operates a reference center for child care information, which includes publications, referrals and other resources for child care, foster care and special programs for children. MWCOG publishes the *Directory of Accredited Child Care Programs in the District of Columbia,* which lists child care providers that have met an established level of quality child care. You can request information over the phone or by visiting the center, which is open Monday through Friday, 1 p.m. to 5 p.m.

National Academy of Early Childhood Programs
800/424-2460, 202/232-8777
1509 16th Street, NW, Washington, DC 20036
The Academy is a service of the National Association for the Education of Young Children (NAEYC) that provides listings of accredited child care facilities in the D.C. area and in other regions of the nation that have met NAEYC's criteria for quality child care services. The Academy also offers guidelines on how to locate quality day care.

SHARE Care
301/320-2321
5606 Knollwood Road, Bethesda, MD 20816
SHARE Care is a service offered by the Parent Connection, Inc. that matches families with similar child care needs through its computerized data bank.

Government Resources

There are a number of state, county and district offices to help parents locate accredited child care services by providing referrals and information. The following is a listing of agencies that will be of assistance in the metropolitan area.

District of Columbia
Department of Consumer and Regulatory Affairs
202/727-7226
614 H Street, NW, Room 1035, Washington, DC 20001

The Department provides referrals for more than 7,000 certified child care services in the District of Columbia. Information can be obtained by phone or by visiting the office Monday through Friday between the hours of 8:15 a.m. and 4:45 p.m.

Washington Child Development Council
202/387-0002
2121 Decatur Place, NW, Washington, DC 20008

The Council is a referral service for licensed child care services in Washington, D.C., including child care centers and child development homes. The Council does not offer recommendations, but gives referrals on accredited programs in the District of Columbia based on parents' specific needs. The Council also helps with securing financial assistance from the government.

Maryland
Baltimore City Dept. of Social Services
Division of Day Care
410/361-2560
1510 Guilford Ave., Baltimore, MD 21202

Provides information and referrals for child care services.

Baltimore County Dept. of Social Services
410/887-2800
620 York Road, Towson, MD 21204

Provides information and referrals for child care services.

Charles County Dept. of Social Services
301/934-2700
PO Box 100, LaPlata, MD 20646

Provides information and referrals for child care services.

Frederick County Child Care Administration
301/695-4508
7470 New Technology Way, Suite P, Frederick, MD 21701
Provides information and referrals for child care services. The referral line is open from 9 a.m. to 2 p.m.

Howard County Child Care Administration
410/872-4200, x298
10176 Baltimore-National Pike, Ellicott City, MD 21042
Provides information and referrals for child care services.

Montgomery County Child Care Connection
301/279-1773
332 W. Edmunson Drive, Rockville, MD 20850
The Connection maintains a listing of nearly 2,000 child care services in Montgomery County. It offers a helpful publication on selecting quality child care services called *Choosing Child Care*. Residents can obtain child care referrals by phone or by visiting the office Monday through Friday between the hours of 9 a.m. and 4 p.m.

Prince George's County Child Care Administration
301/772-8400
425 Brightseat Road, 2nd Floor, # 255, Landover, MD 20785
Provides information and referrals for child care services.

Virginia
Alexandria Office of Early Childhood Development
703/838-0750
2525 Mount Vernon Ave., Unit 2, Alexandria, VA 22301
Provides information and referrals for child care services.

Arlington County Child Care Office
703/358-5101
1801 N. George Mason Drive, Arlington, VA 22207
Provides information and referrals for child care services.

Fairfax County Office for Children
Child Care Information
703/359-5860
3701 Pender Drive, Fairfax, VA 22030
Provides information and referrals for child care services.

Loudoun County
703/777-0353
102 Heritage Way NE, Suite 200, Leesburg, VA 22075
Provides information and referrals for child care services.

Prince William County Department of Social Services
703/792-4300
15941 Cardinal Drive, Woodbridge, VA 22193
Provides information and referrals for child care services.

Child Care Standards

Child care providers are licensed by state and local regulating agencies to ensure that providers meet and maintain certain standards of quality and professionalism. By using the services of a licensed care provider, rather than a neighbor or any other unlicensed child care provider, you can expect:

- Children are inoculated.
- Children receive balanced meals.
- Children receive age-appropriate lessons in structured time that is balanced by unstructured "free" time.
- Caregivers usually have some amount of early childhood education.
- Health and safety inspections of the facility are conducted regularly.

There are different types of child care services to choose from, depending on the type of arrangement that best suits your needs and requirements; you should consider the amount of attention from the caregiver, hours that the service is offered, and the overall environment at the center. A child care center provides regimens based on the different stages of emotional, intellectual and growth needs of the children in a commercial setting. A family day care center provides services in a private home. An infant care center provides care for infants and toddlers.

Licensing standards vary throughout the Washington metropolitan area, based on differing requirements set by regulatory agencies in Washington, D.C., Virginia and Maryland. In its 1996 "State of the States" report on day care in America, *Working Mother* magazine ranked Maryland among the top 10 states in the nation for child care standards, scoring four out of five in each of the categories of quality, safety, availability, and commitment. Surprisingly, the District outscored the Old Dominion with three out of five points in quality and safety, and two each in availability and commitment. Bringing up the rear, Virginia got its highest mark—three points—in availability, and only two points in each of the other categories. Therefore, it is wise for parents to shop around and ask questions.

Finding Quality Child Care

Quality child care helps promote healthy and positive physical, emotional, social and intellectual development in children. To locate quality care, first find out if the caregiver is licensed. Licensing guarantees that the service meets the basic health and safety standards required by your state or local government. However, licensing alone is not enough to ensure that a caregiver provides the most appropriate care for your child. There are other important factors you should take into consideration before making your selection. You can determine how the providers match up to your needs by asking the right questions.

Reliable, consistent care. Does the provider offer a stable daily routine? Is the staff careful and conscientious? Is there a low staff turnover? Does the provider have written policies and procedures? Does the provider have insurance?

Partnership between parent and care giver. Is there ongoing communication between parents and the caregiver? Are parents encouraged to visit the facility at any time?

Adequate supervision. Is there time for individual attention? Is the caregiver accessible throughout the day?

Low child/staff ratio. At child care centers, the ratio should be 10:1 for 3-4 year olds in groups of up to 20, and 4:1 in groups of up to eight infants. In family day care homes, the ratio should be no more than six children per one adult for mixed ages. Does the provider meet this requirement?

Advanced caregiver training. Is the caregiver trained in first aid and CPR? Does the caregiver receive ongoing training in early childhood education?

Appealing use of space. Is the facility attractive, clean and inviting? Are there areas for quiet and active play? Is there an unobstructed view of the children? Is there equipment for physical activity?

Age-specific activities and materials. Does the caregiver have age-appropriate expectations? Are there varied and appropriate play materials and activities for your child's age and stage of development? Does the caregiver offer both free plan and structured activities?

Positive, constructive guidance and discipline. Is the caregiver patient, warm and positive? Is there a flexible, innovative schedule? Is there respect for individuality?

Safe and healthy environment. Does the caregiver have clear policies for illness and emergencies? Does the caregiver encourage frequent hand washing? Is it a nonsmoking environment? Is the access well monitored? Does the caregiver provide nutritional meals? Is the facility equipped with safety devices, such as smoke alarms, fire extinguishers, and child-proof latches for doors and cabinets?

Source: Work and Family Coalition of the Metropolitan Washington Council of Governments

11

For Mothers ONLY!

KellyAnne Gallagher, Consulting Editor
Buffy Beaudoin-Schwartz, Consulting Editor

Networks and Support Groups for Mothers

Mothers Morning Out Program
301/869-5556
Maryland-based group for mothers that meets Monday mornings for activities, support and resource sharing.

Mothers of Preschoolers (MOPS)
303/733-5353, Intl. HQs
MOPS is a national network of mothers of preschool children that is affiliated with Christianity. There are about 10 chapters in the Washington, D.C. metropolitan area, with many located in northern Virginia. To locate a chapter in your area, contact the MOPS international headquarters.

Mothers Support Group
202/244-8871
Membership includes parents of infants and young children. The group meets Monday mornings to share ideas and support each other. Members meet at the Metropolitan Memorial United Methodist Church at 3401 Nebraska Ave., NW, Washington, D.C.

The Parent Connection, Inc.
301/320-2321
5606 Knollwood Road, Bethesda, MD 20816
The Parent Connection, Inc. provides resources, classes and activities to parents and their children, such as parent and child mixers. The

Connection offers "Share Care," a service that matches families with compatible child care needs. Publishes *Washington Parent*.

Single Mothers by Choice (SMC)
212/988-0993, Natl HQs
PO Box 1642, Gracie Square Station, New York, NY 10028

SMC is a support, network and information group for single women who have made the decision to have or adopt a child or are considering single motherhood. SMC has a networking chapter in Washington, D.C. for single mothers to share information, network with one another, gain access to resources, such as donor insemination and adoption, and participate in anonymous research projects. The group offers a "Thinkers Workshop," which explores the possibility and options of becoming a single mother. Contact the national headquarters to locate the local chapter.

Single Parents Raising Kids
301/598-6395

Nonprofit group run entirely by volunteers that offers educational seminars, social events and other activities for single parents with children under the age of 18.

Networks for Working Mothers

Mother's Access to Careers at Home (MATCH)
703/205-9664
PO Box 123, Annandale, VA 22003

MATCH is a network, information, support and advocacy group for mothers who have home-based businesses. MATCH was founded in 1990 and holds monthly meetings with speakers and roundtable discussions.

Office of Workplace Initiatives
202/501-3965
18th & F Streets, NW, Suite 6119, Washington, DC 20405

Provides information and referrals to federal employees about work and family initiatives. The Office is a part of the Government Services Administration.

Balancing Work and Family
by
Michele Ginnerty

The challenge to balance work, family and personal needs can be daunting and may lead to feelings of being overwhelmed and frazzled. Unfortunately, there is no magical formula to make it all work. Creating a comfortable balance means making choices based on your priorities. Think of it as a juggling act. You need to consider not only what you want to juggle, but how much you want up in the air at once. Along with a healthy perspective and a good sense of humor, the following principles can help you chart a course toward a balanced life.

Set Realistic Expectations
- Review your "to do" list. Is it an action plan or a fantasy wish list? Make it a daily ritual to focus on realistic expectations for the day. Focus only on what you're able to do.

Set Limits and Say No
- Don't over commit. Ask yourself, "Does this fit in with my priorities?"
- Let people know what you can and cannot do. If you are not comfortable saying yes, then say no.

Manage Your Time
- Identify the best use of your time and be purposeful. Avoid time-wasting situations. Grocery shopping and banking are much quicker at off peak hours.
- Schedule time for relaxation and fun. If you don't, then something else will most likely get in the way.

Reduce Your Guilt
- Guilt is the conflict between what you want or need to do and what you think you should do. Examine the "shoulds." Are they driven by your values or outside expectations? Remember that taking care of yourself is not selfish, but a necessity.

Communicate
- One person cannot balance everything, it should be a partnership effort with your mate. If you feel like you are pulling more than your fair share, talk about it and ask for help.
- Delegate chores and responsibilities to children, spouses and others, and then step back.

Michele Ginnerty is an independent consultant who specializes in helping parents balance career and family. She is also the mother of a three-year-old.

Alternative Work Schedules

There are a variety of alternative work schedules now offered to help employees meet the demands of family, school or personal needs.

Flex-Time
Flex-time allows employees to alter the hours of their work schedules in order to meet family needs. Employees fulfill their full-time hours but on a nontraditional timeframe.

Part-Time
Part-time status is based on employment of less than 40 hours per week. Part-time schedules may refer to portions of days, weeks, months or years. Oftentimes, part-time employees do not receive health and other employee benefits, such as sick leave.

Voluntary Reduced Time
Known as V-Time, this option allows employees to reduce their work schedule over a set period of time. For example, workers may reduce their work schedule by as much as 50 percent for a specified length of time while retaining their benefits and seniority status.

Job Sharing
Job sharing allows two workers to share the responsibilities of one full-time job. One employee may work 20 hours per week in the mornings while the other employee works 20 hours per week in that same position, but in the afternoons. Job sharing can also refer to two employees in unrelated part-time assignments who share the same budget line.

Telecommuting
As the information age gets fully under way, we are finding more often that work can be done from home with just a telephone, a computer and a modem. Telecommuting allows employees to perform some or all of their work from home. While this may be a good option for working mothers to be near their children, it may also require hiring additional child care assistance in order to perform those duties from home.

Source: U.S. Dept. of Labor, Women's Bureau

The Women's Bureau/U.S. Dept. of Labor
800/827-5335
200 Constitution Ave., NW, Washington, DC 20210
Clearinghouse of information on work and family issues, including resources on work options, child care, and other workplace issues.

Working Mother's Network
410/312-9273
6577 Robin Song, Columbia, MD 21045
The Working Mother's Network offers support meetings, networking opportunities and featured speakers to help mothers or those with an interest in parenting meet the needs of work and family. Members share coping strategies, seek advice and strengthen their parenting skills. The Working Mother's Network is affiliated with the Women's Information Network, a progressive women's professional group.

Groups for Mothers Who Choose to Stay Home

Lawyers at Home
202/785-1540
2000 L Street, NW, Washington, DC 20036
Lawyers at Home provides practical and emotional support to attorneys who are taking time off from the full-time practice of law to spend more time at home with their families. It is affiliated with the Women's Bar Association of the District of Columbia and offers monthly forums and support for part-time and home-based practice. The monthly programs cover professional, personal and parental interests, such as the decision to take time off, maintaining professional skills, reentering the workplace, how to find or negotiate a part-time practice, financial planning, self-esteem and resume gaps.

MOMS Club
301/949-5346, Regional Coordinator
805/526-2725, Natl. HQs
Nonprofit organization that functions as a support and information group and also organizes play groups and babysitting co-ops.

Mothers at Home
703/827-5903
800/783-4666, Order Information
8310A Old Courthouse Road, Vienna, VA 22182
Mothers at Home supports mothers who choose to stay at home to care for their children. The group gives women a voice and offers a variety of

Successful Transitions from Full-Time Career to Full-Time Motherhood

by
Maria Leonard Olsen

So, you've decided to leave the "rat race" and join the "rug rat race." One of the biggest challenges with the transition, however, is maintaining your self-esteem, especially in a city like Washington, where people oftentimes judge you by what you do. Invariably, the decision to forego your career is met with disbelief and derision. Even fellow female colleagues may be disdainful and resentful of your choice. Some will even ask "But what do you DO all day at home?" And cocktail party conversations may seem to end quite abruptly when you state that you work inside the home.

Ironically, like teachers, at-home mothers seem to be undervalued for what is arguably the most valuable contribution to society, raising and nurturing our next generation. Don't let any of this deter you. Instead, learn to cope by focusing on your family and yourself. Here are some things you can do to keep your esteem up and enjoy your time at home.

Develop the right mind set.

Think about it. Many people can perform your job duties at the office. But can someone else better provide for your family full time? You are very fortunate if you are able to care for your children full time. Childhood years are incredibly fleeting and full-time motherhood allows you to make the most of them. Joining a support group is an excellent way to help you enjoy and realize your self-worth as a stay-at-home mother.

Become involved outside the home and maintain contact with other adults.

Don't allow yourself to become socially isolated. Do volunteer work in your community. Many volunteer activities can be done at home, such as making food for a soup kitchen. In addition to the many nonprofit organizations and shelters in the area, almost all counties have volunteer bureaus to get you started.

Start or join a playgroup. Playgroups, especially when your children are young, can serve as wonderful support and information-sharing groups. Many playgroups are started by women who meet at the playground, Gymboree, library or bookstore reading programs, or other children's activities.

Develop interests compatible with child-care needs.

You'll have to use ingenuity to find activities that use your abilities and creativity while raising children full time. For example, enroll in a writing or cooking class that meets on weekends or in the evenings, or work on art projects that can be accomplished during short nap breaks or while your children are close by.

Continue to exercise.

Don't neglect your physical health. Walking is a terrific exercise to do with children. Many moms have walking partners or walking groups. Many area health clubs also provide day care services. Staying in shape will make you feel even better about yourself.

Maintain some type of a schedule.

You'd be surprised at how many things you can neglect by not having a set schedule. While child rearing requires much flexibility, continuing to set and achieve small daily goals will provide some additional and measurable satisfaction.

Take a break.

You will need some time away from your mothering responsibilities to be your best. A break from your daily routine will help you be patient with your children, while allowing you to maintain a healthy relationship with your partner. Find some good babysitters or even trade babysitting time with another mother.

Maria Leonard Olsen, an attorney by profession, is a full-time mother to her daughter, Caroline.

support and information activities, such as development programs for mothers and their children. Mothers at Home publishes a monthly newsletter and some helpful publications, such as *Discovering Motherhood* and *What's a Smart Woman Like You Doing at Home*.

Mothers First
703/827-5922
PO Box 40222, Washington, DC 20016
   Mothers First is a network and support group for mothers who choose to leave the professional environment to raise their children. The group offers educational forums, professional speakers, general support and play activities. There are many committees for specific interests, such as the Older Moms Group.

The Wednesday Morning Group
301/365-8860 (Joan Wolf)
   The Wednesday Morning Group is composed of approximately 60 stay-at-home mothers for the purpose of support, education and networking. The group hosts weekly speakers on a wide variety of topics. The group meets Wednesday mornings at the Cedar Lane Unitarian Church in Kensington, Maryland. Limited babysitting slots are provided on a co-op basis.

Publications for Parents

Baltimore's Child
410/367-5883
11 Dutton Court, Baltimore, MD 21228
http://family.com
e-mail: baltochild@aol.com
   Monthly tabloid containing articles and a listing of upcoming events of interest to parents.

Kidstreet News
410/730-9308
301/596-6180
PO Box 205, Columbia, MD 21045
   Free guide to child-related activities and resources in Washington, D.C. and Maryland.

Maryland Family
410/366-7512
4800 Roland Ave., Suite 300, Baltimore, MD 21210
Monthly tabloid containing articles and a listing of upcoming events of interest to parents.

Parent Resource Guide
703/698-8066
8320 Second Ave., Vienna, VA 22182
The *Parent Resource Guide* contains a comprehensive listing of services, groups and products in all areas of expertise to assist parents. Some of the listings include child care services, new mother resources and nanny services. There are two editions of the guide, one for the Virginia area and one for the Washington, D.C./Maryland region. The guide costs $4.95 and is available through mail order or at some of the major bookstores in Virginia.

Potomac Children
301/656-2133
PO Box 151544
Chevy Chase, MD 20815
Monthly paper containing articles, advice and upcoming events for parents in the D.C. area. Annual subscription rate is $17.85.

Washington Families
703/318-1385
2565 John Milton Drive, # 10, Herndon, VA 22071
Contains parenting news, calendar of events of interest to area parents, and tips and advice on parenting.

Washington Parent
301/320-2321
5606 Knollwood Road, Bethesda, MD 20816
Published by the Parent Connection, this bimonthly paper contains articles, self-help information, upcoming events and classified advertisements.

Part V

Education

12

The Woman College Student

Organizations for College Women

American Association for Higher Education/Women's Caucus
202/293-6440
11 Dupont Circle, Suite 600, Washington, DC 20036
Education, information and networking forum for members interested in women's studies and issues in higher education.

American Association of University Women (AAUW)
202/785-7700
1111 16th Street, NW, Washington, DC 20036
http://www.aauw.org
Students can join as affiliate members of this professional business association. AAUW provides a wealth of gender information on policy, education, business and social issues.

Association for Women in Mathematics (AWM)
301/405-7892
4114 Computer and Space Science Bldg.
University of Maryland, College Park, MD 20742-2461
AWM was established to encourage women to study and have active careers in the mathematical sciences. Students can participate in mentor programs and workshops and have access to information and resources.

Association for Women in Science (AWIS)
202/326-8940, 800/886-AWIS
1522 K Street, NW, Suite 820, Washington, DC 20005
e-mail: awis@awis.org

AWIS offers a mentor program for college science students. It also provides information and other educational opportunities in science.

Girls and Science: Linkages for the Future
202/326-6670
1333 H Street, NW, Washington DC 20005
Program to encourage girls to become involved in science. Sponsored by the American Association for the Advancement of Science and the National Network of Women in Science, this program provides science-related information and educational opportunities to girls and women.

National Association for Women in Education (NAWE)
202/659-9330
1325 18th Street, NW, Suite 210, Washington, DC 20036
NAWE is composed of students and women working in education. NAWE holds conferences for women college students to help improve their leadership skills. NAWE also publishes a newsletter for college students.

National Women's Studies Association
301/403-0525
University of Maryland
7100 Baltimore Ave., Suite 301, College Park, MD 20742
The Association provides information and resources for students and professionals involved in women's studies. The Association publishes a *Women's Studies Program Directory*, which lists colleges, universities and other institutions that offer women's studies programs.

National Women's Students Coalition
202/347-8772
1612 K Street, NW, Suite 510, Washington, DC 20006
The National Women's Students Coalition is a networking, resource and education group affiliated with United States Students Association.

Women's College Coalition
202/234-0443
125 Michigan Ave., NE, Washington, DC 20017
Provides information on women's colleges in the United States as well as research on gender equity and the role of women's colleges.

Women's Studies Electronic Forum and Database
410/455-2040
University of Maryland, Baltimore, MD 21228
e-mail: korenman@umbc2.umbc.edu

http://www.inform.umd.edu:8080/EdRes/Topic/WomensStudies/
These services are provided by the Women's Studies Program at the University of Maryland. The Forum provides networking and resources for women and teachers involved with a women's studies program. The Web site provides a full range of information, resources and links.

Publications for Women College Students

About Women on Campus
202/659-9330
1325 18th Street, NW, Suite 210, Washington, DC 20036-6511
Quarterly newsletter about women on campus, including information on women's colleges, women's studies, student life, women's leadership opportunities, athletics and minority issues. The newsletter is published by the National Association for Women in Education.

Feminist Studies
301/405-7415
2101 Woods Hall, College Park, MD 20742
Journal containing articles on issues relevant to women's studies. The journal also contains book reviews, essays and interviews. It is produced by the University of Maryland.

Women's Colleges and Universities

College of Notre Dame of Maryland
301/435-0100
4701 N. Charles Street, Baltimore, MD 21210-2476
Admissions: 410/532-5330, 800/435-0300
The College of Notre Dame of Maryland is a four-year independent college affiliated with the Roman Catholic Church that offers BA, BS and MA degrees. The school has a student body of more than 3,200 students and a faculty of 85.

Hollins College
703/362-6321
Hollins College, VA 24020
Admissions: 703/362-6401, 800/456-9595
Hollins College is a four-year independent liberal arts college that offers BA and MA degrees. The school has more than 1,070 students and a faculty of 91.

Hood College
301/663-3131
Rosemont Ave., Frederick, MD 21701
Admissions: 301/696-3400, 800/922-1599
Hood College is a four-year independent college affiliated with the Church of Christ that offers BA, BS, MA, MS and MBA degrees. The college has about 2,000 students and a faculty of 130.

Mary Baldwin College
703/887-7000
Staunton, VA 24401
Admissions: 703/887-7023, 800/826-0154
Mary Baldwin College is a four-year independent liberal arts college affiliated with the Presbyterian Church that offers BA and MATeach degrees. The school has about 1,070 students and a faculty of 119.

Mount Vernon College
202/625-4600
2100 Foxhall Road, NW, Washington, DC 20007
Admissions: 202/625-4682
Mount Vernon College is a four-year independent liberal arts college that offers BA and MA degrees. The school has about 430 students and a faculty of 68.

Randolph-Macon Woman's College
804/846-7392
2500 Rivermont Ave., Lynchburg, VA 24503-1094
Admissions: 804/947-8100, 800/745-7692
Randolph-Macon Woman's College is a four-year independent liberal arts college affiliated with the United Methodist Church that offers a BA degree. The college has about 740 students and a faculty of 88.

Sweet Briar College
804/381-6100
Sweet Briar, VA 24595
Admissions: 804/381-6142, 800/947-4300
Sweet Briar College is a four-year private liberal arts college that offers BA and BS degrees. Enrollment is about 560 students with a faculty of 70.

Trinity College
202/939-5000
125 Michigan Ave., NE, Washington, DC 20017

Admissions: 202/939-5040, 800/492-6882

Trinity College is a four-year private college affiliated with the Roman Catholic Church that offers BA, BS, MA, MS and MEd degrees. Total enrollment is about 1,400 students with a faculty of 121.

Women's Studies Programs

Washington, D.C.

The American University (AU): Women and Gender Studies
202/885-2981, 885-2982
223 Gray Hall, College of Arts and Sciences
4400 Massachusetts Ave., NW, Washington, DC 20016-8001
Admissions: 202/885-6000

American University is a four-year private university that offers a Bachelor of Arts degree and a minor in women and gender studies. AU emphasizes interdisciplinary studies and students commonly supplement other majors, such as policy, with courses on women's issues. The minor is often taken in conjunction with a related major, such as public policy.

George Washington University: Women's Studies Program
202/994-6942
2201 G Street, NW, Funger Hall 5061, Washington, DC 20052
e-mail: wstu@gwis2.circ.gwu.edu
Admissions: 202/994-6040, 800/447-3765

George Washington University is a four-year private university, located in the District of Columbia. It is the only local institution that offers a Master of Arts program in women's studies, and one of the few existing on the east coast. The school also offers a Master of Arts in the field of public policy with a concentration in women's studies, which requires an internship with a women's issues public policy group. GW also offers an undergraduate minor in women's studies.

Georgetown University: Women's Studies Program
202/687-3117
Room 586, Intercultural Center, Washington, DC 20057
Admissions: 202/687-3600

Georgetown University is a four-year private university that offers a Bachelor of Arts degree in interdisciplinary studies, with a major in women's studies. Students in any department can minor in women's studies.

Howard University: Women's Studies Program
202/806-6853
2400 Sixth Street, NW, Washington, DC 20059
Howard University is a four-year private university. Women's Studies is a new program that is offered within the Department of Sociology.

Johns Hopkins University: Women's Studies Program
410/516-6166
3400 North Charles Street
300 Jenkins Hall, Baltimore, MD 21218
Admissions: 410/516-8171
Johns Hopkins University is a four-year private university that offers women's studies as a minor to any major at the undergraduate level. The program is based on interdisciplinary studies.

Maryland
Goucher College: Women's Studies Program
410/337-6274
Dulany Valley Road, Baltimore, MD 21204
Admissions: 410/337-6100, 800/GOUCHER
Goucher College is a four-year private liberal arts college that offers a Bachelor of Arts degree in women's studies.

Montgomery College: Women's Studies Program
301/279-5152
51 Mannakee Street, Rockville, MD 20850
Montgomery College is a two-year public community college that offers a certificate program in women's studies. Students must complete four classes to qualify for the certificate. These women's studies courses are transferable to four-year colleges and universities.

University of Maryland at College Park: Women's Studies Program
301/405-6877
2101 Woods Hall, College Park, MD 20742
Admissions: 301/985-7265
University of Maryland at College Park is a four-year public university that offers a Bachelor of Arts degree in women's studies within the College of Arts and Humanities and certificate programs in women's studies at the undergraduate and graduate levels. Students can either take the certificates in conjunction with a degree or obtain "special student" status to complete a certificate program only. The university operates the National Women's Studies Association.

Virginia
George Mason University: Women's Studies Program
703/993-1429
4400 University Drive, Fairfax, VA 22030-4444
Admissions: 703/993-2400/2404
George Mason University is a four-year public university that offers a minor in women's studies. The degree requires 21 hours of course work.

Old Dominion University: Women's Studies Program
804/683-3823
Hampton Blvd., Norfolk, VA 23529-0050
Admissions: 804/683-3637, 800/348-7926
Old Dominion University is a four-year public university that offers a Bachelor of Arts in women's studies and a Bachelor of Science in women's studies. The University also offers a Masters degree with an emphasis in women's studies, and a graduate certificate in women's studies.

University of Richmond: Women's Studies Program
804/289-8298, 804/289-8776
Richmond, VA 23173
Admissions: 804/289-8640
University of Richmond is a four-year private university that offers a women's studies major and a women's studies minor at the undergraduate level.

Virginia Polytechnic Institute and State University: Women's Studies Program
540/231-7615
124 Lane Hall, Blacksburg, VA 24061-0227
Admissions: 703/231-6267
Virginia Polytechnic Institute and State University is a four-year public university that offers an undergraduate minor in women's studies. Students can use women's studies to complement any other major offered at the university. The school is in the process of developing a graduate concentration program in women's studies.

D.C.-Based Correspondence Schools
The Union Institute
202/496-1630, 800/969-6676
1710 Rhode Island Ave., NW, Suite 100, Washington, DC 20036-3007
The Union Institute is a correspondence school that offers a doctoral program with an emphasis in women's studies. The Institute is based in

Cleveland, Ohio, but has a site office in Washington, D.C. The doctoral program consists of three seminars, a 10-day introductory colloquium, 10 peer day meetings and an internship requirement. The Union Institute is accredited by the North Central Association of Colleges and Schools.

13

Internship Opportunities in Washington, D.C.

Internship opportunities abound in Washington, D.C. Whether you're seeking an internship for school credit or simply the opportunity to get your foot in the door in the Washington job market, internships are readily available in all areas of interest in the private, public and nonprofit sectors. You can intern at a congressional office, with a special interest group, media outlet, research institute, the U.S. government, or any of the hundreds of trade or professional associations located in Washington.

If you're interested in an internship with an organization that deals with women's issues, then Washington, D.C., is definitely the hot spot. There are hundreds of options, based on your specific area of interest, whether it's health care, violence against women, education, reproductive issues, social services, human rights or equity in the workplace.

A list of women's groups that offer internship opportunities is listed in this chapter. In addition, the Public Leadership Education Network (PLEN) publishes a helpful guide for women called *Preparing to Lead: A College Woman's Guide to Internships*. PLEN is listed in chapter 4 of this book. Another good source of internship information for women is the Feminist Majority, which operates an internship clearinghouse on its Web site, http://www.feminist.org. You can also target organizations by reviewing the resources listed in other chapters of this book.

Locating an Internship

Advocacy Groups. Refer to chapter 6 for a listing of special interest and research groups that lobby for issues of interest to women and families. Most enlist the services of interns for a variety of tasks, including writing and policy duties.

U.S. Congress. There are hundreds of internship opportunities available in congressional offices and with legislative committees, which rely on interns to respond to constituent mail, attend hearings and perform administrative tasks.

Business and Professional Organizations. Chapter 1 contains more than 150 groups that support the advancement of professional women. You will find that some have intern opportunities for a wide variety of duties, including planning events, legislative affairs and responding to member inquiries.

Political Groups. If you want to intern with a political group that works to expand the participation of women in the political process, then refer to chapter 5 for a listing of Democratic, Republican and nonpartisan groups. Some groups raise money for women candidates while others support and train women for roles in public office.

Government. There are many offices and departments that take on interns for administrative tasks and more substantive duties, such as writing and monitoring legislation. Start with chapter 2 for the personnel contacts and job vacancy hotlines, which also provide information on internship opportunities.

Media. Washington is a hub of media activity. For print opportunities, check into national and regional newspapers, wire services, magazines, trade journals and newsletters. For television, contact local and national news outlets, cable television and news programs with bureaus in Washington. For radio, choose from radio stations and news services.

Social Services. Internship opportunities are available with social service agencies that operate programs such as crisis intervention, battered women's shelters and services for homeless women.

Internships with Women's Organizations

The following organizations focus on issues related to women and offer internship opportunities to students.

American Association of University Women
202/785-7700
1111 15th Street, NW
Washington, DC 20036
    Membership organization for college-degreed women and advocacy group for equity issues.

Association for Women in Communications
703/359-9000
10605 Judicial Drive, Suite A-4
Fairfax, VA 22030-5167
Professional membership group for women working in all areas of communications.

Assn. for Women in Science
202/326-8940
1522 K Street, NW, Suite 820
Washington, DC 20005
e-mail: awis@awis.org
http://www.awis.org/awis
Membership group for professionals and students involved in the field of science.

Catholics for a Free Choice
202/986-6093
1436 U Street, NW, Suite 301
Washington, DC 20009
Special interest group that advocates on behalf of pro-choice Catholics.

Center for Women Policy Studies
202/872-1770
2000 P Street, NW, # 508
Washington, DC 20036
Research and policy organization that advocates for women's equity issues.

DC Commission for Women
202/939-8083
2000 14th Street, NW, Suite 354
Washington, DC 20009
Information and referral center for women, as well as an advocate for issues of interest to women and families.

EMILY's List (Early Money Is Like Yeast)
202/326-1400
805 15th Street, NW, Suite 400
Washington, DC 20005
Political organization that raises money and supports Democratic pro-choice women candidates.

Federally Employed Women
202/898-0994
1400 Eye Street, NW, Suite 425
Washington, DC 20005-2252
Membership association and advocate for women employed by the federal government.

Federation of Organizations for Professional Women
202/328-1415
1825 I Street, NW, Suite 400
Washington, DC 20006
Membership group and advocate for working women.

Feminist Majority
703/522-2214
1600 Wilson Blvd., Suite 801
Arlington, VA 22209
http://www.feminist.org
Special interest group that advocates for feminist issues.

Institute for Women's Policy Research
202/785-5100
1400 20th Street, NW, Suite 104
Washington, DC 20036

Research and policy organization that advocates for equity issues for women.

International Center for Research on Women
202/797-0007
1717 Mass. Ave., NW, # 302
Washington, DC 20036
Research and policy organization that advocates for issues that affect women in the U.S. and abroad.

League of Women Voters
202/429-1965
1730 M Street, NW
Washington, DC 20036
Membership organization that encourages the participation and awareness of women in public policy.

National Abortion Rights Action League (NARAL)
202/973-3000
1156 15th Street, NW, Suite 700
Washington, DC 20005
Special interest group that advocates for pro-choice view.

National Federation of Business and Professional Women's Clubs
202/293-1100
2012 Massachusetts Ave., NW
Washington, DC 20036
Membership group that advocates for workplace equity issues.

National Foundation for Women Legislators, Inc.
202/337-3565
910 16th Street, NW, Suite 100
Washington, DC 20006
Professional membership organization that advocates on behalf of women legislators.

National Organization for Women
202/331-0066
1000 16th Street, NW, # 700
Washington, DC 20036
Membership organization that advocates for progressive women's issues.

National Women's Health Network
202/347-1140
514 10th Street, NW, Suite 400
Washington, DC 20004
Information resource and advocate for women's health issues.

National Women's Law Center
202/588-5180
11 Dupont Circle, Suite 800
Washington, DC 20036
Research and public policy organization that advocates for various women's issues.

National Women's Political Caucus
202/785-1100
1211 Conn. Ave., NW, # 425
Washington, DC 20036
Women's political organization that helps women

become involved in public office.

National Women's Studies Association
301/403-0525
7100 Baltimore Ave., Suite 301
College Park, MD 20742
Membership organization for people involved with women's studies programs.

Older Women's League
202/783-6686
666 11th Street, NW, 7th Floor
Washington, DC 20001
Information and advocacy group for issues affecting older women.

Planned Parenthood Federation of America
202/785-3351
1120 Connecticut Ave., NW
Suite 461
Washington, DC 20036
Advocate for reproductive rights.

Renaissance Women
202/546-4142
205 Third Street, SE
Washington, DC 20003
Special interest group that advocates for conservative issues.

Sisterhood Is Global Institute
301/657-4355
4343 Montgomery Ave., # 201
Bethesda, MD 20814
Special interest group that advocates for international women's rights.

Suited for Change
202/293-0351
1712 I Street, NW, Suite B-100
Washington, DC 20006
Not-for-profit organization that provides professional clothing and career training to low-income women.

The Union Institute Center for Women
202/496-1630
1710 Rhode Island Ave., NW
Washington, DC 20036-20076
Research institute that builds coalitions between scholars and community activists.

Wider Opportunities for Women
202/638-3143
815 15th Street, NW, Suite 916
Washington, DC 20005
Job training and support group that also advocates for women's rights in the workplace.

Women Work!
202/467-6346, 800/235-2732
1625 K Street, NW, # 300
Washington, DC 20006
Job training and support organization that advocates for equal employment rights.

Women's Action for New Directions
202/543-8505
110 Maryland Ave., NE, # 205
Washington, DC 20002
Advocacy group that works to redirect defense money to domestic needs.

Women's Campaign Fund
202/393-8164
734 15th Street, NW, Suite 500
Washington, DC 20005
Nonpartisan organization that raises money and supports progressive women candidates.

Women's Institute for Freedom of the Press
202/966-7783
3306 Ross Place, NW
Washington, DC 20008-3332
Special interest group that advocates the promotion of women in mass media sources.

Women's Legal Defense Fund
202/986-2600
1875 Conn. Ave., NW, # 710
Washington, DC 20009
Research and public policy organization that advocates for various women's issues.

Women's Policy, Inc.
202/554-2323
409 12th Street, SW, Suite 705
Washington, DC 20024
Nonprofit organization that monitors federal policy that affects women and families.

Women's Policy publishes a bi-monthly newsletter and other legislative publications.

Women's Research and Education Institute
202/328-7070
1700 18th Street, NW, 4th Floor
Washington, DC 20009
Research and public policy organization that advocates for various women's issues.

Young Women's Project
202/393-0461
923 F Street, NW, 3rd Floor
Washington, DC 20004
Sponsors projects to help young women develop leadership skills.

YWCA
202/628-3636
624 9th Street, NW, 2nd Floor
Washington, DC 20001
Membership organization that offers recreational and educational activities to young women, and advocates for general issues of interest to women and girls.

Part VI

Social Services

14

Violence Against Women

Denise Snyder, Consulting Editor

Each year, one million women become victims of violence. In fact, according to the U.S. Department of Justice, women are six times more likely to be attacked by intimates than men. And these are just the known cases. Over 80 percent of rape victims know their attacker and nearly one-third of violent crimes (involving a single attacker) are committed by someone with whom the victim had an intimate relationship.

In recent years, tougher state and federal laws have been enacted to provide more stringent punishments for sex offenders and improved assistance for victims. In 1994, Congress approved the Violence Against Women Act, which allocates $1.6 billion for police, prosecution, crime prevention and victim assistance, including increased funding to women's shelters. The Act also gives victims better protection across state lines and requires sex offenders to pay restitution to their victims.

Even though authorities are stepping up efforts to reduce sexual assault attacks, the stigma associated with sexual crimes continues to permeate society. Unfortunately, this results in many women not reporting the crimes and facing victim-blaming attitudes from friends and family. However, there are many groups and services in the Washington metropolitan area intended to help victims get the assistance they need. The crisis and service programs listed in this chapter provide intervention, information, referrals, some counseling, and companion services to help victims through the reporting and healing process.

What to Do If You've Been Raped

Get to a safe place.

Contact someone to help you.
Call a friend, the police, and one of the 24-hour sexual assault crisis lines for help. People are available to accompany you to the hospital and police station, and to provide support and referrals.

Call 911 to report the crime.
If you choose to report the crime, an officer will take your statement and you will be asked to provide a detailed description of the attack. Do not bathe, douche, shower, brush your teeth, eat, drink or change your clothes. These activities destroy physical evidence that may be used to convict the attacker.

Get medical attention.
If you report the crime, you will have to go to the hospital emergency room for an examination to collect evidence. The evidence needs to be collected in the city or county where the rape occurred, not where you live. It's a good idea to go to the emergency room even if you don't want to file a police report immediately because you might have injuries you are unaware of or you may change your mind later about filing a report.

Get some counseling.
Call one of the crisis centers for counseling services or for referrals to other therapists. The more you understand your feelings about the rape and the sooner you discuss them the more likely you are to have a quicker recovery.

Source: DC Rape Crisis Center

Crisis Hotlines

Nearly every county has a 24-hour crisis hotline, with many having separate emergency programs for sexual abuse and domestic violence. Most hotlines offer crisis intervention and referrals for counseling, emergency shelter and legal assistance. Many of the hotlines have staff available to accompany victims to the hospital or police department following a sex crime. The following crisis lines are in operation 24 hours a day, unless otherwise noted.

Washington, D.C.

	Sexual Abuse/Violence	202/333-RAPE
	Crisis and Referral Hotline	202/223-2255
	Crisis Line	202/561-7000

Maryland

Charles Co.	Rape/Abuse Hotline	301/645-3336
Frederick Area	Crisis	301/662-2255
Montgomery Co.	Crisis	301/738-2255
	Sexual Assault	301/656-9420
	Mobile Crisis Team	301/652-8849
Prince George's Co.	Crisis	301/577-4866
	Sexual Assault	301/618-3154

Virginia

Alexandria	Crisis (2 pm - 10 pm)	703/751-0123
	Domestic Violence	703/838-4911
	Sexual Assault	703/683-7273
Arlington Co.	Victims of Violence (8 am-6 pm)	703/358-5150
	Victims of Violence (6 pm-8 am)	703/358-4848
Fairfax Co.	Sex Abuse and Assault	703/360-7273
Northern Virginia		703/527-4077

National Domestic Violence Hotline		800/799-SAFE
	(TDD)	800/787-3224

Shelters and Services for Battered and Abused Women

District of Columbia

Bethany Women's Center
202/483-3739
1226 Vermont Ave., NW
Washington, DC 20005
Day center that provides counseling, career and educational services, referrals and activities.

DC Coalition Against Domestic Violence
202/783-5332
513 U Street, NW
Washington, DC 20001
The Coalition is mainly an advocacy group, but also provides referrals to domestic violence programs.

DC Crime Victim's Assistance Program (CVAP)
202/842-8467
65 Eye St., SW, Randall Bldg. Suite 116
Washington, DC
CVAP offers 24-hour crisis intervention, counseling and referrals for battered and abused women.

DC Rape Crisis Center
202/232-0789
202/333-RAPE, 24-hour hotline
202/328-1371, TDD
PO Box 34125
Washington, DC 20043-4125

Offers emergency intervention, individual and group counseling, referrals, and other services for rape victims and adult survivors of childhood sexual assault. The Center offers a companion program, self-defense classes and other programs.

Hermanas Unidas @ Ayuda
202/387-4848
1736 Columbia Road, NW
Washington, DC 20009
Legal education and support group for battered Latinas.

Her Space
202/347-2777, 202/667-7001
5 Thomas Circle, NW (Admn.)
Washington, DC 20005
Confidential safe house and 24-hour shelter for victims of domestic violence. Other services include counseling, legal advice, referrals and support groups.

My Sister's Place
202/529-5991
PO Box 29596
Washington, DC 20017
Operates a 24-hour shelter and crisis hotline for battered women and their children. Other services include legal and job assistance.

Virginia

Alexandria Office on Women Sexual Assault Response and Awareness Program
703/838-5030
703/683-RAPE, 24-hour crisis
110 N. Royal Street, #201
Alexandria, VA 22314
Provides emergency intervention, referrals, counseling, information, treatment programs and counseling for abusers, self-defense classes and a Hispanic Women's Support Group.

Arlington County Safehouse for Battered Women
703/237-0881
PO Box 1285
Arlington, VA 22210
The Safehouse is a 24-hour emergency shelter for battered women and their children. Other services include counseling, legal assistance and referrals.

Arlington County Victims of Violence Program
703/358-5150 (8 a.m. - 6 p.m.)
202/358-4256 (6 p.m. - 8 a.m.)
1725 North George Mason Dr.
Arlington, VA 22205
Offers emergency intervention and support services, counseling, general assistance and referrals.

Fairfax County Victim's Assistance Network
703/360-7273
Provides resources, referrals and other crisis and non-emergency assistance for victims of domestic violence and sexual assault in Fairfax County.

Fairfax County Women's Shelter
703/435-4940
PO Box 1174
Vienna, VA 22183
Provides a 24-hour emergency shelter, counseling, referrals, meals and other services for battered women and their families.

Maryland

Charles County Center for Abused Persons
301/843-1110
301/645-3336, 24-hour crisis
Emergency and non-emergency assistance for victims of rape, sexual assault or domestic violence.

Family Crisis Center of Prince George's County
301/779-2100
301/864 -9101, 24-hour hotline
Provides emergency shelter for women and their children, counseling, legal and educational assistance to residents of Prince George's County.

Heartly House Domestic Violence Program
301/662-8800, 24-hour hotline
Provides crisis and non-emergency services for victims of domestic violence, rape and assault. Services include shelter, counseling and daytime programs.

Helping Hands Shelter
301/340-2796
622 N Horners Lane
Rockville, MD 20850

Overnight shelter for abused and homeless women and their infants. Other services include counseling, job and educational services, and day programs.

Montgomery County
301/654-1881, Abuse
301/652-8849 Sexual Assault
301/652-8849 (4 p.m.-midnight)

Provides emergency and nonemergency services for victims of domestic violence, rape and assault. Other services include individual and group counseling, legal assistance and referrals.

National Programs

Battered Women's Justice Project
800/903-0111

Health Resource Center on Domestic Violence
800/313-1310

National Council on Child Abuse and Family Violence
800/222-2000

National Resource Center on Domestic Violence
800/537-2238

Safety Tips for Women

It is wise for women to take safety precautions both when out in society and while at home. The more knowledgeable and aware women are, the better their chances are of warding off danger. Classes are available to teach safety techniques to ward off an attacker and also to better inform women about what safety devices are available and the pros and cons of using such devices.

Self-Defense

Self-defense classes are a good way to help protect yourself against a possible attacker. It's better to know how to react in situations that could put your life in jeopardy. Self-defense courses are offered by the DC Rape Crisis Center and the Alexandria Sexual Assault and Awareness Program and through other violence awareness programs. Some County Departments of Recreation and Parks offer classes on self-defense as do martial arts studios.

Self-defense classes teach women techniques on how to fend off an attacker to bide time to get away. The classes also teach women general awareness tips with the intent of deflecting an attack before it even occurs. The combination of these skills is intended to build a woman's self-confidence in order to make her less vulnerable to an attack.

Public Awareness Tips for Women

- The key to warding off an attack is being aware of your surroundings at all times and acting with a sense of confidence. The Alexandria Office on Women recommends that women take note of the following safety precautions.

- When walking, use a steady, confident pace and avoid walking through dark or deserted areas.

- Vary your travel routes from time to time.

- Carry a whistle or keys in your hands.

- Be wary of giving your name, address or place of business in restaurants and other public places.

- Don't overload yourself with packages.

- If you're driving and anyone tries to enter the car, sound your horn in short blasts until the police or others come to your assistance.

- If you're driving and two cars try to box you in and you fear for your safety, sound your horn until help arrives.

- If you're riding public transportation try to sit near the driver and don't fall asleep. If you believe that someone is following you, stay on the bus or train until after the suspect gets off. On a bus, ask the driver to let you off at a safe place.

Safety Tips for Your Home

Lights, locks and common sense are the key components to ward off intruders to your home. The Alexandria Office on Women recommends that women be aware of the following safety precautions.

- Make sure you have strong locks on all doors and windows. Don't rely on door chains for protection from anyone seeking entry.

- Use extra locks for windows near fire escapes. If you live in a basement or first floor apartment, install releasable bars on the windows. Curtains or blinds should be on every window.

- Report any suspicious activities that occur in your neighborhood to the police and to your landlord.

- Be sure lights are installed and working in dark walkways, driveways and yards.

- Be aware of places where assailants might hide under stairs, between buildings and in bushes.

- Don't let strangers into your home.

- Request identification from service personnel, or call their company to verify their employment before you open the door.

- Report unusual phone calls to the police.

- Meet your neighbors and know which ones you could trust in an emergency.

- When returning home at night, have your keys ready before you get to the door.

- If someone is watching or following you, go to a neighbor's house or a public place to call the police.

- Never hide a key outside of your home.

- Hang bells or wind chimes on entryways and place cans or house plants on the top or in the tracks of windows so that they will be disturbed by anyone who tries to break in.

- When you leave your home, use light timers, one inside and one outside, and rotate the light you leave on at night.

- Have a lock on your bedroom door and a phone by your bed, with emergency numbers written so you can read them without glasses.

15

Housing

Housing has increasingly become a women's issue, especially for single mothers. Nowhere is that more evident than the District of Columbia, where limited affordable housing is pushing many women—even moderate-income women—into homelessness. Although assistance is available, services such as homeless shelters and transitional housing facilities are greatly impacted. Waiting lists are only getting longer. To meet the demand, nonprofit organizations and private companies are creating more affordable housing options, some specifically for women.

This chapter provides an overview of some low-cost housing options that are available to various groups of women, including women with children, single women, women with HIV/AIDS, women in recovery from substance abuse, and mentally ill women. This chapter also includes emergency housing options and social services for women who are homeless or are on the verge of becoming homeless.

Low-Cost Housing for Women and Families

ARCH
202/889-6344
2427 Martin Luther King, Jr. Ave., SE
Washington, DC 20020
   Apartment situations. Rent is $350-$550.

Hope and a Home
202/462-8686
1711 14th Street, NW

Washington, DC 20009
   Transitional housing. Rent is $250-$350.

Jubilee Housing
202/667-5400
1750 Columbia Road, NW
Washington, DC 20009
   Various locations in northwest D.C.

Marshall Heights Dev. Corp.
202/396-1200
3917 Minnesota Ave., NE
Washington, DC 20019

Mary House
202/635-0534
4303 13th Street, NE
Washington, DC 20017
    Apartment situations for predominantly homeless and low-income Latinos.

Partner Arms
202/829-5614
935 Kennedy Street, NW
Washington, DC 20011
    Transitional housing. Renters pay 30 percent of their income.

Salvation Army Transitional Family Program
202/783-4054
424 Ridge Street, NW
Washington, DC
    Transitional housing. Renters pay 30 percent of their income.

TEN Program
202/635-9215

1438 Rhode Island Ave., NE
Washington, DC 20018
    TEN pays the first six months rent in this transitional housing program.

Thea Bowman House
202/399-1385
4065 Minnesota Ave., NE
Washington, DC 20019-3503
    Transitional housing for employed people. Section 8 subsidies are accepted.

Trenton Park
202/562-7401
3647 6th Street, SE
Washington, DC 20032
    Trenton Park has 259 low-income units. Section 8 is accepted. Applicants can apply on Tuesdays and Thursdays.

Trinity Housing
202/347-0511, ext. 313
305 E Street, NW
Washington, DC 20001
    Two-year transitional housing for homeless families. Renters pay 30 percent of their income.

Low-Cost Housing for Single Women

Aged Women's Home
202/333-4385
1255 Wisconsin Ave., NW
Washington, DC 20007
    Group home for women 62 years or older and able to care for themselves. Houses 11 women and is free of charge to women who are living near the poverty line or below. Offers private rooms, shared bath, and washer and dryer. The house is funded by the Female Union Benevolence Society.

Women and Housing
by
Lisa Hutchins, Housing Specialist

Limited affordable housing in the District of Columbia poses a serious threat to the housing stability of many moderate- and low-income residents. Although most of the homeless are single men, in the early 1980's women and children began joining their ranks and eventually outpaced them. Sadly, women with children have emerged as the fastest-growing segment of the homeless population. Nearly half of single mothers with dependent children are now living below the poverty line.

As a group, women are at greater risk for homelessness based on their economic standing, their wage earnings and the shrinking availability of federal assistance programs. Overall, women live in greater poverty than the general population. Women of color, and especially those with children, are at the greatest risk of homelessness. Women generally earn less than men. Although the wage gap is slowly narrowing, on average women still earn approximately 75 cents for every dollar earned by men.

Moreover, shrinking federal assistance for housing and general assistance has had a detrimental affect on women, leaving them cash-strapped and vulnerable to homelessness. Since 1970, AFDC benefits have declined by 43 percent. Currently, 43 percent of residents in the District cannot afford a one-bedroom apartment, based on formulas that dedicate at least 30 percent of their income to housing. And federal money for housing has dramatically declined over the last two decades. In 1996, funding from the Department for Housing and Urban Development for the construction of new housing units was reduced to zero. This number is staggering when you consider that in the 1970s, an average of 400,000 new units per year were constructed, a number that was reduced to 36,000 new units per year in the 1990s and then eventually zero. Funding for Section 8, housing subsidies, which assist nearly three million low-income residents, has always been vulnerable to cutbacks. In 1996, the U.S. Congress stopped expansion of the Section 8 program even though waiting lists for Section 8 assistance were excessively long and have gotten even longer.

In lieu of cutbacks, the federal government is redirecting its funds to the non-profit sector to build and operate housing. This innovative approach to providing housing assistance is beneficial in many ways, but comes up short in results. Currently, there is a gap of five million affordable housing units relative to the need. Unfortunately, nonprofits are only able to produce about 50,000 housing units per year—an insufficient number to meet the need.

Still, local nonprofit organizations are responding even further by providing shelter and by developing an innovative response to the homeless crisis, the "continuum of care" model, which moves homeless people from emergency situations to transitional shelter and finally on to permanent housing. Although limited, Washington has a good network of permanent and transitional housing for people needing assistance.

Capital Hill House
202/628-5390
1338 Constitution Ave., NE
Washington, DC 20002
　　Transitional housing for single women without children. Residents must be employed or in a situation in which they will be earning a salary shortly. Rent is $300 per month.

Harvest House
202/797-8806
71 O Street, NW
Washington, DC 20001
　　The Harvest House is a new transitional housing and job training program to help women reenter the job market.

Phyllis Wheatley YWCA
202/667-9100
901 Rhode Island Ave.
Washington, DC 20001
　　Women must be self-sufficient. Rent is $250 monthly.

Susanna Wesley House
202/347-1577, x314
4622 12th Street, NE
Washington, DC 20001
　　Transitional housing for employed single women. Rent is based on income.

Thompson-Markward Hall
202/667-9100
235 Second Street, NE
Washington, DC 20002
　　Transitional housing for predominantly women that offers single rooms and a central bathroom.

Housing for Women with HIV/AIDS

Miriam's House
202/667-1758
PO Box 73618
Washington, DC 20056
　　Group home for HIV positive homeless women and their children. Nursing services and hospice care are available. Rent is based on income.

Whitman Walker Clinic
Schwartz Housing Services
202/797-3555
1407 S Street, NW
Washington, DC 20009
　　Several group homes and apartments for HIV-positive mothers and their children. Rent is 25 percent of income over $400 per month and no charge for women who earn less.

Housing for Women in Recovery from Substance Abuse

Hannah House
THEIRS Program
202/289-4840
612 M Street, NW
Washington, DC 20001
Women must be clean for at least 30 days. Rent is nominal.

Jeremiah House
202/832-3451
18th Street, SE, # 2
Washington, DC 20013
Tenants must be employed and have a Section 8 certificate.

Lazarus House
202/667-8026
2523 14th Street, NW
Washington, DC 20009
Transitional group housing for singles and families who have been sober for at least six months.

Maya Angelou House
202/797-8806
71 O Street, NW
Washington, DC 20001
A 90-day substance abuse treatment center for women, located in West Virginia.

Micah House
202/387-0002
PO Box 28285
Washington, DC 20038-8285
Group house for single women in recovery from substance abuse. Residents must participate in weekly meetings.

Oxford Houses
202/829-2650
1387 Locust Road, NW
Washington, DC 20012
Group homes for women in recovery from substance abuse. Residents must attend weekly meetings.

Susanna Wesley House
202/347-1577, x314
4622 12th Street, NE
Washington, DC 20001
Transitional housing for single women, including women in recovery from substance abuse and those with a mental illness. Residents must be employed and meet regularly with a case manager.

St. Martin's House
202/526-5426
116 T Street, NE
Washington, DC 20002
A transitional treatment program for homeless women and their families.

Tabitha's House
202/667-0405
5620 Colorado Ave., NW
Washington, DC 20011
Transitional housing for people who have been sober for at least six months.

Social worker helps client with housing application at Hannah House.
Photo: Lisa Cashman

Housing and Services for Homeless Women

Washington, D.C.

Calvary Women's Shelter
202/783-6651
928 5th Street, NW
Washington, DC 20001
   Provides emergency shelter, psychiatric services, referrals and social services.

Dinner Program for Homeless Women
202/737-9311
945 G Street, NW
Washington, DC 20001
   Provides meals and other social services to homeless women. Dinner is served Sunday-Thursday, 4 p.m.-7 p.m.

Hannah House
202/289-4840
612 M Street, NW
Washington, DC 20001
   Transitional living center for up to six months that offers counseling, meals, recovery workshops and personal improvement programs.

House of Imagine
202/797-7460
PO Box 1493
Washington, DC 20013
   Provides shelter for homeless and battered women and other social services.

House of Ruth
202/667-7001
202/544-1134, Mothers Program
202/547-2600, Shelter
5 Thomas Circle, NW (Admn.)
Washington, DC 20005
Provides emergency shelter and assistance to homeless women, including pregnant and new mothers.

Luther Place Night Shelter
202/387-5464
1226 Vermont Avenue, NW
Washington, DC 20005
Shelter, counseling and social services.

Mount Carmel House
202/289-6315
471 G Place, NW
Washington, DC 20001
Provides 24-hour shelter with counseling, day programs, educational services, employment assistance and referrals.

New Endeavors by Women
202/682-5825
611 N Street, NW
Washington, DC 20001
Transitional shelter for homeless women and services such as counseling, education and employment training, health and social services.

Rachael's Women's Center
202/682-1005
1222 11th Street, NW
Washington, DC 20001
Daytime shelter open between 8:30 a.m. and 4 p.m. that provides career and personal counseling, meals, health programs, and a variety of social services.

Suited for Change
202/293-0351
1712 I Street, NW, Suite B-100
Washington, DC 20006
Provides career clothing and professional development training to homeless or low-income women who are seeking employment.

Maryland
Dorothy Day Place
301/762-8314
251 N. Stone Street Ave.
Rockville, MD 20850
Provides general assistance, including transitional living, job and social services, counseling, health and meals.

Helping Hands Shelter
301/340-2796
622 N. Horners Lane
Rockville, MD 20850
Overnight shelter and other services, such as counseling, job and educational services and day programs.

House of Imagine
301/420-2663
PO Box 1493
Washington, DC 20013

Shelters for homeless and battered women. Women must have a referral from a social services agency.

Volunteer of America Shepherd's Cove Homeless Shelter
301/322-3093, 301/350-4717
1400 Doewood Lane
Capitol Heights, MD 20743

Homeless shelter for women and children for up to six weeks. The shelter also provides a variety of daytime services, including stress management work-shops, case management, pre-school, job service, housing assistance and health care.

Virginia

Arlington Community Temporary Shelter for Women
703/237-1147
PO Box 1285
Arlington, VA 22210

Shelter for homeless women and their children. Arlington residents receive preference, but others are also admitted. Provides counseling, referrals and other assistance.

*Housing list compiled with the assistance of Carey Schneider and Lisa Hutchinson.

Social Service Departments

Social Service Departments provide assistance to needy residents. In addition to information on how to apply for housing assistance, you can also get information about AFDC, food stamps, and child care supplements.

District of Columbia	202/727-5930
Maryland	
Charles County	301/870-3665
Montgomery County	301/217-6980
Prince George's County	301/422-5000
Virginia	
Arlington County	703/358-5051
Alexandria	703/838-0900
Fairfax County	703/324-7500
Loudoun County	703/777-0353

Angie

Angie is one of five homeless or formerly homeless women in the District of Columbia whose work is featured in *I Have Arrived Before My Words: The Autobiographical Writings of Homeless Women* (Charles River Press, January 1997) by Deborah Pugh and Jeanie Tietjen. The following excerpt is her story.

I am no longer homeless, but I have been through the experience. I write this in the beginning days of 1996 and have had my own shelter since the summer of 1992. The after shocks of having been homeless would still come back to haunt me just until the recent past. I still feel a shudder now and then. To be alone without one of life's basic requirements—shelter—is a traumatic event.

I define homelessness as not having a roof over one's head to call her own—in other words, the lack of a physical space to call home. But at least for me, there was an added dimension to being homeless. I experienced an internal feeling of emptiness, an aching that at times felt like it would never, ever go away. It was like a living puzzle: how did I get in this predicament anyway? This catastrophe wasn't supposed to happen *to me.*

In the spring of 1991, I had to give up a large, two-bedroom apartment in which I had lived for 22 years. I had reared my two sons there, first as a working single parent and then as an unemployed disabled mother trying to eke out an existence on extremely limited means. I could no longer postpone the inevitable. I couldn't pay the rent. I would have to move. I think that I was in a state of shock for a while.

I had become disabled after a bout with breast cancer in 1973. Complications developed from the radiation therapy and I spent six months in the hospital. When I physically recovered from radiation burns, I would from time to time smile a little to myself and wonder just how "therapeutic" it had been in the face of the ensuing physical damage and disability. Also, during those years, I suffered periodic psychotic episodes associated with manic-depressive illness. Usually I was depressed. I had been hospitalized for mental illness several times, but was not correctly diagnosed until 1992 after my homeless experience. In that year, I was finally placed on the correct medication and continued psychotherapy.

Today I am stabilized, balanced, feeling more in control of myself and what concerns me; I am looking forward to the future...

A new season dawns
Now, a sunny place
        and space
of her own—after a season of streets.
Yes, a light at the end of a tunnel—
        it is not a speeding train.
Welcome home, Serenity,
Welcome home, Peace—
A place to call my own.

Reprinted with the permission of Charles River Press. For more information on the book, check your local bookstore or call the publisher at 703/519-9197.

16

Legal Assistance

Women have made significant advancements in recent years, but unfortunately, discrimination still exists. In the workforce, women are sometimes subjected to biases such as pay inequity and sexual harassment. In society and home life, women continue to become victims of rape and domestic violence. Even though these crimes have become more acceptable to discuss, the stigma associated with reporting them still permeates society, resulting in many crimes going unreported. However, there are many legal options available to women in the areas of employment discrimination, domestic violence and sexual assault. This chapter identifies the resources to help women find relief when they are put in unfair or harmful situations.

Employment Discrimination

Women experience different types of discrimination in the workforce, including wage inequity, bias in hiring and promotions, pregnancy-related discrimination, job assignment bias and sexual harassment. However, there are laws to protect against these discriminatory acts. The Civil Rights Act ensures all workers equal pay and equal treatment. The Equal Pay Act of 1963 makes wage discrimination based on gender illegal. The Family and Medical Leave Act of 1993 allows parents to take up to 12 weeks of annual unpaid leave for family and individual health needs. The Pregnancy Discrimination Act, an amendment to the Civil Rights Act of 1964, ensures employment rights for pregnant women.

If you believe you have been discriminated against at work or on a job interview, you can get advice on how to proceed from the resources listed in this section.

Business and Professional Women (BPW)
202/293-1200
2012 Massachusetts Ave., NW, Washington, DC 20036
BPW offers information on employment discrimination and counseling services. BPW is a membership organization that works for pay equity and integrating women into all sectors of the workforce.

Equal Employment Opportunity Commission (EEOC)
202/275-7377, 800/669-4000
1400 L Street, NW, Suite 200, Washington, DC 20005
You can file an employment discrimination complaint with the EEOC, as well as obtain information on fair employment and workplace. The EEOC provides referrals to other resources and agencies.

Federally Employed Women (FEW)
202/898-0994
1400 Eye Street, NW, Washington, DC 20005
FEW assists women employed by the federal government with employment discrimination issues by providing legal referrals and information packets.

Federation of Organizations for Professional Women (FOPW)
202/328-1415
2001 S Street, NW, Washington, DC 20009
FOPW, a nonprofit membership group that supports working women, operates the Professional Women's Legal Fund to assist women with job discrimination.

Feminist Majority Foundation, Sexual Harassment Hotline
703/522-2501
Hours: M-F, 9 a.m. - 6 p.m.
The Sexual Harassment Hotline provides information, referrals, links to state resources and feminist strategies to rectify sexual harassment situations in the workforce.

Georgetown University Law Center/Sex Discrimination Clinic
202/662-9640
111 F Street, NW, Room 334, Washington, DC 20001
The Sex Discrimination Clinic offers legal assistance and referrals to assist people with sex discrimination cases. Services are provided by third-year law students under the supervision of attorneys and professors.

Employment Discrimination Hot Lines

9 am-6 pm	Sexual Harassment Hot Line	703/522-2501
	Feminist Majority	
6 pm-9 pm	WERC Hot Line	202/659-WERC
	Women's Employment Resource Center	
10 am-4 pm	Job Survival Hot Line	800/522-0925
	National Assn. of Working Women	

9 to 5, National Association of Working Women
800/522-0925
Hours: 10 a.m. - 4 p.m.
This national membership association operates the *Job Survival Hotline*, which provides information and referrals on all types of employment discrimination.

Women's Bureau, U.S. Dept. of Labor
Clearinghouse for Work and Family Issues
800/827-5335
200 Constitution Ave., NW, Washington, DC 20210
The Clearinghouse offers information and publications on job rights, discrimination and federal policies such as the Family Medical Leave Act and the Pregnancy Discrimination Act.

Women's Employment Resource Center (WERC) Hotline
202/659-WERC
PO Box 65883, Washington, DC 20035
Resource and referral service for women who have experienced employment discrimination. WERC helps women locate legal representation and a support network of other women who have had similar experiences. The service is provided by the Metropolitan Women's Organizing Project, a group of professionals and community activists who want to improve the working conditions for low-income women. The service is in operation Monday through Friday between the hours of 6 p.m. and 9 p.m. On Saturdays, the hotline is in operation from 9 a.m. to 1 p.m. If you cannot call during these times, leave a message and your call will be returned.

What to Do If You Experience Job Discrimination

Write down what happened to make you think you're being discriminated against.
Include the date, time and place of the incident. Include what was said and who was there. Be specific. Keep your notes in a safe place at home, not at the office. If you have experienced sexual harassment, then your first step is to say "no" clearly at the time of the incident. Tell the harasser that you do not want the sexual attention. If it happens again, send a letter telling that person to stop and keep a copy for yourself.

Get emotional support from friends and family.
It can be very upsetting to feel you have been treated unfairly at work. Take care of yourself. Consider what you want to do and get help to do it.

If you belong to a union, talk to your representative.
Union rules often allow you to file a grievance and try to resolve what has happened to you. If you don't have a union, call a women's group or a civil rights organization for help.

Talk to your employer.
Some companies may have informal ways to handle discrimination problems. A personnel or EEO/Affirmative Action officer should have this information available. Explain your complaint to supervisors and administrators in writing. Your company may be as eager as you are to solve the problem without going through the formal complaint process.

Find out how other women have been treated at your office.
Talk to any women at work who may have had the same problem. You may want to share information and conjure ways to improve working conditions.

Keep doing a good job and keep a record of your work.
Keep copies of your job evaluations and any letters or memos that show that you do a good job at work. Keep these copies at home. Your boss may criticize your job performance later on in his or her defense.

You have a right to file a charge.
You can file a charge with the Equal Employment Opportunity Commission (EEOC). Most states and local governments also have fair employment practices agencies, which also register complaints.

Source: US. Dept. of Labor, Women's Bureau.

Filing a Charge with the EEOC

The U.S. Equal Employment Opportunity Commission (EEOC) enforces the laws that ensure equal treatment in the workplace. There are two main laws that ensure equal treatment: *Title VII of the Civil Rights Act of 1964*, which prohibits employment discrimination based on gender, race, color, religion, sex or national origin; and the *Equal Pay Act of 1963*, which prohibits discrimination on the basis of sex in the payment of wages.

• You can file a discrimination charge in person, by mail or telephone with the nearest EEOC office. If you are a federal employee, then contact your EEO counselor, who will try to resolve the matter informally before charges are filed. The EEOC has strict time frames in which charges must be filed. *Title VII* charges must be filed within 180 days of the alleged discriminatory act. In states or localities where there is an anti-discrimination law, a charge must also be presented to that agency. An Equal Pay Act lawsuit must be filed within two years (or three years for willful violations) of the discriminatory act.

• You will be interviewed, and if all legal jurisdictional requirements are met, the EEOC will draft a charge.

• EEOC notifies the employer about the charge and undertakes an investigation that involves requesting information from the employer and interviewing any witnesses.

• If it is believed discrimination had occurred, the EEOC conciliates or attempts to persuade the employer to voluntarily eliminate or remedy the discrimination, which may include reinstatement of a job or back pay, or restoration of lost benefits. In federal cases, the EEOC administrative judge submits findings and conclusions to the federal agency, which in turn issues the final decision.

• If conciliatory efforts fail, the EEOC could file a lawsuit in federal district court on behalf of the complainant. Applicants may enlist the services of private counsel in lieu of EEOC litigation.

• If the complainant is unhappy with the outcome, she may file an appeal with the EEOC's Office of Federal Operations. This can be done in writing by contacting: Director, Office of Federal Operations, EEOC, PO Box 19848, Washington, DC 20036.

Source: U.S. Equal Employment Opportunity Commission

Sexual Abuse/Domestic Violence

The following resources offer legal assistance for crimes of physical abuse and sexual assault. For emergency assistance, contact a 24-hour crisis center (see those listed at the beginning of chapter 14).

DC Coalition Against Domestic Violence
202/387-5630
513 U Street, NW, Washington, DC 20001
Offers support services for victims in criminal and civil domestic violence cases. Workers will accompany victims to court, explain procedures and give advice on legal representation.

DC Rape Crisis Center
202/232-0789
PO Box 34125, Washington, DC 20043-4125
The DC Rape Crisis Center provides a 24-hour companion program to assist women with reporting the crime and going through the court process, information and referrals.

Domestic Violence Advocacy Project
George Washington University
202/994-7463
2000 G Street, NW, Suite 200, Washington, DC 20052
The Project provides information and legal assistance to low-income victims of domestic violence. Services are performed by third-year law students under the supervision of professors and attorneys. Nearly all clients go through the D.C. Superior Court system.

Emergency Domestic Relations Project
Georgetown University Law Center
202/393-6290
500 Indiana Ave., Room 4465, NW, Washington, DC 20004
The Emergency Domestic Relations Project is a good resource for acquiring legal representation for domestic violence cases. Clients can also get assistance with filing a claim.

Hermanas Unidas/Ayuda
202/387-4848
1736 Columbia Road, NW, Washington, DC 20009
Legal education and support group for battered Latinas.

Domestic Violence Knows No Boundaries
by
Herma-Joze Whalen-Blaauwgeers

By the time you finish reading this short article, six women in the United States will have suffered an injury as a result of domestic violence. Some will even die. If you think this figure is just another statistic to be filed and forgotten, come with me on a short journey into the dark and terrifying world of domestic violence.

There is a common notion that most victims of domestic violence are poor minorities, but this crime—and abuse is a crime—knows no boundaries. It occurs in families from every ethnic, economic, religious, social and educational background. But because this crime is committed almost exclusively against women (and their children) in the privacy of their homes, it has not been taken seriously. Traditionally, the abuse of a wife by her husband has been considered "a husband's prerogative." Characteristically, victims of domestic violence remain isolated and silent. They do not reach out for help largely because they have been shamed by their abusers into believing that they are to blame for what is happening to them. They become trapped in the cycle of abuse and can see no avenue of escape.

The effects of domestic abuse on our society are enormous and the costs, both financial and emotional, are staggering. In the workplace alone, businesses forfeit at least $100 million annually in lost wages, sick leaves, absenteeism and non-productivity. But worst of all, 91 percent of female homicide victims in the U.S. are killed by their partners, many at work.

What can we do to stop domestic violence? First, we must become more alert to the signs of an abuse victim. Then we must be willing to intervene and take action to protect and remove the woman and her children from the abusive situation. And we must ensure that these women have access to the legal assistance they need to break the cycle of abuse forever.

Many women cannot, however, afford to pay a lawyer and do not know where to go for help. Although President Clinton has signed the Violence Against Women Act, no funds have been appropriated for legal aid. Under many existing state laws, women are either not eligible for legal services or waiting lists are too long to be of any use.

LAAW (Legal Aid for Abused Women and Children) has been established to fill this void and to provide educational and awareness programs designed to prevent abuse. We know that a good lawyer can make the difference between a woman losing everything—her job, home and children—and receiving timely protection, a decent settlement, etc. LAAW is committed to working directly with the business community and has developed an Anti-Abuse Package designed to assist employers in spotting abuse victims in the workplace and information on how to help them. Abuse awareness is every individual's responsibility.

Herma-Joze Whalen-Blaauwgeers is the founder and executive director of Legal Aid for Abused Women and Children (LAAW).

Legal Aid for Abused Women and Children (LAAW)
703/820-8393
3524 South Utah, Arlington, VA 22206
Nonprofit organization staffed by volunteers that assists women and their children who have been victims of domestic violence. LAAW provides legal representation for women who do not qualify for any federal, state or local services, but still need assistance.

Sexual Assault and Awareness Program
Alexandria Office on Women
703/838-5030
110 N. Royal Street, # 201, Alexandria, VA 22314
The Sexual Assault and Awareness Program offers legal advice and a companion service to assist women with filing charges against their attacker. The program also offers crisis support and other forms of assistance for victims of sexual assault.

Women in the Law Clinic
American University
202/274-4140
4801 Massachusetts Ave., NW, Washington, DC 20016
The Women in the Law Clinic offers information, referrals and some representation to indigent women in cases of abuse, family law, child support, domestic violence and neglect. The Clinic is not a walk-in center. Services are provided by third-year law students under the supervision of attorneys and professors.

Women's Resource Center
703/771-3397
9 Loudoun Street, SE, Leesburg, VA 20175
Provides legal advice, information and representation for low-income victims of domestic violence who are residents of Loudoun County. The Center also provides crisis services for victims of domestic violence.

Pension Rights for Women

Women make up 60 percent of the population over 65 years old, but represent nearly 75 percent of the elderly poor. One reason women face a greater risk of poverty in old age is that they are less likely than men to receive adequate pensions. That's why it's important for women to understand how pensions work early in life. The Women's Pension

Project at the Pension Rights Center operates a clearinghouse on pensions and divorce. Here are the answers to some of the most common questions about pensions.

Q. Who is included in a company pension plan?
A. An employer's pension plan doesn't always cover all employees. You will have to check with your personnel office to find out if you are included. Some employers don't offer pension plans for their employees. If this is the case, you may ask your employer to consider sponsoring a pension plan.

Q. How many years of service are required for employees to be covered by a pension plan?
A. Most plans provide benefits to employees who have worked for a minimum of five years for the company. Some, however, still require employees to have up to seven years of on-the-job service.

Q. How much money will the pension yield?
A. How much you receive depends on what type of pension plan you have and how many years you have worked under the plan. Generally, you can figure the dollar amount of a pension by multiplying the number of years you have worked by a certain dollar amount.

Q. How does the pension plan affect social security benefits?
A. Some pension plans take social security benefits into account when deciding on how much the pension will yield. This plan will subtract part of the employees' social security benefits from their pension.

Q. When do pension plans go into effect?
A. You can start collecting on a pension when you retire, usually at age 65. However, if you choose to collect the pension at an earlier time, the payments will be much smaller.

Q. What happens to the pension benefits if the employee changes jobs?
A. In most cases, your pension stays with the plan until you reach retirement age. Some plans, however, allow employees the option of taking a lump sum payment from the plan with them when they leave the job. Check into your options.

Your Pension Rights at Divorce

It is estimated that 80 percent of widows living in poverty were not poor before their husbands died. In case of death or divorce, women should take note of their own pension plans and those of their spouses. According to the Women's Pension Project at the Pension Rights Center, here are some points you should know.

- A pension earned during marriage is part of the marital property.
- Your spouse may have more than one pension.
- A pension actuary or accountant can estimate the value of the pension.
- You may receive your share of the pension directly from the pension plan.
- Ask the plan administrator what to include in the court order, divorce decree or property settlement so that the plan will pay you directly.
- Your court order must be specific about the amount and when the payments are to start and stop.
- You may trade off your share of the pension for another asset in the settlement.
- Arrange for your pension share to be divided at the time of divorce. In most states, it is almost impossible and extremely expensive to get it after the divorce.
- Ask what will happen if you remarry or if your ex-spouse dies.
- Ask about social security benefits as a divorced spouse.

Pension Rights Center
Women's Pension Project
918 16th Street, NW
Suite 704
Washington, DC 20006

Women's Institute for a
Secure Retirement
202/393-1246
1201 Pennsylvania Ave., # 619
Washington, DC 20004

Part VII

Sports and Leisure

17

Sports and Fitness

Doralie Denenberg Segal, M.S.
Certified Program Director, ACSM, Consulting Editor

Research has shown that playing sports not only has significant health benefits for women, but it contributes to better self-esteem and improved self-confidence. The good news is that women are actively participating in sports and fitness. Since the landmark passage of Title IX, which requires athletic equality at federally funded schools, more women than ever before are getting involved in sports and at earlier ages. The effect of this legislation is already being seen in the quantity and quality of female athletes. At the 1994 Winter Olympics, women won nine of the 13 U.S. medals. That's significant when compared to early Olympic games where women were not even allowed to compete. And at the 1996 Olympic Games in Atlanta, all eyes were on the women athletes: track and field stars Jackie Joyner-Kersee and Gail Devers, swimmer Amy Van Dyken, the U.S. Women's Basketball Team, the U.S. Women's Soccer Team and Softball Team. The Olympics were a clear sign that girls were beginning to have a wide variety of female athletes as role models.

Washington, D.C., is an image of that upward trend. In addition to a vast number of coed sports leagues and teams in the Washington area, there is a whole host of sports groups for women, including specialized areas, such as rock climbing, rugby, outdoor adventure sports, sailing and ice hockey.

But if organized sports aren't your thing, there are many other activities you can do to maintain a healthy lifestyle, such as walking, jogging or aerobics. Maintaining a healthy lifestyle helps you to look and feel great, and it could add years to your life. This chapter identifies athletic opportunities for women and offers basic guidelines to maintaining a healthy lifestyle.

Sports Groups for Women

Adventure (Outdoor)

Becoming an Outdoors Woman
410/974-3545
580 Taylor Ave., D-4, Annapolis, MD 21410
http://gacc.com/dnr/Hot/outdoorw.htm
The Department of Natural Resources sponsors this weekend excursion in which women are taught outdoor skills such as hunting, fishing, canoeing, orienteering, and backpacking. No skill level is required to participate. This program was started by the University of Wisconsin and is offered by many state departments throughout the nation.

Chesapeake Outdoors Women
410/827-7029
9930 Ferndale Ave., Columbia, MD 21046
Fishing club, primarily fly fishing, for women living in the metro area and beyond. Members go on local fishing trips and attend meetings. Beginners can learn how to fly fish from more skilled members.

Expanding Horizons
703/685-0805
PO Box 3753, Arlington, VA 22203
Expanding Horizons offers women all types of outdoor adventure activities, such as hiking, kayaking, rock climbing, white-water rafting, orienteering, bicycling and camping trips. Many activities are one-day adventures, but there are also two- to five-day trips for canoeing, backpacking and rock climbing. Expanding Horizons also offers leadership training based on the outdoor challenge. The course is held in two sessions and is intended to improve self-confidence and group interaction skills. There is also a day camp for ages 8 to 18.

Outward Bound Program/Adventure Programs for Women
800/341-1744
1900 Eagle Drive, Baltimore, MD 21207
Outward Bound offers several adventure programs for women which are taught by women, including backpacking, canoeing and sailing.

Virginia Women in the Outdoors
757-253-4180
Williamsburg, VA

The Virginia Department of Game and Inland Fishing sponsors a variety of outdoor skills workshops and weekend hunting excursions. The programs teach women skills such as hunting, fishing, canoeing, and orienteering. No skill level is required to participate. Weekend workshops for deer hunting and turkey hunting are also offered.

Washington Women Outdoors, Inc. (WWO)
301/864-3070
PO Box 345, Riverdale, MD 20738
WWO offers a variety of adventure activities for women to develop competence and comfort in the outdoors. Day and weekend activities are offered, such as canoeing, rock climbing, hiking, cross-country skiing, backpacking, white-water rafting, kayaking, bicycling, and map and compass courses. WWO is open to individuals and groups of women. WWO also offers leadership training courses, which teach first aid, group facilitator skills and group dynamics.

Baseball

Washington Metropolitan Women's Baseball League
703/313-9615
The League consists of five teams of competitive play, but is open to women of all skill levels. The season is from June to September, with games and practices held in Montgomery County and Fairfax County.

Golf

Executive Women's Golf League
202/310-1599
800/407-1477, National HQs
The League provides a unique networking opportunity and support system for women who want to play golf in an encouraging environment. The League helps women learn or improve their golf skills so they can develop the confidence to play in a corporate golf setting. Members receive touring information and discounts at host courses.

Ice Hockey

Washington Women's Ice Hockey Club
800/505-1644, 703/506-8503

Women practice and play ice hockey in two leagues: beginning-intermediate and advanced-intermediate. Hockey season goes from October to April.

Motorcycle Clubs

LadyRider, Inc.
703/237-2824
1015 Madison Lane, Falls Church, VA 22046
LadyRider is a female motorcycle club (with associate male members) that gathers for monthly rides and meetings. Women of all ages and with all sizes of motorcycles are encouraged to ride.

Women on Wheels
301/942-2312, Montgomery County Chapter
800/322-1969, Natl. HQs
Women on Wheels is a motorcycle club open to professional women with any type of motorcycle. There are about a dozen chapters located in the Washington metropolitan area that plan weekend rides and social activities. Call the national headquarters to locate a club in your area.

Rock Climbing

Sheclimbs, Inc.
703/360-4710
503/244-6735, Natl. HQs
e-mail: sheclimbs@aol.com
Sheclimbs, Inc. fosters personal growth, self-reliance, self-esteem and confidence through participation in the sport of climbing. Women of all climbing abilities are welcome to join, but must have a basic level of knowledge about climbing and safety. Members participate in climbs and service-oriented functions such as crag clean-ups. The D.C. chapter of this national organization plans events for local members.

Rugby

Chesapeake Women's Rugby
410/594-1643
rugby30@aol.com
Individuals and teams can play in this women's rugby club.

Maryland Women's Rugby
301/942-6704, 301/652-RUGBY, hotline
Rugby for women of all ages and skill levels. Teams practice and play in Hyattsville.

Potomac Rugby Union
202/543-6862, hotline
703/802-0564
Rugby teams for women of all ages and skill levels in the metropolitan area. Teams for adults, high school students and college students.

Women's Rugby
202/544-8310
Individuals and teams can participate in this women's rugby club. Competitive play and tournaments.

Running

Washington RunHers
PO Box 5622, Arlington, VA 22205
Women's running club that meets for weekend runs, evening runs and other events. For more information write to the above address.

Soccer

Sports Network
703/631-5123
8320 Quarry Road, Manassas, VA 22110
Indoor multi-sports center that offers soccer teams for women over 30.

Washington Area Women's Soccer League
703/827-7907
A competitive soccer league that offers Fall and Spring season play. Teams participate in local and state tournaments.

Volleyball

Senior Women Volleyball
301/384-9524
Players include women 50 and over who compete on age-specific teams. Players compete in local games, USVA nationals and the Maryland

Senior Olympics. In 1996, two teams, the 50 and older team and the 60 and older team, won gold medals at these games.

USA Volleyball
301/270-0710
USAV is composed of 70 women's volleyball teams that practice and play throughout the Washington metropolitan area. The league is competitive with tournament play. Teams and individuals can join.

Water Sports

Potomac Boat Club
202/333-9737
3530 Water Street, NW, Washington, DC 20007
The Potomac Boat Club offers several women's rowing teams, including master's sweep, open women's sweep and competitive.

National Capital Area Women's Paddling Assn., Inc. (NCAWPA)
301/421-9456
17405 Rockey Gorge Court, Silver Spring, MD 20905
e-mail: dw3mao1@erols.com
The Association offers canoeing, kayaking and other paddle sports for women. Women can participate in Dragon Boat Racing, a large boat with 20 paddlers, outrigger canoe racing, marathon canoe racing, and Olympic-style flatwater kayaking. Members participate in competitions in the United States and internationally. The group is affiliated with the Washington Canoe Club and launches from Water Street in Georgetown.

Womanship
410/267-6661, 800/342-9295
410 Severn Avenue, Annapolis, MD 21403
c-mail: Womanship@aol.com
Womanship comprises female sailing enthusiasts and those wanting to learn or improve their boating skills. Womanship offers courses, clinics and camaraderie in sailing on the Chesapeake Bay and other locations. Womanship organizes weekend sails to Florida and New England as well as foreign destinations, such as two-week trips to Greece, New Zealand and Ireland. Members can also join the Women's International Sailing Association (WISA) through Womanship. WISA, organized in 1987 by Womanship alumni members, provides an international network for boating expeditions, seminars and other activities.

Members of the Washington Women's Dragon Boat Team of the NCAWPA paddle
hard to the beat of the drum.   © Marcie J. Pacilli

Organized Team Sports

Departments of recreation and parks offer women-only teams in
volleyball, basketball, softball, and soccer. Players are responsible for
creating teams, but oftentimes the departments help players find existing
teams in need of players.

Washington, D.C.
District of Columbia Dept. of Recreation and Parks   202/645-3944
3149 16th Street, NW, Washington, DC 20010

Virginia
Alexandria Dept. of Recreation and Parks   703/838-5003
1108 Jefferson Street, Alexandria, VA 22314
Arlington County Dept. of Recreation and Parks   703/358-4710
2100 Clarendon Blvd., Suite 414, Arlington, VA 22210
Fairfax County Dept. of Recreation and Parks   703/324-5522
12011 Govt. Center Pkwy, # 1050, Fairfax, VA 20902
Falls Church Dept. of Recreation and Parks   703/241-5077
223 Little Falls Street, Falls Church, VA 22046
Herndon Parks and Recreation Dept.   703/435-6868
814 Ferndale Ave., Herndon, VA 22070

Vienna Parks and Recreation Dept.   703/255-6360
120 Cherry Street, SE, Vienna, VA 22180

Maryland

Gaithersburg Dept. of Parks and Recreation   301/258-6350
502 South Frederick Ave., Gaithersburg, MD 20877
Montgomery County Dept. of Recreation   301/217-6790
12210 Bushey Drive, Room 306, Silver Spring, MD 20902
Prince Georges County Dept. of Recreation and Parks 301/217-6790
6600 Kenilworth Ave., Riverdale, MD 20737
Rockville Dept. of Recreation and Parks   301/309-3340
111 Maryland Ave., Rockville, MD 20850
Takoma Park Recreation Dept.   301/270-4048
7500 Maple Ave., Takoma Park, MD 20912
Wheaton Recreation Center   301/217-6790
11711 Georgia Ave., Wheaton, MD 20902

Exercise

Regular exercise is good for your mind and body, and it could add years to your life. Exercise improves your cardiovascular (the main cause of death for American women) and musculoskeletal (a major source of disability in older women) systems. By keeping your bones, muscles, and joints strong and flexible in the early years, you can reduce your risk of osteoporosis and other debilitating conditions in the later years. Additionally, physical activity improves self-esteem, elevates mood and dissipates tension.

For health benefits, the Centers for Disease Control and Prevention and the American College of Sports Medicine recommend that people engage in moderate endurance exercise for at least 30 minutes on most days of the week. To achieve this goal, it is not necessary to engage in high-endurance activities such as jogging or high-impact aerobics. Many other activities give you similar health benefits, such as bicycling, rope skipping, rowing, stair climbing, swimming and brisk walking.

It is also important to supplement your aerobic workouts with weight training to strengthen muscles and maintain bone mass. Weight training should be performed at least twice a week using the major muscle groups. During each session, complete two to three sets of eight to 12 repetitions.

To improve your health and maintain a fit body, women should strive to burn a minimum of 200 calories beyond normal everyday activities. If you are exercising for health benefits only, then your goal should be regular, moderate exercise, which uses about 150 calories of energy and can be accomplished in as little as 15 minutes.

Activities That Burn 150 Calories

Stair walking	15 minutes
Jogging (at least 1½ miles)	15 minutes
Jumping rope	15 minutes
Bicycling (at least 4 miles)	15 minutes
Basketball (competitive)	15-20 minutes
Swimming	20 minutes
Water aerobics	30 minutes
Walking (15 min/mile)	30 minutes
Raking leaves	30 minutes
Dancing (fast dancing)	30 minutes
Bicycling (at least 5 miles)	30 minutes
Gardening	30-45 minutes
Touch football	30-45 minutes
Volleyball	45 minutes
Washing the car	45-60 minutes

Source: Surgeon General's Report on Physical Activity and Health

Exercise Wisely

In order to derive the most benefits from your exercise program, it's important to work out on a regular and progressive basis, which sometimes results in injury. You can prevent this from happening by exercising wisely.

• Build gradually to your exercise regimen. Weekend warrior tactics can cause more than achy muscles.

• Before you exercise, warm up by performing the activity itself or a low-intensity level activity that uses the same muscles as the activity.

• Slowly stretch your muscles, holding for about 30 seconds per stretch. Do at least two or three repetitions of each stretch. DO NOT bounce. It is also important to repeat these stretches after you have completed your workout.

• Increase the duration or distance of your activity by no more than 10 percent on any given day.

• Make certain you are well hydrated, not just in the warm weather but also in winter.

- If you're exercising outdoors, it's safest to exercise with a friend or two, especially if you're in an unpopulated area. Do not wear headphones! You need all your senses to stay fully aware of your surroundings.

- Alternate difficult workouts with easier ones. Don't be afraid to take at least one rest day a week. This might be a time to try another form of exercise, such as some contra or folk dancing.

- When you finish working out, do not stop abruptly. You can cool down by slowing the activity itself. For example, if you've been jogging, continue at a much slower pace and gradually come to a walk. The cool down process should take about five minutes.

Women's Fitness Centers

If you're looking for women-only fitness centers, there is a good selection in the Washington metropolitan area. Most offer aerobics classes, weights, exercise equipment, personal training and nutritional counseling.

YWCA

District of Columbia Center
202/626-0710
624 Ninth Street, NW
Washington, DC 20001

Northern Virginia Center
703/560-1111
Wolftrap & Gallows Road
Dunn Loring, VA 22027

YWCA Fitness Centers offer aerobics classes, a heated indoor pool, saunas, weight-training equipment and a gymnasium. Swimming lessons and classes, such as Water Exercise for Arthritis (WEA) are offered. There are two locations in the D.C. metropolitan area.

Fitness for Women
202/364-1190
4250 Connecticut Avenue, NW
Washington, DC 20008

800/385-3348
26 Parole Plaza
Annapolis, MD 21401

301/913-9652
4825 Bethesda Avenue
Bethesda, MD 20814

Spa Lady
703/247-2174
2052-A Albemarle Street
Arlington, VA 22207

301/540-5700
12964 Middlebrook Road
Germantown, MD 20874

703/823-0037
256 S. Van Dorn
Alexandria, VA 22304

703/768-4497
1632 Bellevue Blvd.
Alexandria, VA 22307

703/913-4911
6230 Rolling Road
Springfield, VA 22152

The Women's Club
703/817-0700
14175 Sullyfield Circle
Chantilly, VA 20151

Membership Groups

American Alliance for Health, Physical Education, Rec. and Dance
703/476-3400
1900 Association Drive, Reston, VA 22091
The Alliance is made up of six national associations to help promote good health and recreation.

American Running and Fitness Association
301/913-9517
The Association is an information, resource and networking group for people interested in jogging, running or other physical fitness activities. You can get recommendations on good aerobics programs and running paths, as well as advice on sports physicians and nutrition.

Consumer Nutrition Hotline
800/366-1655
The Consumer Nutrition Hotline is a service provided by the American Dietetic Association.

Food and Nutrition Information Center
National Agriculture Library
301/504-5719
10301 Baltimore Blvd., Room 304, Beltsville, MD 20705
http://fnic@nal.usda.gov
Offers information and publications on food and nutrition.

National Association for Girls and Women in Sport (NAGWS)
703/476-3450
1900 Association Drive, Reston, VA 22091
NAGWS is an association for girls and women involved with sports, including students, coaches, trainers and officials. Members have access to the latest information about girls and women in the sports field, such as

clinics for athletes and trainers, guidelines and rule books and Title IX enforcement. Members can participate in leadership training seminars.

U.S. Department of Agriculture
Center for Nutrition Policy and Promotion
202/418-2312
1120 20th Street, NW, Suite 200, Washington, DC 20036
   Information and referrals on nutrition.

Women's Sports Foundation
800/227-3988, 212/516-4700
Eisenhower Park, East Meadow, NY 11554
e-mail: wosport@aol.com
   The Women's Sports Foundation is a support, resource and networking organization for female athletes. The Foundation maintains the International Women's Sports Hall of Fame, provides a speakers bureau and a variety of support services for women involved in all levels of sports.

18

Arts and Literature

Art Groups for Women

Americans for the Arts
202/371-2830
927 15th Street, NW 12th Floor, Washington, DC 20005
This national organization represents artists and arts organizations, including many women members and groups. Provides information, resources and referrals.

Cultural Alliance of Greater Washington
202/638-2406
410 Eighth Street, NW, Suite 600, Washington, DC 20004
The Cultural Alliance offers a variety of programs and services for artists, including networking events, management assistance, professional development, a job bank and reduced-cost health care coverage.

National Association of Women Artists
212/675-1616
41 Union Square West, New York, NY 10003
The Association offers networking opportunities, support and development programs and resources for female artists. It serves as a forum for women in the visual arts by seeking exhibition space and creating opportunities for women painters, printmakers, photographers and sculptors. It also promotes educational and cultural programs through lectures, workshops, school programs and videos. The headquarters is located in New York, with members in Washington, D.C.

National Women's Caucus for Art
215/854-0922
1920 Race Street, Philadelphia, PA 19103-1178

http://www.mit.edu.../ahannan/WCA6.html
The Caucus works to increase the participation of women in the visual arts by creating opportunities for women to produce, exhibit and promote their work. The group functions as a voice for female artists at the national level.

Roadwork
202/234-9308
Nonprofit group that promotes emerging female artists in the D.C. metro area through support, networking and activities for women artists.

Women in Museums Network
202/357-3300
WiMN is an informal network of women who meet for monthly luncheons at the Smithsonian's American History Museum to listen to museum professionals speak on a variety of art topics. About half of the members are Smithsonian employees. There are no membership fees to join. Members benefit from networking opportunities, job leads, bi-monthly mailings and access to an annual membership directory.

Agencies for the Arts

Local government arts agencies provide support services, information, referrals, workshops and programs to support or showcase local talent.

Alexandria Cmsn. for the Arts
703/838-6348
1108 Jefferson Street
Alexandria, VA 22314

Arlington County Cultural Affairs Division
703/358-6960
2700 S. Lang Street
Arlington, VA 22206

DC Commission on the Arts and Humanities
202/724-5613
1111 E Street, NW, Suite B-500
Washington, DC 20005

Fairfax Co. Council of the Arts
703/642-0862
4022 Hummer Road
Annandale, VA 22003

Maryland Arts Division
301/864-2929
6611 Kenilworth Ave., # 215
Riverdale, MD 20737

Montgomery County Commission on the Humanities
301/217-7900
100 Maryland Ave.
Rockville, MD 20850

The National Museum of Women in the Arts

Frida Kahlo, *Self-Portrait Dedicated to Leon Trotsky*, 1937.

The National Museum of Women in the Arts houses the most important collection of art in the world by women, including pieces by Mary Cassatt, Rachel Ruysch, Camille Claudel and Georgia O'Keeffe, spanning from the Renaissance period to the present.

The museum was created by Wilhelmina and Wallace Holladay, who collected art by women and realized the need for a museum to showcase works by women artists. Their collection became the largest assemblage of women's art and eventually became the base for the National Museum of Women in the Arts. Even before the downtown museum became a reality, the Holladays offered tours of their home so that people could view their collection.

The permanent collection features approximately 500 artists and more than 2,000 art works, including paintings, sculptures and photographs. The collection spans the Renaissance period all the way up to the present day. Based on membership, the National Museum of Women in the Arts is one of the largest museums in the world.

The National Museum of Women in the Arts is located at 1250 New York Ave., NW, Washington, DC 20005, 202/783-5000. Hours are Monday through Saturday 10 a.m. to 5 p.m., Sunday noon to 5 p.m.

Music/Dance Groups

Bowie Sounds of Music
301/262-5471
13319 Yarland Lane, Bowie, MD 20715
Bowie Sounds of Music is a group composed of women who sing patriotic, easy listening and religious songs. The group performs at garden shows, local events, churches and nursing homes throughout the Washington metro area.

Golden Rays
703/370-1466
Golden Rays is a tap dance group for women who are 55 years and older. The group practices and performs tap dance shows for special events. The troupe is well known for its elaborate costumes.

International Alliance for Women in Music (IAWM)
202/994-6338
Music Department, George Washington Univ., Washington, DC 20052
http://music.acu.edu
IAWM is a coalition of composers, conductors, performers, musicologists, educators, librarians and lovers of music. IAWM encourages the dissemination of music by women composers. The group also functions as a network, professional development and information resource for women musicians. IAWM promotes female artists through concerts, festivals, recordings, annual score calls, awards presentations and publications. IAWM was created in 1995 through the uniting of the International Congress on Women in Music, the American Women Composers and the International League of Women Composers.

National Women's Symphony
301/983-8113
PO Box 42803, Washington, DC 20015
The National Women's Symphony is a professional orchestra that features the music of women composers. The Symphony performs two to three times each year and is made up of female and male musicians. Performances include works by contemporary women composers, historical women composers and standard repertoire, such as Beethoven, Mozart and Brahms. Contemporary composers often appear at the concerts to share their feelings about their works with the audience. Performances by the National Women's Symphony are listed in the Lively Arts section of the *Washington Post*.

New Dimension Singers
301/572-7364
2827 Calverton Blvd., Silver Spring, MD 20904

New Dimension Singers is composed of female singers who perform show tunes, ballads and blues music. All shows are choreographed and are based on three-part music scores. The group commonly performs at churches and retirement homes and frequently as the after-dinner entertainment for various functions.

Sweet Adelines, Intl.
918/622-1444

Sweet Adelines has 600 choruses around the country with over a dozen chapters located in Virginia and Maryland. Sweet Adelines comprises female singers who practice and perform four-part barbershop harmony. Each chapter is independent and competes regionally and nationally. For a chapter chorus in your immediate area, contact the international headquarters and request local contact information.

Women's Committee for the National Symphony Orchestra
202/416-8150
The Kennedy Center, Washington, DC 20566-0002

The Women's Committee holds educational and fundraising events throughout the year to support the National Symphony Orchestra. Membership is open to all women who share a love of music and an interest in the National Symphony. Some of the educational activities include traveling to schools as docents to acquaint students with music and instruments, and operating a children's instrument "petting zoo." The group also holds several fundraising events throughout the year, including a holiday showcase. There are over 1,000 members in six chapters of the Women's Committee throughout the metropolitan area.

Writing Groups for Women

International Women's Writing Guild
212/737-7536
PO Box 810, Gracie Station, New York, NY 10028

The Guild is a support and networking group for women writers, with many members located in the Washington area. The Guild offers professional development programs and resources, global networking opportunities and encouragement for women to succeed in all areas of the writing profession.

Bikewoman in Washington Rush Hour
by
Marguerite Beck-Rex

Bicycle messengers, compact and bright-limbed,
zip through the stalled traffic,
while larger than life, men on horseback
are frozen in motion.

You, too, larger than life and bright-limbed,
surge through the deadlock,
whistling and singing,
riding each spoke of the wheels of the city.

There, at each hub, loom the great dead,
old heroes and horses of glorious
battles and triumph,
laurel-crowned and immobile as history.

On car-clogged streets, today's battleground,
each hero and horse inches forward on four wheels,
crawling toward history at some other circle,
while agile and two-wheeled you pump through the city,
alive and unhindered.

You are crowned with a helmet.
Your history stretches before you.

Local editors and writers discuss their books as part of a program series sponsored by the Women's National Book Association, Washington Chapter.

National League of American Pen Women
202/785-1997
1300 17th Street, NW, Washington, DC 20036
The League comprises writers, composers, artists and other professional women in the arts. Networking and resource group informs members of upcoming shows and exhibitions; publishes newsletter.

Women's National Book Association
703/587-4023
212/675-7805, Natl. HQs
3101 Ravensworth Place, Alexandria, VA 22302
http://www.bentoni.com/wnba
WNBA supports and promotes women working as authors, booksellers, librarians, editors, publishers or related positions, as well as women who love to read. WNBA sponsors book-related programs and hosts networking brunches. The book programs strike a balance between literary, business development and book industry topics. WNBA's newsletter, *Signature*, contains articles of interest to book lovers and women working in the book industry. Members are encouraged to publish articles in the newsletter.

Women's Poetry Group
301/565-9112
220 Woodward Building, 733 15th Street, NW, Washington, DC
The Women's Poetry Group consists of women who want to write poetry based on their own lives. The group provides a forum for members to read their poetry, and get feedback and encouragement.

Women's Journals

Belles Lettres
804/984-5226
1243 Maple View Drive, Charlottesville, VA 22902
Belles Lettres is a book review journal by women. It is published three times per year.

Feminist Studies
301/405-7415
2101 Woods Hall, College Park, MD 20742
Journal of articles on issues relevant to women's studies, book reviews, essays and interviews. Published by the University of Maryland.

Women's Bookstores

Lambda Rising
202/462-6969
1625 Connecticut Ave., NW, Washington, DC 20009
Lesbian bookstore.

Lammas Women's Bookstore
202/775-8218
1426 21st Street, NW, Washington, DC 20036
Feminist bookstore that offers publications in most areas of interest to women. Lammas also sponsors events, programs and book groups.

Sisterspace and Books
202/332-3433
1354 U Street, NW, Washington, DC 20009
Specializes in books by and about African-American women. The bookstore sponsors programs and discussions on book topics, such as literacy groups and a resource center.

19

Volunteer Opportunities

There are many ways to donate your time or money to help out a good cause in the Washington community, whether it's assisting at a homeless shelter or crisis center, helping to build a new home for a needy family, or becoming a mentor to an at-risk girl. If you would like to specifically help other women, there are many organizations that could use your assistance. Even if your time is scarce, you will find that many groups are willing to work around busy schedules.

Community Service Groups

Community service groups are a great way to become involved with a variety of volunteer projects, events and programs. Some groups focus on specific areas, such as Her House, which builds homes for single-parent families. However, most of the groups will give you access to a variety of projects.

The Coalition of 100 Black Women of DC Inc.
202/862-3903
1730 K Street, NW, Suite 304, Washington, DC 20006
   The Coalition consists of women who are dedicated to improving the quality of life for the African-American community. The Coalition is involved with partnerships, raising money for scholarships, awards programs and fundraisers.

General Federation of Women's Clubs
202/347-3168
1734 N Street, NW, Washington, DC 20036
   International organization made up of women volunteers for service in the D.C. community and at the national and international levels.

Her House
202/563-2172
PO Box 30884, Washington, DC 20030
Her House is a network of women of all professions who build homes for low-income women and their families. A partner of DC Habitat for Humanity, Her House is made up of women's construction groups and individual skilled and unskilled volunteers who build homes from start to finish.

International Council of African Women
202/546-8459
PO Box 91812, Washington, DC 20090
The International Council of African Women offers volunteerism and networking through diaspora and a variety of community programs.

Junior League of Washington
202/337-2001
3039 M Street, NW, Washington, DC 20007
Junior League promotes volunteerism and community improvement through a variety of service projects, events and activities. Junior League is involved with short-term and long-term projects, including fundraising events to benefit needy residents in Washington, D.C.

The Links, Inc.
202/842-8686
1200 Massachusetts Ave., NW, Washington, DC 20005
The Links, Inc., is committed to educational, civic and cultural activities that are central to the well-being of African-Americans. Volunteers can participate in a wide variety of service projects in the D.C. community and at the national and international levels.

National Association of Colored Women's Clubs
202/726-2044
5808 16th Street, NW, Washington, DC 20011
The Association is a service group dedicated to "raising to the highest plane the home-life, moral standards, and civic life of our race" through community service projects, such as raising scholarship money.

National Council of Negro Women, Inc.
202/737-0120
633 Pennsylvania Ave., NW, Washington, DC 20004

Members can participate in a variety of long-term and short-term community service projects to improve the conditions for the black community in Washington and in other regions of the nation.

National Association of Negro Business and Professional Women's Clubs, Inc. (NANBPW)
202/483-4206
1806 New Hampshire Avenue, NW, Washington, DC 20009
NANBPW is a coalition of 350 groups that works to improve the welfare of African-Americans. NANBPW provides employment and economic development, professional training, and a variety of community service activities that relate to family, housing and discrimination.

Soroptimist International
800/942-4629
10 Center Plaza, # 1000, Philadelphia, PA 19102-1883
Soroptimist International is a service organization for executive and professional women that offers community service projects in the areas of health, education, environment, economic and social development, human rights and international understanding. To locate your local chapter office, contact the international headquarters.

Suited for Change
202/232-0351
1712 I Street, NW, Suite B-100, Washington, DC 20006
Suited for Change provides career clothing and professional development seminars to low-income women who are seeking employment. Volunteers are needed in several capacities: to help women select appropriate clothing for job interviews, to assist with clothing drives, to plan or conduct professional development seminars and to assist with fundraising or other outreach projects.

Women in Community Service (WICS)
202/393-1188, DC
703/671-0500, Natl. HQs
815 15th Street, NW, Suite 836, Washington, DC 20005
WICS is a network of volunteers who provide support and guidance to at-risk young women. WICS volunteers can become mentors or perform various administrative duties. To become a mentor, volunteers must devote at least two hours per week for at least six months. WICS works in partnership with the Job Corps to provide job placement services.

Women's Committee for the National Symphony Orchestra
202/416-8150
The Kennedy Center, Washington, DC 20566-0002
The Women's Committee supports the National Symphony Orchestra through community service, education and fundraising. Membership is open to women who share a love of music and an interest in the National Symphony. Activities include traveling to schools to acquaint students with music and instruments, and operating a children's instrument "petting zoo" which allows kids to test various instruments. The Women's Committee has over 1,000 members in six chapters throughout the metropolitan area.

Zonta Club
301/652-2866
e-mail: judgeme@msn.com
The Zonta Club is an international organization of professionals dedicated to promoting the status of women through community service. Community projects include assisting at women's shelters and with literacy projects, offering career services to homeless and low-income women, and mentoring students. There are nine chapters of the Zonta Club located throughout the Washington metropolitan area.

Social Service Agencies

The social services depend heavily on community assistance. Women can get involved by donating their time, money or professional skills at homeless shelters, soup kitchens and crisis centers. There are several 24-hour crisis hotlines that are always in need of additional assistance. Homeless shelters need volunteers for assistance in a wide range of areas, including teaching residents how to read, helping prepare meals or staffing the overnight shelter. Refer to chapters 14 and 15 for descriptions of the social service agencies listed in this section.

Social Services for Homeless Women

Washington, D.C.

Calvary Women's Shelter	202/783-6651
Dinner Program for Homeless Women	202/737-9311
Hannah House	202/289-4840
House of Ruth	202/667-7001

Luther Place Night Shelter	202/387-5464
Mount Carmel House	202/289-6315
New Endeavors by Women	202/682-5825
Rachael's Women's Center	202/682-1005
Suited for Change	202/232-1097

Maryland

Dorothy Day Place	301/762-8314
Helping Hands Shelter	301/340-2796
Volunteers of America	301/322-3093

Virginia

Arlington Community Temp. Shelter for Women	703/237-1147

Social Services for Battered Women

Washington, D.C.

Bethany Women's Center	202/483-3739
DC Coalition Against Domestic Violence	202/783-5332
DC Crime Victim's Assistance Program	202/842-8467
DC Rape Crisis Center	202/232-0789
Hermanas Unidas/Ayuda	202/387-4848
Her Space	202/347-2777
My Sister's Place	202/529-5991

Virginia

Arlington County Safehouse for Battered Women	703/237-0881
Arlington County Victims of Violence Program	703/358-5150
Fairfax County Victim's Assistance Network	703/360-7273
Fairfax County Women's Shelter	703/435-4940
Sexual Assault Response and Awareness Program	703/838-5030

Maryland

Charles County Center for Abused Persons	301/843-1110
Family Crisis Center of Prince George's County	301/779-2100
Heartly House Domestic Violence Program	301/662-8800
Helping Hands Shelter	301/340-2796
Montgomery County Abused Persons Programs	301/654-1881

Volunteer Clearinghouses

Volunteer clearinghouses are a great point of entry to community service. The clearinghouses provide the linkage to opportunities with hundreds of organizations and causes that are in need of volunteers. By simply calling a clearinghouse, you can find out about all the different volunteer options and the appropriate contacts to get you started helping out. If you are interested in donating your time or money to a group that benefits women, then make your request to the volunteer coordinator.

Alexandria Volunteer Bureau	703/836-2176
Arlington Co. Volunteer Office	703/358-3222
Greater DC Cares	202/289-7378
Loudoun Co. Volunteer Center	703/777-0113
Montgomery County Volunteer Center	301/217-4949
Prince George's County Voluntary Action Center	301/699-2800
Voluntary Action Center of Prince William County	703/369-5292
Volunteer Center of Fairfax County	703/246-3460

Mentor Opportunities

There are a number of groups in need of female role models to benefit the next generation of emerging women. Groups such as Women in Community Service and Big Sisters are always looking for women in the community to serve as role models to girls and young women in need of guidance. Be aware that some groups require mentors to commit to several months of interaction.

Big Sisters of the Washington Metropolitan Area
202/244-1012
4000 Albermarle Street, NW, # 303, Washington, DC 20016
   Big Sisters matches local girls with responsible women, who serve as mentors and friends. The relationships are intended to provide counseling, support and friendship for the girls to help guide them into adulthood.

Girl Scout Council of the Nation's Capital
202/337-4300, 800/523-7898
2233 Wisconsin Ave., NW, 410, Washington, DC 20007

The Girl Scouts has troops all over the D.C. metropolitan area that rely on volunteers for troop leadership roles and staffing summer day camps. Positions include director, assistant leaders, special events coordinator, recruiters, volunteer trainers and activities director. Girl Scouts promotes honesty, respect and community service.

Metro MANA
202/833-0060
725 K Street, NW, Suite 501, Washington, DC 20006
Metro MANA offers a mentoring program for Latina teens that encourages girls to stay in school while exposing them to different types of professions and resources. The mentor program matches career women with junior high and high school students. MANA is the Mexican-American Women's National Association.

Sasha Bruce Youthwork
202/675-9340
1022 Maryland Ave., NE, Washington, DC 20002
Sasha Bruce Youthwork operates a number of programs to improve the lives of at-risk children. Volunteers can participate in the Big Sister Program, which provides mentoring relationships to at-risk girls. Volunteers can also take part in the Teen Mothers Program, which offers educational guidance, employment and legal assistance, parenting counseling and other services to teenage moms.

YWCA
202/667-9100
901 Rhode Island Ave., NW, Washington, DC 20001
Volunteers are needed to tutor children between the ages six and 13 in English and other school studies. Volunteers would need to be available in the afternoon hours.

Women's Centers

Women's centers offer professional and personal resources, programs and referrals to women. Volunteers can participate in various activities such as staffing a career center, helping create a flyer to publicize an event or responding to inquiries from women. Recent budget cuts have left some women's centers relying more heavily on volunteers than in the past.

Alexandria Office on Women
703/838-5030
110 N. Royal Street, Room 201, Alexandria, VA 22314
The Alexandria Office on Women provides career and personal services to women, and operates domestic violence and sexual assault response programs. The Office trains volunteers for all programs and services. Volunteers can help staff the emergency response programs or career workshops, or help provide general services to women. Volunteers can also assist with public education programs and respond to telephone inquiries.

DC Commission for Women
202/939-8083
2000 14th Street, NW, Suite 354, Washington, DC 20009
Due to a lack of government funding in recent years, the DC Commission for Women is open part-time and operates almost entirely on volunteers. Volunteers can participate in community education, public relations, research, special events planning, legislation and administration.

Fairfax County Office for Women
703/324-5730
12000 Government Center Parkway, Suite 318, Fairfax, VA 22035
The Fairfax County Office for Women is a career resource and life skills center for women of Fairfax County. Volunteers are needed for various administrative duties, including responding to telephone inquiries and, occasionally, research and writing projects for women's policy issues.

Montgomery County Commission for Women
301/279-1800
255 North Washington Street, Rockville, MD 20850
Montgomery County Commission for Women is a personal counseling and career development center that accepts volunteers for varying duties. Volunteers can participate as information referral specialists for the career center, as well as perform administrative duties that relate to activities, seminars and workshops offered by the Commission.

Prince William County Office for Women
703/792-6611
4370 Ridgewood Center Drive, Suite D, Woodbridge, VA 22192
Volunteers are needed to staff the Employment Center and the Computer Center. Volunteers are trained to help women access job and employment information by computer and administrative duties.

The Women's Center
703/281-2657
133 Park Street, NE, Vienna, VA 22180
The Women's Center is a nonprofit career development and psychotherapy center for women that also functions as a general resource center for women. The Women's Center accepts volunteers for duties in the areas of public relations, fundraising, data processing and bookkeeping. Women can also volunteer to assist with Saturday career workshops, special events and staffing the information and referral desk.

The Women's Center, Prince William County
703/281-4928, x397
Pinekirk Presbyterian Church
13428 Dumfried Road, Manassas, VA 22111
Volunteers are needed to staff the career center as well as provide a variety of administrative duties to maintain this walk-in career and personal development center.

The Women's Center and Referral Service
301/937-5265
3215 Powder Mill Road, Adelphi, MD 20783
An all-volunteer center that assists women with career and personal growth through programs, seminars, networks and support groups. Volunteers are needed in all areas of service delivery.

Political Volunteerism

Get involved in the political process by volunteering your time supporting a candidate or initiative or becoming involved with a voting project. For a more detailed listing of groups that promote women in public office, refer to chapter 5. You can also get involved in the political process by volunteering your time to advance a cause you believe in. Refer to chapter 6 for a listing of advocacy groups.

League of Women Voters of the National Capital Area
703/522-8196
1730 M Street, NW, Washington, DC 20036
The League of Women Voters holds voter registration drives and other political activities to educate and inform voters about policy issues and candidates. There are several chapters in the metropolitan area.

National Federation of Republican Women
703/548-9688
124 North Alfred Street, Alexandria, VA 22314
Networking, political and educational group for Republican women, which offers a variety of community service projects.

National Political Congress of Black Women, Inc. (NPCBW)
202/338-0800
600 New Hampshire Ave., NW, Suite 1125, Washington, DC 20037
NPCBW works to increase the role of African-Americans in the political process through leadership development, mentor programs, political support, advocacy and networking. Volunteers are needed for various projects and events.

National Women's Political Caucus (NWPC)
202/785-1100
1211 Connecticut Ave., NW, Suite 425, Washington, DC 20036
NWPC works to empower women in the political process. Volunteers can contribute time or money to the promotion of women candidates on the national and local levels.

Sewall-Belmont House
202/546-3989
144 Constitution Ave., NE, Washington, DC 20002
The Sewall-Belmont house is a museum of the women's suffrage movement, which gave American women the legal right to vote. Volunteers are needed in all areas to keep the museum operating, including for receptions, educational outreach projects, research, administrative tasks, grounds maintenance and archiving events.

Woman's National Democratic Club
202/232-7363
1526 New Hampshire Ave., NW, Washington, DC 20036
Networking, political and educational group for Democratic women. The group offers community service projects, such as adult literacy programs and assistance at local shelters.

Index

About Women on Campus, 171
Action Bulletin for Women's Rights,
110
advocacy groups, 99
Advocates for Youth, 99
AFL-CIO: Women's Rights Project,
99; Standing Committee on
Salaried and Professional
Women, 34
Aged Women's Home, 194
Alan Guttmacher Institute, 99
Alcohol, Drugs and Pregnancy
Healthline, 125
Alert, 110
Alexandria Chamber of Commerce,
62
Alexandria Commission for the
Arts, 230
Alexandria Hospital, 115
Alexandria Office on Women, 38,
99, 189, 210, 242
Alexandria Professional Women's
Network, 8
Alexandria Volunteer Bureau, 240
Alexandria Women's Health Clinic,
117
Allen, Susan Au, 87
Alzheimers Association of Greater
Washington, 126
American Alliance for Health,
Physical Education, Recreation
and Dance, 225
American Anorexia, Bulimia
Association, 131
American Association for Higher
Education, Women's Caucus,
12, 169
American Association for the
Advancement of Science, 28

American Association for Women
Radiologists, 18
American Association of
Immunologists, Committee on
the Status of Women, 18
American Association of University
Women, 12, 99, 169, 178
American Association of Women
Dentists, 18
American Association of Women
Emergency Physicians, 18
American Astronomical Society,
Committee on the Status of
Women, 28
American Bar Association,
Commission on Women in the
Profession, 23
American Business Women's
Association, 8
American Cancer Society, 126, 127
American Chemical Society,
Women Chemists Committee,
31
American College of Nurse-
Midwives, 18, 99, 139
American College of Obstetricians
and Gynecologists, 18-19, 127
American Council for Drug
Education, 125
American Council on Education,
Women's Office, 12, 99
American Counseling Association,
Committee on Women, 27
American Federation of
Government. Employees,
Women's Dept., 15, 99
American Federation of State,
County and Municipal
Employees, 16

American Federation of Teachers, Women's Rights Committee, 12
American Heart Association, 132
American Institute of Architects, Women's Committee, 6
American Lung Association, 127
American Medical Women's Association, 19, 99
American Mental Health Counselor Association, Women's Committee, 27
American News Women's Club, 22
American Nurses Association, 19, 99
American Pharmaceutical Association, Committee on Women's Affairs, 19
American Physical Society, Committee on the Status of Women, 31
American Physiological Society, Women in Physiology Committee, 31
American Psychiatric Association, Committee on Women, 27
American Psychological Association, Committee on Women in Psychology, 27
American Public Health Association, Women's Caucus, 19
American Running and Fitness Association, 225
American Society for Cell Biology, Women in Cell Biology Committee, 31
American Society for Microbiology, Committee on the Status of Women, 31
American Society for Public Administration, Section on Women, 16
American Society for Training and Development, Women's Network, 20
American Society of Bio-Chemistry and Molecular Biology, 31

American Society of Women Accountants, 14
American Sociological Association, Committee on the Status of Women, 27
American Statistical Association, Committee on Women in Statistics, 31
American University, 173; Women in the Law Clinic, 210
American Women in Radio and Television Inc., 22
American Women's Society of Certified Public Accountants, 15
Americans for the Arts, 227
Amnesty International Women's Program, 99
Annandale Women and Family Center, 117
Anxiety Disorders Association of America, 134
APSO/Lamaze, 143
ARCH, 193
Arlington Chamber of Commerce, 62
Arlington Community Temporary Shelter for Women, 200, 239
Arlington County Cultural Affairs Division, 228
Arlington County Safehouse for Battered Women, 189, 239
Arlington County Victims of Violence Program, 189, 239
Arlington County Volunteer Office, 239
Arlington Hospital Cancer Center, 127
Armstrong, Alexandra, 35
arts, 227; agencies, 228; groups, 227; music/dance, 230
Association for Women in Communications, 11, 179
Association for Women in Computing, 12
Association for Women in Development, 37, 48
Association for Women in Mathematics, 32, 169

Association for Women in Science, 32, 102, 169, 179
Association for Women Veterinarians, 19
Association of American Geographers, Committee on the Status of Women, 31
Association of American Law Schools, Women in Legal Education, 21
Association of American Law Schools, Women in Legal Education, 14
Association of Junior Leagues, 102
Association of Women in International Trade, 20, 48
Association of Women Surgeons, 19
Association of Women's Health, Obstetrics and Neonatal Nurses, 19

Bailey's Health Center, 115
Battered Women's Justice Project, 190
Becoming an Outdoors Woman, 216
Behrensmeyer, Anna K., 29
Belles Lettres, 234
Bethany Women's Center, 188, 239
Big Sisters of the Washington Metropolitan Area, 240
Biophysical Society, Committee on Professional Opportunities for Women, 32
Black Women United for Action, 102
Black Women's Agenda Inc., 102
Black Women's Roundtable on Voter Participation, 86
Blum, Barbara Davis, 9
Bowie Sounds of Music, 230
Breast Cancer Resource Committee, 128
Breast-Feeding Consultants of NOVA, 144
Breast-Feeding Counseling Services, 144

business, 56; loan assistance, 64; loan tips, 67; marketing, 61; procurement, 68; starting or expanding, 56
Business and Professional Women, 8, 204. See also National Federation of Business and Professional Women, Inc.
Business Women's Network, 8

Calvary Women's Shelter, 198, 238
Capital Baby, 141
Capital Hill House, 196
Capitol Hill Women's Political Caucus, 26, 43, 86
Capitol Women's Center, 117
Caring and Sharing, 128
CASA of Maryland Center for Employment and Training, 38
Catholics for a Free Choice, 102, 179
Center for Advancement of Public Policy, 102
Center for Development and Population Activities, 102
Center for Law and Social Policy, 102
Center for Nutrition Policy and Promotion, 226
Center for Policy Alternatives, Women's Economic Justice Program, 102
Center for Women Policy Studies, 102, 179
Center of Concern Women's Project, 102
chambers of commerce, 60
Charles County Center for Abused Persons, 189, 239
Chesapeake Outdoors Women, 216
Chesapeake Women's Rugby, 218
child care, 149; resources, 150-150; standards, 153
Child Care Aware, 150
Child Welfare League of America, Inc., 102
Children's Defense Fund, 102
Children's Foundation, 102

Church Women United, 103
Clearinghouse on Women's Issues,
103
Clinton, Hillary Rodham, 95
Coalition for America's Children,
103
Coalition of Labor Union Women,
36, 103
Coalition of 100 Black Women of
DC Inc., 235
college, 169; organizations, 169;
publications, 171; women's
studies, 173
Columbia Hospital for Women, 115,
116, 127, 146
Commerce Business Daily, 69
Commonwealth Women's Clinic,
117
Community of Caring, 146
Concerned Women for America,
103
Confinement Line Telephone
Support Network, 140
Consumer Nutrition Hotline, 225
Council of Presidents, 103
crisis hotlines, 187
Cultural Alliance of Greater
Washington, 227
CWI Newsletter, 110

DC AIDS Information Line, 132
DC Coalition Against Domestic
Violence, 103, 188, 208, 239
DC Commission for Women, 103,
242
DC Commission on the Arts and
Humanities, 228
DC Crime Victim's Assistance
Program, 188, 239
DC Rape Crisis Center, 188, 208
DC Webgrrls, 12
Democratic Congressional
Campaign Committee, 44
Democratic National Committee,
44; Women's Division, 90, 103
Democratic Women of Capitol Hill,
27, 90

Department of Commerce, 55, 59;
Minority Business Development
Agency, 60
Department of Labor, Women's
Bureau, 205
Depression After Delivery, 145
Depression and Related Affective
Disorders Association, 134
Dingman Center for
Entrepreneurship, 64
Dinner Program for Homeless
Women, 198, 238
District of Columbia Chamber of
Commerce, 60
District of Columbia Commission of
Public Health, 133
District of Columbia Nurses
Association, 20
Dorothy Day Place, 199, 239

Eagle Forum, 103
Eating Disorder Program,
Washington Adventist Hospital,
131
Edelman, Marian Wright, 97
Edward C. Mazique Parent Child
Center, 146
Eleanor Roosevelt Institute, 103
employment, 38, 42; capitol hill,
43; congressional, 42;
discrimination, 203, 206-207;
federal job information, 45-46;
government, 44; informational
interviews, 52; international,
47; internship, 53; job search,
49, 51; networking, 49; public
policy, 41
Emily's List, 90, 103, 179
ERA Summit, Americans for
Democratic Action, 103
Erbe, Bonnie, 87
Equal Employment Opportunity
Commission, 204, 207
Executive Women in Government,
16
Executive Women's Golf League,
219

exercise, 222; membership groups, 225; women's fitness centers, 224
Expanding Horizons, 216

Fairfax County Chamber of Commerce, 62
Fairfax County Council of the Arts, 228
Fairfax County Office for Women, 38, 62, 103, 242
Fairfax County Victim's Assistance Network, 189, 239
Fairfax County Women's Shelter, 189, 239
Fairfax Hospital, Life with Cancer, 128
Family Crisis Center of Prince George's County, 189, 239
Family Life and Maternity Education, 143
Family Medical Leave Act, 93
Family Place, 146
Federally Employed Women, 16, 103, 179, 204
Federation of Organizations for Professional Women, 8, 104, 179, 204
Feminist Majority, 104, 179, 204
Feminist Studies, 171, 234
Feminists for Life, 104
Femme Care Medical Center for Women, 117
Ferguson, Anita Perez, 84
Ferraro, Geraldine, 87
Fifty plus One, 72, 86
Financial Women International Inc., 15
Food and Nutrition Information Center, 225

General Federation of Women's Clubs, 104, 235
George Mason University, 175
George Washington University, 173; Domestic Violence Advocacy Project, 208; Emergency, Domestic Relations Project, 208; Sex Discrimination Clinic, 204
Gillian Rudd Leadership Institute for Women Business Owners, 72
Ginsburg, Justice Ruth Bader, 100
Girl Scout Council of the Nation's Capital, 240
Girls, Incorporated, 104
Golden Rays, 230
Goucher College, 174
Greater Bethesda-Chevy Chase Chamber of Commerce, 60
Greater Bowie Chamber of Commerce, 60
Greater DC Cares, 240
Greater Gaithersburg Chamber of Commerce, 60
Greater Southeast Community Hospital, 116
Greater Washington Coalition for Cancer Survivorship, 128

Hannah House, 197, 198, 238
Harrison Center for Career Education, 38
Harvest House, 296
health, 136; alcohol/drugs, 125; autoimmune diseases, 126; breast cancer, 127; cancer, 126; centers, 116; coverage, 118; eating disorders, 131; finding a physician; heart disease, 131; HIV/AIDS, 132; immunization, 133; medicaid, 119; mental health, 134; older women, 135; osteoporosis, 136; reproductive, 113; resources, 123; tests, 114
Health Insurance Association of America, 119
Health Resource Center on Domestic Violence, 190
Healthy Mothers, Healthy Babies, 104
Heartly House Domestic Violence Program, 189, 239
Helping Hands Shelter, 190, 199, 239

Her House, 236
Her Space, 188, 239
Hermanas Unidas, Ayuda, 188, 208, 239
Hill, The, 44
Hillcrest Women's Surgi-Center, 117
Holladay, Wilhelmina Cole, 7
Hollins College, 171
Hood College, 172
Hope and a Home, 193
House Action Reports, 44
House of Imagine, 198, 200
House of Ruth, 199, 238
housing, 193; and services for homeless women, 198; for women in recovery from substance abuse, 197; for women with HIV/AIDS, 196; low-cost for single women, 194; low-cost for women and families, 193
Howard University, 174; Cancer Center, 130
Human Rights Campaign Fund, 104
Human Rights Watch, Women's Rights Project, 104

I Have Arrived Before My Words: The Autobiographical Writings of Homeless Women, 201
Independent Women's Forum, 104
International Black Women's Congress, 104
International Center for Research on Women, 104
Institute for Women's Policy Research, 104, 179
Institute of Electrical and Electronic Engineers, Task Force on Women, 33
Insurance Professionals of Washington, DC, 15
International Alliance for Women in Music, 6, 230
International Association of Women Judges, 21

International Career Employment Opportunities, 48
International Council of African Women, 236
International Women's Forum, 20
International Women's Media Foundation, 22
International Women's Writing Guild, 36, 231
internships, 177; locating, 177; with women's organizations, 178

Jacobs Institute of Women's Health, 105
Jeremiah House, 197
Jewish Social Service Agency, 39, 145
Jewish Women International, 105
Johns Hopkins University, 174
Jubilee Housing, 193
Junior League of Washington, 236

Kidd, Susan, 24
Kidstreet News, 164
Krebs, Martha, 30

La Leche League International, 144
LadyRider, Inc., 218
Lambda Rising, 234
Lammas Women's Bookstore, 234
Latin American Youth Center, Teen Parenting Program, 146
Lawyers at Home, 161
Lazarus House, 197
leadership: programs, 72; for college women, 79; for young women, 77; tips for women, 74
Leadership America, Inc., 72, 75
League of Republican Women of the District of Columbia, 92
League of Women Voters, 26, 86, 87, 91, 105, 180, 243
legal, 205; employment discrimination, 203-207; pension rights, 210; sexual abuse/domestic violence, 208

Legal Aid for Abused Women and
  Children, 209
Legal and Business Information
  Center, 64
Linguistic Society of America,
  Committee on the Status of
  Women, 14
Links, Inc., 236
literature, 227; women's
  bookstores, 234; women's
  journals, 234; writing groups
  for women, 231
Local Leadership Roundtable, 73
Lombardi Cancer Helplink, 130
Loudoun County Volunteer Center,
  240
Lupus Foundation of Greater
  Washington, 126
Luther Place Night Shelter, 199,
  239

mammography, 115-116
Marshall Heights Dev. Corp., 194
Mary Baldwin College, 172
Mary House, 194
Maryland Arts Division, 228
Maryland Chamber of Commerce,
  60
Maryland Family, 165
Maryland Insurance Administration,
  119
Maryland Network Against
  Domestic Violence, 105
Maryland Women's Rugby, 219
*Maternity and Infant Resource
  Guide*, 141
Maternity Center, 145
Matthews, Kathleen, 25
Mautner Project for Lesbians with
  Cancer, 130
Maya Angelou House, 197
Metro MANA, 241
Metropolitan Washington Council
  of Governments, 150
Metropolitan Women's Organizing
  Project, 105
Mexican American Women's
  National Association, 105

Micah House, 197
Minority Business Development
  Agency, 69
Miriam's House, 196
Miscarriage, Infant Death and
  Stillbirth, 145
M.O.M. Program, 140
MOMS Club, 161
Montgomery College, 174
Montgomery County Abused
  Persons Program, 239
Montgomery County Chamber of
  Commerce, 60
Montgomery County Commission
  for Women, 39, 62, 105
Montgomery County Commission
  on the Humanities, 228
Montgomery County Health Dept.,
  116
Montgomery County Volunteer
  Center, 240
motherhood, 157; alternative work
  schedules, 160; at-home, 161;
  balancing work and family,
  159; networks, 157;
  publications, 164; transition to
  full-time motherhood, 162;
  working mothers, 158
Mother's Access to Careers at
  Home, 36
Mothers at Home, 161
Mothers First, 164
Mother's Matters, 144
Mothers Morning Out Program,
  157
Mount Carmel House, 199, 239
My Image After Breast Cancer, 130
My Sister's Place, 188, 239

National Abortion Federation, 105
National Abortion Rights Action
  League, 105, 180
National Academy of Early
  Childhood Programs, 150
National Academy of Sciences
  Committee on Women in
  Science, 32

National AIDS Hotline, Centers for Disease Control and Prevention, 132
National AIDS Information Clearinghouse, 132
National Alliance for the Mentally Ill, 134
National Association for Girls and Women in Sport, 33, 105, 225
National Association for Women in Education, 14, 170
National Association of Anorexia Nervosa and Associated Disorders, 131
National Association of Black Women Attorneys, 21
National Association of Child Advocates, 105
National Association of Colored Women's Clubs, Inc., 8, 236
National Association of Home Builders, Women's Council, 33
National Association of M.B.A. Women, 8
National Association of Minority Contractors, 33
National Association of Minority Political Women, 88
National Association of Negro Business and Professional Women's Clubs, 10, 105, 237
National Association of People with AIDS, 132
National Association of Professional Mortgage Women, 15
National Association of Professional Saleswomen, 28
National Association of Railway Business Women, 34
National Association of Women Artists, 227
National Association of Women Business Owners, 10, 106
National Association of Women in Construction, 33-34
National Association of Women Judges, 22

National Bar Association, Women Lawyers Division, 22
National Black Nurses Association, 20
National Black Women's Health Project, 106, 123
National Breast Cancer Coalition, 106
National Cancer Institute, 127, 130
National Capital Area Women's Paddling Association, Inc., 220
National Chamber of Commerce for Women, 62
National Child Support Advocacy Coalition, 106
National Clearinghouse for Alcohol and Drug Information, 125
National Clearinghouse for Leadership Programs, 78
National Coalition Against Domestic Violence, 106
National Coalition for Cancer Survivorship, 106
National Committee for Quality Assurance, 119
National Committee on Pay Equity, 106
National Conference for College Women Leaders, 78
National Conference of Puerto Rican Women, 106
National Council for International Health, 48
National Council of Catholic Women, 106
National Council of Jewish Women, 106
National Council of Negro Women, Inc., 106, 2386
National Council on Child Abuse and Family Violence, 106, 190
National Domestic Violence Hotline, 188
National Drug Information Treatment and Referral Line, 125

National Education Association, Women's Caucus, 14, 106
National Family Planning and Reproductive Health Association, 106
National Federation of Black Women Business Owners, 10
National Federation of Business and Professional Women, Inc., 107, 180. *See also* Business and Professional Women
National Federation of Press Women, 22
National Federation of Republican Women, 26, 92, 107, 233, 244
National Foundation for Women Business Owners, 55
National Foundation for Women Legislators, Inc., 73, 180
National Gay and Lesbian Task Force, 107
National Heart, Lung and Blood Institute Information Center, 132
National Hispana Leadership Institute, 73
National Immunization Information Hotline, 133
National Institute for Mental Health, 134
National Institute of Aging, 135
National Institute of Arthritis and Musculoskeletal and Skin Diseases, 126
National Institute of Mental Health, 131
National Leadership Institute, 73
National League of American Pen Women, 67
National League of Cities, Women in Municipal Government, 16
National Maternal and Child Health Clearinghouse, 123, 140
National Minority AIDS Council, 133
National Multiple Sclerosis Society, 126

National Museum of Women in the Arts, 231
National Network of Commercial Real Estate Women, 33
National Network to End Domestic Violence, 107
National Order of Women Legislators, 26
National Organization for Women, 93, 107, 180
National Osteoporosis Foundation, 136
National Political Congress of Black Women, 26, 76, 88, 107, 244
National Race for the Cure, 129
National Republican Congressional Committee, 44
National Resource Center on Domestic Violence, 190
National Right to Life Committee, 107
National Symphony Orchestra, 238; Women's Committee, 231
National Woman's Party, 88
National Women's Business Center, 57
National Women's Caucus for Art, 227
National Women's Economic Alliance Foundation, 76
National Women's Health Information Center, 124
National Women's Health Network, 107, 124, 180
National Women's Health Resource Center, 124, 130
National Women's Law Center, 107
National Women's Political Caucus, 27, 83, 84, 88, 93, 107, 180
National Women's Students Coalition, 170
National Women's Studies Association, 170, 181
National Women's Symphony, 230
NE Place Health Center, 147
Network of Entrepreneurial Women, 10

networking, 34;
advertising/marketing, 6;
art/design, 6;
business/entrepreneur , 8;
communications/public
relations, 11; computers/data
processing, 12; education, 12;
environment/energy, 14;
finance/banking, 14;
government, 15; health
care/pharmaceuticals, 18; human
resources, 20; international, 20;
legal, 21; media , 22; politics,
26; psychology/sociology, 27;
real estate, 28; sales, 28; science
and technology, 28; sports, 33;
tips, 4; trade professions, 33;
transportation, 34; working
mothers, 36; writing/publishing,
36
New Dimension Singers, 231
New Endeavors by Women, 199,
239
New Summit Medical Center, 117
"9 to 5," National Association of
Working Women, 8, 99
Norton, Eleanor Holmes, 87
Nova Women's Medical Center,
117
NOW Legal Defense and
Education Fund, 107

Office of Government Contracting,
69
Office of Minority Health Resource
Center, 124
Office of Nutrition Programs,
Women and Infant Children's
Program, 144
Office of Personnel Management,
46
Office of Women Business
Ownership, 57, 58
Office of Workplace Initiatives, 158
Offices of Small and Disadvantaged
Business Utilization, 69
Old Dominion University, 175

Older Women's League, 107, 135,
181
Organization of Chinese-American
Women, 107
Organization of Women in
International Trade, 21, 48
Outreach for Parent Teens, 147
Outward Bound, 216
Oxford Houses, 197

Panic Disorder Education Program,
134
Parent Resource Guide, 165
Partner Arms, 194
Pension Rights Center, Women's
Pension Project, 108, 213
Perinatal Loss Support Group, 145
P-FLAG, 107
Phyllis Wheatley YWCA, 196
Planned Parenthood, 108, 117
Policy Leaders Action Network, 76
Political Woman Hotline, 110
politics: democratic groups, 90;
getting involved, 84;
nonpartisan/bipartisan groups,
86; republican groups, 92
Potomac Boat Club, 220
Potomac Chamber of Commerce, 60
Potomac Children, 165
Potomac Family Planning Center,
118
Potomac Rugby Union, 219
pregnancy, 139; bereavement, 145;
breast-feeding, 144; childbirth
education, 143; hospitals, 141;
nutrition, 144; postpartum, 145;
resources, 139; teens, 146
Prince George's County Chamber of
Commerce, 60
Prince George's County Voluntary
Action Center, 240
Prince George's Hospital Center,
116
Prince George's Reproductive
Health Services, 118
Prince William County Commission
for Women, 63, 108

Prince William County Office for
Women, 40, 63, 242
Prince William County—Greater
Manassas Chamber of
Commerce, 62
Professional Women Controllers, 34
Professional Women in
Construction, 34
Pro-Life Alliance of Gays and
Lesbians, 108
Providence Hospital's Wellness
Institute, 130
Public Leadership Education
Network, 78, 79
Public Relations Society of
America, Women in Public
Relations Committee, 11

Rachael's Women's Center, 199,
239
Randolph-Macon Woman's
College, 172
Rehm, Diane, 23
Religious Coalition for
Reproductive Choice, 108
Renaissance Women, 108, 181
Republican National Committee,
44; Women's Division, 92
Republican Network to Elect
Women, 92
Republicans for Choice, 92, 108
Roadwork, 228
Rockville Chamber of Commerce,
60
Roll Call, 44

Salvation Army Transitional Family
Program, 194
Sasha Bruce Youthwork, 241; Teen
Mothers Program, 147
Self-Help Clearinghouse of Greater
Washington, 135
Senior Women Volleyball, 219
Service Corps of Retired
Executives, 57
Sewall-Belmont House, 89, 246
Shady Grove Adventist Hospital,
116

Shady Grove Eating Disorder
Center, 131
Sheclimbs, Inc., 220
Small Business Administration, 55,
56; Business Information
Center, 58; loans, 65; Office of
Women Business Ownership,
57; SBA OnLine, 58; Service
Corps of Retired Executives, 57;
Small Business Answer Desk,
57; Small Business
Development Centers, 59;
Washington, D.C., office, 56
SHARE Care, 150
Single Mothers by Choice, 158
Single Parents Raising Kids, 158
Sisterhood Is Global Institute, 108,
181
Sisterspace and Books, 234
social service departments, 200
Society for International
Development, 48
Society for the Advancement of
Women's Health Research, 108
Society of Women Engineers, 33
Society of Woman Geographers, 33
Soroptimist International, 237
The Source, 110
Speech Communications
Association, Women's Caucus,
11
sports, 215; adventure, 216;
baseball, 217; golf, 217; groups
for women, 217, 225; ice
hockey, 217; motorcycle clubs,
218; organized team, 221; rock
climbing, 218; rugby, 218;
soccer, 219; volleyball, 219;
water, 220
Sports Network, 219
St. Martin's House, 197
Suited for Change, 39, 40, 181,
199, 237, 239
Susan B. Anthony, 88
Susanna Wesley House, 196, 197
Sweet Adelines International, 231
Sweet Briar College, 172

Tabitha's House, 197
Takoma Women's Health Center, 118
Tarr-Whelan, Linda, 98
Teen AIDS Hotline, 131
TEN Program, 194
Thea Bowman House, 194
Thompson-Markward Hall, 196
To The Contrary, 87
Trenton Park, 194
Trinity College, 172
Trinity Housing, 194

Union Institute, 176, 181
United Food and Commercial Workers International Union, 36
University of Maryland at College Park, 174
University of Richmond, 175
U.S. Business Advisor, 58
U.S. Chamber of Commerce, 62
U.S. House of Representatives Placement Office, 44
U.S. Senate Placement Office, 44
USA Volleyball, 220

violence, 185; crisis hotlines, 187; rape, 186; safety tips, 190-192; services for battered and abused women, 188
Virginia Association of Female Executives, 10
Virginia Bureau of Insurance, 119
Virginia Chamber of Commerce, 62
Virginia Polytechnic Institute and State University, 175
Virginia Women in the Outdoors, 216
Virginia Women's Network, 108
Voluntary Action Center of Prince William County, 240
volunteer, 235; clearinghouses, 240; community service groups, 235; mentor opportunities, 240; political, 243; social service agencies, 238; women's centers, 241

Volunteer Center of Fairfax County, 240
Volunteers of America, 239; Shepherd's Cove Homeless Shelter, 200
Voters for Choice, 108

Washington Adventist Hospital, 116
Washington Area Council on Alcohol and Drug Abuse, 125
Washington Area Women's Soccer League, 219
Washington Families, 165
Washington Feminist Faxnet, 110
Washington Free Clinic, 118
Washington International Trade Association, 48
Washington Metropolitan Women's Baseball League, 217
Washington RunHers, 219
Washington Surgi-Clinic, 118
Washington Women in Public Relations, 11
Washington Women Outdoors, Inc., 217
Washington Women's Ice Hockey Club, 217
Wednesday Morning Group, 164
Wheaton Chamber of Commerce, 60
Whitman-Walker Clinics, 133, 196
Wider Opportunities for Women, 40, 77, 108, 181
Widnall, Sheila E., 17
WISH List, 92
Woman Activist Fund, 108
Woman Care of Washington, 118
Woman's National Democratic Club, 27, 90
Womanship, 2220
Women As Leaders Seminar, 78
Women Business Owners of Montgomery County, 10
Women Construction Owners and Executives, 34
Women Executives in State Government, 16

Women in Advertising and Marketing, 6
Women in Aerospace, 32
Women in Cable and Television, 11
Women in Community Service, 237
Women in Film and Video, 26
Women in Government, 16, 109
Women in Government Relations, 18, 109
Women in Housing and Finance, 15
Women in International Security, 21, 48
Women in Midlife and Menopause, 135
Women in Museums Network, 6, 228
Women in Technology, Inc., 33
Women Leaders Online, 109
Women Life Underwriters Confederation, 15
Women of Washington, Inc., 10, 13
Women Officials of the National Association of County Officials, 18
Women on Wheels, 218
Women Work! The National Network for Women's Employment, 40, 181
Women's Action for Good Employment Standards, 109
Women's Action for New Directions, 109, 181
Women's Alliance for Theology, Ethics & Ritual, 109
Women's American ORT, 109
Women's Bar Association of the District of Columbia, 22
Women's Campaign Fund, 83, 88
Women's Campaign Research Fund, 77
Women's Caucus for the Arts, 6
Women's Center, 41, 63, 72, 243
Women's Center and Referral Service, 41, 63, 243
Women's Center of Prince William County, 41, 243
Women's Clinic, 118

Women's College Coalition, 109, 170
Women's Comprehensive Health Center, 118
Women's Council, 133
Women's Council of the Democratic Senatorial Campaign Committee, 90
Women's Council of Realtors, 29
Women's Council on Energy and the Environment, 14
Women's Direct Response Group, 6
Women's Employment Resource Center, 207
Women's Federation for World Peace, 109
Women's Foreign Policy Group, 21
Women's Health Information Clearinghouse, 124
Women's HR Network, 20
Women's Information Network, 11, 90
Women's Institute for a Secure Retirement, 213
Women's Institute for Freedom of the Press, 109, 182
Women's Legal Defense Fund, 109
Women's National Book Association, 36, 233
Women's Policy, Inc., 183
Women's Quarterly, 110
Women's Research and Education Institute, 183
Women's Resource Center, 210
Women's Rugby, 219
Women's Services Center, 125
Women's Sports Foundation, 226
Women's Studies Electronic Forum and Database, 170
Women's Transportation Seminar, 34
Working Mother's Network, 36, 161

Young Parents Network, 148
Young Women's Project, 78
YWCA, 183, 241

Zonta Club, 238

About the Author

Jacci Duncan is a communications advisor to women's groups in Washington, D.C. She has spent six years working as a print and television journalist and a freelance writer in California. She has written on a range of topics, including gender issues, politics, health care, economics, and business issues. She is a graduate of the University of California at Los Angeles.

She began writing *Washington for Women* after accumulating an incredible number of resources for women in Washington, D.C., and seeing firsthand the need in the community for a comprehensive guide for women.